ST. NORBERT COLLEGE
301.161016 G65m
Gordon, Thomas Frank,
Mass communication effects and processes

1007 7816 5

D0464167

301.161016
G65m

Mass Communication Effects and Processes

A Comprehensive Bibliography, 1950~1975

Thomas F. Gordon
and
Mary Ellen Verna

 SAGE Publications   Beverly Hills   London

Copyright © 1978 by Sage Publications, Inc.

A,l rights reserved. No part of this book may be reproduced or utilized in any form or by any means, electronic or mechanical, including photocopying, recording or by any information storage and retrieval system, without permission in writing from the publisher.

For information address:

SAGE PUBLICATIONS, INC.
275 South Beverly Drive
Beverly Hills, California 90212

SAGE PUBLICATIONS LTD
28 Banner Street
London ECIY 8QE

Printed in the United States of America

Library of Congress Cataloging in Publication Data

Gordon, Thomas Frank, 1944-
   Mass communication effects and processes

Includes indexes.
1. Mass media—Psychological aspects—Bibliography
2. Mass media—Social aspects—Bibliography
3. Television and children—Bibliography. I. Verna, Mary Ellen joint author. II. Title
Z5630.G67   [HM258]   016.30116'1   77-26094
ISBN 0-8039-0903-9

   FIRST PRINTING

Kochen

MASS COMMUNICATION
EFFECTS AND PROCESSES

PREFACE

This research bibliography grew out of the authors' continuing interest in the socialization effects of the mass media. In 1973 a smaller bibliography on this topic was prepared as background for other research projects underway at that time (see entry 1028). From that initial experience it became clear that the media-effects- literature was scattered throughout a variety of academic journals and reference sources. Furthermore, because of the pervasiveness and complexity of the socialization problem, it became evident that there was more relevant literature available than we had anticipated. Thus, to grasp the full extent of this effects-related literature we decided to do an extensive search dating from 1950. The present volume is the result of that search for the 25 year period through 1975. The present intent is to update this collection at two to three year intervals.

Although our primary interest was in social-psychological effects, deciding what was or was not relevant to a particular effect became increasingly difficult, due to the complex interactive nature of the various problem areas and processes. Thus, when in doubt the rule was to include rather than exclude. Similarly, because many of the citations dealt with multiple topic or content areas, the decision was to alphabetize the entire set and provide a complex, cross-referenced subject index, rather than to attempt to group the citations by common subtopics.

Roughly 200 of the citations have been given brief annotations. In most cases the annotations have been added to elaborate on a short or unclear title, to indicate the scope or size of a bibliography, or to indicate the basic conclusions of what were perceived to be key studies. When the latter was the case, annotations were usually made for works that may be less readily available than others. For example, works from the five volume *Television and Social Behavior* series, stemming from the Surgeon General's violence research, were not annotated because the reports will be available in most major libraries and other sources have reviewed and summarized them (see items 89, 466, 1846, 2141).

The authors wish to express their gratitude to Shawn Cannon who assisted with segments of the search process and contributed significantly to the manuscript preparation, and also to Mona Astra and Teresa Maxson for their assistance with manuscript preparation. Finally, we wish to thank Rhoda Blecker of Sage Publications for her assistance and encouragement throughout the project.

Thomas F. Gordon
Mary Ellen Verna

CONTENTS

To time and the search . . .
a combination eternal.

And to my parents with love,
James and Julia Gordon.

TFG

To the people who make life worth living:
Maryann Michele Papanier-Wells
brother Carl and Dr. Carl.

MEV

THE SEARCH PROCESS

BIBLIOGRAPHIES

The present volume originated as a working research bibliography (see entry 1028). Given the decision to do a thorough search of the 1950–1975 period, the *Bibliographic Index* and the *World Bibliography of Bibliographies* were consulted for related bibliographic works. The present subject index (see Bibliographies) details the collection of 68 related bibliographies. Of these 68, 28 deal almost exclusively with media, television, or radio (as listed under those headings in the index). Of these 28, the following 18 could be located and were searched: 2, 90, 289, 573, 576, 577, 621, 1028, 1163, 1322, 1651, 1847, 2208, 2373, 2374, 2375, 2376, 2473.

Furthermore, the bibliographies of literally hundreds of individual books and articles, too extensive to enumerate, were searched. These included the bibliographies associated with the major reviews listed in the reviews section of the subject index, as well as major books, articles, and the bibliographies of every research report in the multi-volume government research series associated with the violence and pornography commission programs of study. Also, *Cumulative Book Index* (1950–1975) was searched under the headings of: Mass Media, Moving Pictures, Television, Violence, Politics, Socialization.

ABSTRACTING SERVICES

From the primary abstracting services, *Psychological Abstracts* (1950–1975) were searched under the topics of: Communication, Communication/Mass, Socialization, Television, Film. Similarily, *Sociological Abstracts* (1953–1975) were searched under: Communication, Media, Mass Media, Television, Socialization. *Journalism Abstracts* (1963–1975) were

9

searched under the topics of: Advertising, Audience Analysis, Communication Theory/Process and Effects, Content Analysis, Public Opinion, Public Relations, Radio-Television-Film, Visual Communication. *Dissertation Abstracts* (1950–1975) were searched under the headings of: Media, Television, Socialization. As well, a bibliographic collection of roughly 2000 theses and dissertations in broadcasting, assembled for publication by Professor Kittross, Tempie University, was searched for relevant dissertation items. This computerized collection stemmed from searches of other bibliographies of theses and dissertations in broadcasting and a direct mail survey soliciting citations from major broadcasting-related departments around the country. Lastly, the entire index for *Mass Media Booknotes* (1969-1975) was searched.

INDIVIDUAL JOURNALS

Besides the abstracting services, the subject indices of the following journals were individually searched from 1950 (or date of inception) through 1975. If a name change occured for the journal (e.g. *Educational Broadcasting Review* became *Public Telecommunications Review*) the predecessor was also searched:
— Journal of Advertising Research
— Journal of Marketing Research
— AV Communications Review
— Journal of Broadcasting
— Communication
— Communication Research
— Human Communication Research
— Journal of Communication
— Journalism Monographs
— Journalism Quarterly
— Mass Comm Review
— Public Opinion Quarterly
— Telecommunications Review
— Television Quarterly

Given the social-psychological emphasis, media areas routinely excluded were law and regulation, historical development, economics and business, technical operations, management and professional training. Methodological references were included only if they seemed particularly relevant to the socialization process, or were unique to assessment in a particular effects area. Given our research emphasis, citations from the popular press were also excluded. Lastly, convention papers were excluded because of the frequent inability to judge their nature and quality.

LITERATURE OVERVIEW

This overview of the literature will provide a general conceptual or organizational scheme with examples of representative studies in each category. The first section will present studies related to media processes and effects—first societal processes, then effects processes. This will be followed by the content analytic studies which represent how people and/or behaviors/ activities are presented in the media. These studies characterize the information being presented to (received by) the audience. The next section will overview how audience members use the media by way of usage patterns and functions/gratification derived from that usage. The final major section will overview the studies of media effects relative to particular subgroups of the audience.

In general, the overview is structured as follows, with each of the categories subdivided relative to the dominant content, use, subgroup, or effect-area emphasized in the literature:

I. General Societal Processes
    (A) The Socialization Perspective
    (B) General (Non-Media) Socialization Influences
    (C) Specific Aspects of the Socialization Process
    (D) Socialization of Particular Subgroups
        (1) Children and Adolescents
        (2) Women
        (3) Social Class Differences
        (4) Cross Cultural Differences
II. Media Processes and Effects
    (A) Societal Processes
        (1) Advertising
        (2) The Audience
        (3) Censorship
        (4) Culture
        (5) Diffusion
        (6) Functions

11

        (7)   Interpersonal Relations
        (8)   Influence of Media on Each Other
        (9)   Influence of Media on Living Patterns
        (10) Politics
        (11) Violence
        (12) International
    (B) Effects Processes
        (1)   Arousal
        (2)   Catharsis
        (3)   Identification
        (4)   Imitation/Modeling
        (5)   Learning
III.   Media Content
    (A) Presentation of People/Subgroups
        (1)   The Aged
        (2)   Blacks
        (3)   Children (Sex-Role Images)
        (4)   The Poor
        (5)   Women
    (B) Presentation of Activities/Behaviors/Events
        (1)   Advertising
        (2)   Mental Illness
        (3)   Alcohol
        (4)   Drugs
        (5)   Sexual Behavior
        (6)   Music
        (7)   Occupational Roles
        (8)   Violence/Crime
IV.   Media Use
    (A) Use Processes
        (1)   Selective Exposure
        (2)   Information Seeking
        (3)   Selective Perception
    (B) Media Functions
    (C) Media Use by Subgroups
        (1)   Adolescents
        (2)   Children
        (3)   Blacks
        (4)   The Aged
        (5)   The Poor
V.   Media Effects
    (A) Adolescents
    (B) Children
    (C) Blacks
    (D) The Aged/The Poor/Women

I. GENERAL SOCIETAL PROCESSES

(A) The Socialization Perspective

Most media researchers recognize the importance of conceptualizing media processes and effects within their broader sociocultural context. The increasingly popular orientation with this emphasis is the socialization perspective. The term socialization refers to the process of preparing an individual for entry into a given social system. That individual may be child, adolescent, or adult, and the social system may be anything from a club or peer group to the more abstract society at large. Comstock and Lindsey (577), in their overview of current and projected research efforts, listed television and the socialization of young persons as the number one research priority for the scientific community.

The socialization perspective recognizes the complexity of the preparatory process. Numerous agents of influence may be involved in bestowing the experiences (knowledge), norms, values, and skills expected of accepted members of the system. This becomes increasingly true as societies move from primitive or traditional states to more complex modern and industrial states. With this evolution it is inevitable that the influence processes which were predominantly interpersonal in nature will become involved in mass communication processes. Thus, the problem of the modern media researchers is not only to conceptualize the processes and effects within the context of other agents of influence, but also to discern the complex interactions that eventually produce the final result.

(B) General NonMedia Socialization Influences

In the present collection of references numerous citations have been included which deal with the generalized process of human socialization and development. It should be noted, however, that because the literature dealing with sociological and psychological systems, as well as with child development in general, is so vast, a systematic search of these areas was beyond the scope of the present collection. Thus the items included either turned up in the other searches — primarily because they had the term socialization in their title — or were known through other references to be particularly relevant. These items range from Goslin's *Handbook of Socialization* (1030) to works on socialization and development by Clausen (530, 531), McNeal (1675), White and Watts (2598), Williams (2629), and the more recent overview of influences on development by Bronfenbrenner and Mahone (370).

(C) Specific Aspects of the Socialization Process

Several of the citations included deal with specific aspects of the socialization process rather than with the total scheme. Represented among these would be works concentrating on conscience (75), psychological needs (73), the development of motives and values (241), and the interplay of child rearing and the development of moral structures (1333).

Language behavior and meaning has received notable attention as a specific subprocess. Hence, Leopold (1527) provides a bibliography of literature related to children and language development. Other recent works focus on language and meaning in a social context (510), social class differences in maternal language styles relative to social control (588), social class differences in general language and communication styles (340), and the relationship between language, socialization, and delinquency (1447).

(D) Socialization of Particular Subgroups.

(1) *Children and Adolescents.* Although a great deal of attention has been focused on the child socialization process, other subgroups have also come under scrutiny. This is especially true with increased interest in the role of women in society and the plight of the elderly and the poor. In the child socialization category, notable works include Capecchi and Livolsi (438), Danziger (623), Edge (758), Elkin (784), Hoppe, et al. (1240), and Richards (2054). For the somewhat older adolescent, Elder (1968) reviews adolescent socialization and personality development, while Thomas (1974) details the family role in adolescent socialization. For adults, as noted earlier, the socialization process does not end at adulthood. Brim (350), Brim and Wheeler (351), and Wright and Turk (2679) provide perspectives on adult socialization. Rosow (2125) details the process of socialization to old age.

(2) *Women.* Much attention has been focused in recent years on the sex-role socialization of young girls and women. Here, Astin (81) provides a bibliography of sex role references and Stoll (2384) provides a thorough comparison of differences in male-female abilities, physical and psychological characteristics, potentials, and socialization stereotypes. Stein and Bailey (1973) detail the achievement socialization of females, while Gersoni-Staun (980) reviews sexism and youth.

(3) *Social Class Differences.* In the area of social class differences, the orientations range from family life style differences and the social world of the slum child (1371) to social class and ethnic differences in

socialization (368, 1199, 1376). Ziegler provides a general review of social class and the socialization process (2694).

(4) *Cross-Cultural Comparisons.* A limited number of cross-cultural comparisons of differences in general socialization processes are provided. For example, the work of Wilson (2633) in contrasting the political socialization of Chinese vs. American children and Bronfenbrenner's (369) comparison of American and Russian differences in the socialization process are notable. The majority of cross-cultural comparisons in this literature are media specific such as Furu's (921) assessment of the role of the media in socialization of the Japanese child.

II. MEDIA PROCESSES AND EFFECTS.

(A) Societal Processes

In the present bibliography, generalized mass media and society texts and readers were, for the most part, excluded. For an overview and comparison of texts of this type, appropriate for an introductory mass media and society course, see Sterling (1974). References included which deal with societal processes include primarily works emphasizing the impact of media systems on social processes (e.g., 98, 1957, 1679, 1681).

(1) *Advertising.* The advertising area is pervasive in that it has been studied from a variety of perspectives. Those references exemplifying societal concerns include works by Barmash (172) emphasizing the overall psychology of today's consumerism. Buzzi (410) assesses the cultural and political ramifications of our advertising system. Similarly, Howard and Hulbert (1251) discuss advertising in the public interest. Steiner (2361) provides a survey of public attitudes toward advertising while Wright and Mertes offer perspectives on advertising's role in society (2680).

(2) *The Audience.* Analyses of audiences have tended to be complementary to the study of other variables. However, generalized studies of particular channels of communication for specific audiences are evident (2206, 2133, 2360, 2438). The second major category of audience studies relates to general audience attitudes and preferences (185, 186, 187, 1973).

(3) *Censorship.* The majority of censorship studies (599, 1133) have dealt with books or movie censorship related to pornographic material (e.g., 447, 804, 1905). Control in broadcasting becomes a regulatory matter which is primarily under the jurisdiction of the Federal

Communications Commission. Given the social/psychological emphasis of the present bibliography, the literature related to the regulatory and legal aspects of broadcast media control have not been covered. The limited works which are represented relate primarily to the control of sex and violence on television (e.g., 578, 966, 976, 1127, 2260) or the specific presentation of mental illness (966, 976).

(4) *Culture.* The question of the relationship between cultural change and media has been posed from the early days of media research. Relatively few theories of popular culture (342) and/or mass behavior (1678) have been offered to explain the relationship, however. Usually, the intent has been to explain the interplay between media and mass culture (27, 1503, 2350), in most cases emphasizing the entertainment aspects of the medium (1746).

Social change as an aspect of cultural processes has received the bulk of attention (see for example: 5, 464, 647, 790, 825, 1679, 1681, 1738, 1962, 2675). Also, with the increasing evidence of media influence on fads and pop art, studies of popular culture have shown a recent increase (2062, 928, 442, 1469).

(5) *Diffusion.* The study of diffusion relative to societal processes concentrated primarily on the diffusion of innovations (72, 1107, 1484, 1759) or the diffusion of information or news throughout a given system (629, 653, 1345, 2082). The work of Rogers and Shoemaker (2101) provides an excellent review of the diffusion of innovations research. News diffusion has received considerable attention in the literature, from predictive models (914) and regulatory patterns (1214) to the role of interpersonal processes (1062, 1489, 1744) and visual impact (1918). Rosengren (2116) provides an overview of the news diffusion research.

(6) *Functions.* Althought the emphasis of functional approaches to the study of media have tended to assess functions for individuals, broader societal conceptions are available (634, 829, 1301, 1493, 1605, 2118, 2673, 2674). More specifically, Mendelsohn (1743, 1752) examines the interplay of the functional approach and its potential for policy decisions. With the increased government demand for research which can contribute to policy decisions, this latter area appears to be a particularly important area of future concern. The uses and gratifications studies will be overviewed under the individual processes and effects categories to follow.

(7) *Interpersonal relations.* The role of the mass media in social and interpersonal interaction has received attention primarily from the functional perspective (348, 898, 1316, 1584, 2276, 2325). Chaffee (478) and Rogers (2098) offer evidence and provide reviews of the

research related to the media–interpersonal interface. This interface takes on particular importance in the modernization cycle (1997, 2150) and in the diffusion of innovations relative to the two-step flow hypothesis (36, 72, 1342, 1345, 2059, 1721, 2678).

(8) *Influence of Media on Each Other.* Relative to the use of individual media and the influence of one medium on another, most of the attention has been focused on the impact of television. Masson (1722) and Robinson and Converse (2091) provide overall reviews on TV's impact on other media. Belson (212) and Parker (1951) examine the impact of television on newspaper and magazine use, while Curran (614) assesses TV's impact on newspaper use over the period 1945–1968. Studies of television's impact on news media preferences (615) and on movie-going (209) are also evident. Lastly, assessments of media as institutions provide an overall view (927, 963, 964, 2676).

(9) *Influence of Media on Living Patterns.* Most of the research on media influences on living patterns has concentrated on the use of leisure time in general (584, 655, 656, 1039, 1329, 1368, 1400, 1482, 1779, 1781, 2086, 2209). Of the various media, television's influence on leisure time has been the primary focus of research efforts (305, 602, 994, 1241, 1402, 1609, 1779, 1781, 2086, 2087). Relative to family interaction processes, the same holds true (see: Media-Family; Television and Family, in the subject index).

(10) *Politics.* Of the societal processes in which media play a role, politics has been one of the most researched. The studies range from attitudes toward the role of the media (49) to media usage (198, 671, 1632, 2050) candidate perceptions (810, 1209, 1642, 2274, 2685), advertising (675, 1963, 1964, 2134, 2135) and a host of general media and television effects studies. As would be expected, given the pervasiveness of television, the majority of studies have concentrated on that medium.

(11) *Violence.* Without a doubt, violence in the media has been the most researched content and effects area. Roughly 120 studies on television violence are evident for children and adolescents alone. Another 225 studies are listed under the general television violence heading, which means the title made no reference to children or adolescents. Furthermore, roughly 50 studies are classified under media violence, because the title makes no reference to a particular medium or subgroup. Thus, in the present collection nearly 400 references deal with violence and the media.

Fortunately, reviews of much of that research are available (e.g., 220, 1018, 1054, 1156, 1261, 1939, 2506) including reviews of the more recent Surgeon General's violence research (89, 313, 465, 466, 575, 798, 1230, 1846, 1939, 2141).

(12) *International.* In the international category of the subject index items have been included only if they made direct reference to a foreign country or a cross-cultural or international process. No attempt was made to categorize items based on point of publication. Thus, the international label refers to content being dealt with by the referred work, not its origin of publication.

Also, to reiterate, because there was no systematic search of the foreign literature, the references included here resulted from the search process described earlier.

The international citations emphasize cross-cultural process (550, 960, 962, 1274, 2015, 2091, 2165), the general role of the media in international communication (670, 817, 1306, 1524, 1806, 2087) and propaganda processes (1117, 1232, 1247, 1306). For references on the role of the media in national development, the reader is referred to the subject index under Media-National Development.

(B) Effects Processes

The following categorization of literature relates to mechanisms or processes by which effects take place. These studies are more concerned with how the results were produced than with the particular content or context constraints.

(1) *Arousal.* As an explanatory mechanism, arousal has received increasing attention. Various studies have posited the role of arousal in aggressive behavior (707, 945, 1692, 1693, 2315). Most notably, Tannenbaum has emphasized the generalized role of arousal in aggressive response, whether that arousal is generated by an aggressive stimulus or some other stimulus such as erotic material (2416, 2419, 2427). Zillman (2697, 2698, 2700, 2701) has pursued a similar line of inquiry. Within the literature on effects of pornography, arousal has most often been studied as an end result of exposure rather than an intervening variable (589, 600, 2174). In both cases, however, the proposition being pursued is that increased arousal produces an increased response and that the response will be linked to cue properties of the arousing stimulus and the available response situation.

(2) *Catharsis.* As a possible explanatory mechanism, catharsis has been studied most heavily in an aggression context (239, 243, 431, 939, 1229, 1431, 1712, 2315, 2702). The work of Feshbach (843–854) has been instrumental in attempting to discern the conditions under which exposure to aggressive content will decrease vs. increase the likelihood of

an aggressive response. Goranson (1017) provides a review of the two opposing views on catharsis. An informative and critical dialogue on the catharsis question is also available between Liebert, et al. (1571, 1567) and Feshbach and Singer (854, 852) steming from research done under the Surgeon General's program.

(3) *Identification*. The role of identification in effects processes has been studied most often among children (28, 42, 830, 831, 1262, 1767, 1868, 1887). The predominant contextual situation in these studies and others (721, 2421, 2479) has been aggressive or violent content. For a theoretic view with an aggressive slant, Bandura (130) provides a social learning theory of identification processes. Other identification studies have emphasized incidental learning (134), observational learning (1691), identification with an underdog (2223), the role of race in identification (457, 514, 721, 1868, 1874) and generalized community identity (314).

(4) *Imitation/Modeling*. In the imitation/modeling research, Bandura (128) provides a review of the conflicting theories, while Kuhn (1444) reviews imitation theory from a cognitive developmental perspective. Liebert (1557) reviews modeling and the media. The modeling research deals with processes of inhibition or disinhibition of particular responses (e.g., 1532, 1563, 1570, 2532, 2533, 2534, 2535). In most cases these involve processes of reinforcement (127, 141, 981, 1532, 1563, 2441, 2442) or self rewards (133, 136, 138, 981). Race has also been examined as a factor in the imitation/modeling process (1570, 1868, 1874, 1875, 2441). The most popular context for the study of imitative processes has again been aggression (eg., 126, 143, 144, 174, 175, 1141, 1207, 2179). However, the imitation of positive or prosocial behaviors is receiving increased attention (e.g., 16, 563, 903, 904, 1569, 2119, 2143; see Media Effects: Prosocial Behavior).

(5) *Learning*. The concept of learning is broad and pervades many of the previous categories. Since, in the present collection, no attempt was made to survey the literature on learning in general or instructional media, the learning references included relate directly to mass media. In most cases, the emphasis has been on children's learning from television (e.g., 560, 652, 756, 1331, 1356, 1442, 1888, 2007, 2217) and to a lesser extent other media, including film (66, 1691, 1729, 1785, 2070). As specific aspects of the learning process, works are evident on social learning (129, 130, 131, 140, 223, 1157), incidental learning (134, 1116, 1170), and observational learning (1521, 1558, 1691, 1927).

Television's potential as an educational medium has been recognized, perhaps too idealistically, from its introduction. Schramm, et. al. (2220)

provide an assessment of public attitudes toward educational television in the early 1960s and Lyle (1610) offers evidence concerning the question of why people do or do not watch educational television. In a theoretic view, Ide (1282) reviews the potentials and limitations of television as an educational medium. Overall, television as an instrument for adult education has not received a great deal of attention (25, 224, 321, 509, 927, 940). For those more specific details on instructional television, usually equated with classroom use, Schramm (2213) provides a review and overview of the research.

III. MEDIA CONTENT

(A) Presentation of People/Subgroups

(1) *The Aged.* Research on the image of elderly people in the media has shown a recent increase. In the past, the key emphasis in media studies was on use of available free time — as devoted to media in general (461, 1040, 1041, 1225, 2205) and more specifically to television (430, 628, 629, 630, 631, 632, 2185). The more recent emphasis is on the image or stereotype as present in advertising (890) or television programming (76, 1197, 1980).

(2) *Blacks.* Of the minority groups (including women), black images and preferences have been the most studied. In media advertising, the research emphasis has been on black images in magazine advertising (237, 553, 598, 837, 990, 2281). As an overview, Kassarjian (1335) characterizes the use of blacks in American advertising between the years 1946–1967.

Studies of reactions to blacks in advertisements extend the advertising content analytic studies. Here the questions have involved advertisement effects on product use or purchase (1850), black reactions to the ads (1032, 1981), white reactions to the ads (279), or comparisons of black vs. white reactions (151, 152).

In media content other than advertising the research emphasis has been on the image of blacks in TV programming (702, 705, 1220, 1705, 1900, 2065) and, to a much lesser extent, print fiction (166) and television newscasts (2066). Also, the image of blacks in motion pictures has received considerable attention (284, 316, 606, 1506, 1713, 1731, 1844, 2004).

(3) *Children (Sex-Role Images).* The research on children has focused primarily on media use patterns or on effects of particular types of content. Very few studies of the image of the child in media have been done. Of those available, the dominant focus of concern has been with

gender or sex-role stereotyping — on prime time TV (45, 755, 1588, 1708), in children's Saturday morning or children's programming in general (405, 406, 1920, 2378), on educational shows intended for children (694), in preschool picture books (769) or elementary school primers (403), or in advertising directed toward children (2511).

(4) *The Poor.* None of the research compiled dealt specifically with the image of the poor as presented in media. Studies of the poor have concentrated on media use patterns and the most effective ways to reach them (see Use Patterns).

(5) *Women.* A considerable amount of interest and research has been generated relative to the image of woman as portrayed in the media. Advertising in general (409, 1421, 1620) has been scrutinized and more specifically, magazine advertising (593, 1804) and television advertising (168, 594, 703).

The majority of research, however, has been concentrated on role images in television (730, 895, 1325, 1588, 1674, 1708, 1719, 1863, 1900, 2253, 2254, 2255). Other media aspects given less attention include treatment of women and feminism in newspapers (1800, 1826, 2031), women heroines in magazines (101), and women in television news and public affairs presentations (1864, 2385).

(B) Presentation of Activities/Behaviors/Events

(1) *Advertising.* Aside from the people stereotypes discussed above, the content analyses of advertising have tended to concentrate on children's commercials in general (158, 162, 164, 427, 728, 835, 1295) or on questions of merchandising and nutrition in children's commercials (505, 506, 507, 2489, 2490).

(2) *Mental Illness.* The media presentation of images related to mental illness, and the control of those images has received very little attention in the literature. Nunnally (1903, 1904) and Taylor (2430) offer early attempts to assess the imagery aspects, while Gerbner (966) and Gerbner and Tannenbaum (976) present early studies related to the control and regulation question.

(3) *Alcohol.* Very few content studies dealing with the imagery or use of alcohol exist in the literature. Pfantz (1983) presents an analysis of the image of alcohol in popular fiction between the years 1900–1904 and 1946–1950. Dillon (685, 686, 687) assesses how alcohol is dealt with on television relative to the NAB code and comparison of TV vs. real world alcohol consumption.

(4) *Drugs.* Grant money stemming from congressional concern over the problems of drug addiction and trafficking has stimulated several

recent studies in this area. One general question pursued has been the nature of imagery offered by commercial drug advertisements and their role in fostering a drug dependent mentality (167, 1185, 1326, 1793, 2382, 2613, 2643). Other studies have emphasized drug use or depiction in media content or programming (222, 1136, 1137, 2641, 2642).

(5) *Sexual Behavior.* Most of the content studies of sex related behaviors have been limited to pornographic materials. In these cases the emphasis has been on trafficking and distribution, rather than specific behaviors (1384, 2168) or availability and/or desirability of particular types of material (359, 1351, 1453). In the studies related to general mass media, the emphasis has been on types of content carried in the newspapers, popular magazines, or romance magazines (1934, 1935, 1936, 2344). Fuchs and Lyle (911) and Whitehead (2602) provide general characterizations of sex and violence in the popular media.

(6) *Music.* Content analytic studies of music have been of general interest because of the apparent relationship between music and cultural change (1172, 1820, 1843, 2616). Cole (551) provides a content analysis of the lyrics from popular songs of the 1960s. Courtship patterns are characterized by Carey (439) and Harton (1243), while Schwartz, et al. (2226) examine drug lyrics in popular music.

(7) *Occupational Roles.* The analysis of occupational roles has tended to focus on sex-role differences (see Children and Women), or roles portrayed by blacks (see Blacks). DeFleur (650) provides a general content analysis of occupational roles portrayed on television and Seggar (2255) assesses ethnic and sex representation in television roles. An obvious lack of attention to generalized occupational role images and presentations is evident.

(8) *Violence/Crime.* Again, the violence/crime area has been one of the most heavily researched media content areas (see subject index under Media-Violence; Television-Violence). The most substantial and consistent content analysis effort has been the work of Gerbner and colleagues (974, 975) in providing longitudinal analyses of violent acts, aggressor characteristics, victim characteristics, etc., occuring in network programming over the years 1967–1975. This effort has not been without controversy, and the literature offers major critical attacks (543, 544, 1937) and replies to those attacks (780, 781, 954). Other major characterizations of violence in American media are provided by Baker and Ball (109) Dominick (696), Greenberg (1054), and Simmons (2303).

IV. MEDIA USE

(A) Use Processes

The areas to follow deal with processes related to media use rather than particular patterns or subgroups.

(1) *Selective Exposure.* The process of selective exposure to media content has been recognized as an important variable in the understanding of media use and effects. Here, Katz (1339), McQuire (1648), and Sears (2244, 2245) provide reviews of the selective exposure research and attempt to place the process within the total context of media use, perception, interpretation and effects. Lowin (1596) provides a comparison of the approach vs. avoidance models of selective exposure. The importance of selective exposure to the understanding of use patterns has carried over to a variety of subareas, primarily associating use with attitudes toward the particular media content in question (680, 1038, 1385). Other areas of concern include entertainment programming such as "All in the Family" (2512), news (271, 2588), politics (84, 171, 1635), interpersonal influences (1374), and sex differences in selective exposure (2114).

(2) *Information Seeking.* The research emphasizing information seeking behavior provides evidence related to the concept of selective exposure (83, 484, 668, 715, 716, 2040). The orientations here include information seeking motivations (408, 716, 1596), the role played by attitude intensity (527), anxiety (267) and arousal (988) in the seeking process. Relative to particular areas, information seeking about political content is the best represented (e.g., 199, 1630). Overall, Dervin's (667, 668) work on generalized information seeking provides an important theory and model base from which to conceptualize the process.

(3) *Selective Perception.* The selective perception items in the current collection are media specific and do not reflect a search of the psychological literature under that concept. The emphasis reflects the role of ego-involvement in the selective perception process (1832), the communication process in general (2250), in educational processes (2457), in television viewing in general (219), and in specific entertainment television programs (2106).

(B) Media Functions

Research on media functions has shown a significant increase in recent years. Media scholars have recognized the potential explanatory power of looking at media use relative to the functions, needs, or gratifications that may be fulfilled through such use (647, 1493, 1605, 1893, 2673, 2674). As such, much of this emphasis has taken a uses and gratifications orientation with the medium of television as the center of attention (847, 1446, 2088).

The work of Katz, et al. (295, 1346, 1347, 1348, 1349) probably best exemplifies this body of research. The functional orientation to television has extended from an examination of basic need satisfaction (473, 1096, 1550), to political functions (1655), functions of television news (1621), and the functions of television following a major assassination (1805). Similar orientations have been extended to children (380, 1058, 1953) as well as adolescents (920, 921, 2404, 2568).

Another key area of interest has been that of the agenda setting function of the media. Here, McCombs and Shaw (1631) and McLeod, Becker, and Byrnes (1660) conceptualize and overview this research. Although studies in this area have assessed behavioral implications of agenda setting (262) and new approaches to the study of agenda setting (20), the primary area of interest has been the political arena (1644, 2456), including Watergate (2564).

(C) Media Use by Subgroups

(1) *Adolescents.* Of the subgroups to be studied relative to media usage, children and adolescents have received the greatest attention. Although some of the adolescent studies have concentrated on media in general (660, 1285, 1625, 2326), or reading ability and media use (1311), most have focused on television (e.g., 121, 482, 1068, 1659, 1871). Also, although content areas such as drug abuse (1793, 2466) and politics (412, 1754) have received attention, the dominant focus of concern has been the use of violent or aggressive media content (579, 658, 700, 1760, 1792, 2670, 1849). Considering the popularity and availability of radio among adolescents, relatively few studies have concentrated on this medium (698, 1211, 2568).

(2) *Children.* The media use habits of children have been more heavily studied than any other subgroup (102, 1587, 1764, 1845, 1851, 2151). Lyle and Hoffman (1611) provide a summary of the research on children's use of television and other media, which includes their own major research effort for the Surgeon General's violence studies. Again, television has been the primary medium of interest (1065, 1194, 1419, 1851, 1907, 2023, 2235, 2241, 2656). To a lesser extent, the usage patterns of the preschool child have also been examined (70, 832, 925).

Lyle and Hoffman (1612) and Stevenson (2380) provide major characterizations of television and the preschooler. Violence and the preschooler has also received limited attention (1411, 1932, 2379).

One factor that must be considered relative to children's usage patterns is the role of the parent in determining those patterns. These efforts have taken two primary lines, first being an assessment of the extent to which control is exercised (159, 160, 432, 2145) and the second being a more aggressive advocacy of control with specific recommendations (891, 1364, 2156).

(3) *Blacks.* Considering the amount of evidence noted above dealing with images of blacks in various media, relatively few studies of general usage patterns exist (39, 309, 441, 1068, 1335). Most commonly, these have involved urban poor blacks as noted in the work of Dervin, Greenberg, and colleagues (667, 669, 1067, 1068, 1069, 1072, 1085). Where evident, the emphasis has been on youth rather than adults (721, 871, 1625) or on use of specific types of content such as politics (1628) or news (1607).

(4) *The Aged.* Several studies of how the elderly use their leisure time in general have been conducted (597, 656, 1167, 1399, 1872, 2209, 2515). These studies provide a basis from which to consider the studies which examine the more specific role of the media in their lives (430, 1225, 2185, 2205). In a few cases, the emphasis has been on specific aspects of behavior such as the role of the media in social disengagement (461) or the use of media as substitute activity (1040, 1041). Although this research on media and the elderly includes television, it is the work of Davis which concentrates most specifically on that medium (628, 629, 630, 631, 632).

(5) *The Poor.* Most of the media research on the poor has dealt primarily with the urban poor (278, 667, 669, 1067, 1748). As noted above, this often involved a large component of low income blacks. A few studies have characterized the "working class" (308, 658, 660), or, as with the work of Williams (2623, 2624) and Greenberg (1068, 1069, 1072, 1085), provided comparisons of lower vs. middle socioeconomic groups. At another extreme from the urban poor, several studies of the rural poor in Appalachia provide an interesting contrast (708, 712, 713, 1308, 2369). For summary purposes, Wade (2520) offers a review of the research on media and the disadvantaged.

(6) *Women.* With the increased interest in women and the media, most of the studies have focused on the images of women — as noted above. In the present collection of citations, of the roughly 70 studies

dealing specifically with women, only one relates to media use patterns. In this case, television viewing preferences were related to women's self-concepts (1108).

V. MEDIA EFFECTS

The research in this section represents the end of the content-use-effects sequence. Thus, studies in the following subcategories are limited only to effects items. These usually take the form of experimental studies but may also be of a review or discussion nature.

Numerous references in the present collection are titled "effects" without further specification and thus may deal with a variety of effects areas — usually in a review fashion (e.g., 470, 1119, 1249, 1679, 1681, 1718, 2069, 2359). The more notable of such works would be those of Catton (469), Klapper (1390, 1391, 1392, 1394, 1397), Kline (1403), Larson (1485), Schramm and Roberts (2216), Tannenbaum and Greenberg (2422), and the review articles by Weiss (2570, 2571).

Other major effects areas of note include *learning* (918, 1047, 1698, 1785, 1927, 2005, 2166, 2468, 2600, 2620, 2668), media effects on *prejudice* (997, 1073, 1159, 1160, 1574, 2113, 2188, 2476, 2512), and generalized media effects on *public opinion* (52, 344, 750, 1281, 1889, 2109, 2393). Numerous generalized studies of media effects on *politics* are evident also (e.g., 474, 1119, 1121, 1289, 1627, 1084, 2110, 2135, 2246, 2259). Within the political area more specific effects studies concentrate on perceptions of candidates (554, 1209, 1642, 1919, 2685) and media effects on voting behavior (671, 991, 1066, 1470, 1476, 1756, 2135). More specific still are the studies of the effects of election day broadcasts on voting turnout and behavior (908, 909, 910, 1801, 2475). The effects of broadcasting political conventions (303, 382, 604, 1941, 2536) and television's general role in politics have also proven to be popular areas of study (e.g., 294, 298, 419, 590, 986, 1676, 1784, 1809, 1964, 2136, 2283, 2447, 2469, 2639, 2685).

Aside from the violence area, which is dealt with in the subgroups below, the antisocial effects area to command the most attention has been *pornography* (e.g., 534, 1254, 1350, 1833, 1835). The effects emphasized have ranged from general reactions to such content (82, 627, 2635), to specific arousal states produced by the content (589, 600, 707, 2174), and, more commonly, to the role of pornography in sexually deviant behavior (626, 1006, 1007, 1008, 1315, 2450, 2523). General discussion of the social consequences of the availability of pornographic materials provide a societal perspective (1710, 2636, 2651). The Pornography Commission report presents the results of the governmentally funded studies (565).

(A) Adolescents

The effects studies on adolescents have concentrated, for the most part, on the violence area. This holds for items classified under media in general (e.g., 658, 1130, 1186, 1190, 1191, 2227) and under television more specifically (e.g., 87, 480, 579, 1792, 2449). In most cases the dependent variable of interest has been aggressive behavior although to a lesser extent attitudes were of interest (700, 1760), verbal rather than physical aggression (2671), or desensitization to violence (733).

Relative to other areas, the number of effects studies is quite limited. The effects of advertising on adolescents has received some attention, as reflected in the work of Ward and colleagues (2544, 2545, 2546, 2552, 2556). Wade (2518) provides an exploratory look at creativity and the media, while Schramm (2208) overviews general media effects on adolescents.

(B) Children

(1) *Violence.* Many more effects studies are available for children than for adolescents. Again, violence tops the list with more than 100 effects-related studies (see the subject index under Children-media and Children-television-violence). For someone wishing to obtain a quick familiarity with this body of evidence, the natural place to start is with the report of the President's Advisory Commission on Television and Social Behavior (2506), followed by some of the excellent reviews available (e.g., 853, 1020, 1130, 1261, 1559, 1566, 1568, 2318).

(2) *Advertising.* The effects of advertising on children has sparked considerable recent controversy resulting in scholarly condemnations of puffery and economic exploitation (1740, 2008, 2545), legal and parental pursuit from groups like Action for Children's Television (9, 10, 11) and the Council on Children, Media, and Merchandising (504, 505), and governmental hearings (see 2008, 2490). The present collection of effects studies deal primarily with effects on attitudes and product preferences (79, 402, 998, 2074, 2129, 2130, 2265), or on the not so subtle pressure which children may exert on parental buying (1842, 2550). Again, the work of Ward and colleagues represents the most concerted research effort dealing with children and advertising (2542, 2544, 2546, 2551, 2555, 2556, 2557).

(3) *Learning.* Another key effects area of research on children relates to learning from the media (557, 559, 560, 1331, 2007). These studies have focused on a variety of areas including social and personality factors (756), the learning of political content (893), learning of occupational roles (646, 650, 652, 2577), generalized passive learning from television (1442), the learning of peripheral or incidental content (1116, 1170), and the effects of color vs. black and white television on learning (1356, 1357). Schramm, Lyle and Parker (2217) provide an early (dated 1961) review of children's learning from television, while the *Television and Social Behavior* volumes provide a collection of studies related to television violence and social learning (1848). Along this same line, Siegel (2287) reviews the research on the effects of media violence on social learning.

(4) *Modeling.* Related to learning but more behavioral in orientation is the research on modeling effects (1767, 2278, 2461, 2462). Here interest has varied from female models (1708), to race (721, 1053, 1570, 1868, 1874, 1875), social withdrawal (1908), the effects of adult vs. peer models (1410, 1875), and live vs. symbolic or mediated models (38, 1966, 2661). Liebert (1557) provides a review of the modeling research.

(5) *Language.* Several studies have examined the role of media in the language learning process (592, 1456, 1479, 1629, 1727). Aside from research on *Sesame Street* and *The Electric Company* (114, 115, 116, 117, 118, 119, 315, 1538, 2041, 2169), perhaps the most comprehensive look at the effects of television on language learning is reflected in the work of Sherrington (2273).

(D) The Aged/The Poor/Women

For each of these three areas the research has been predominantly content analytic in nature or studies of use patterns. No studies in the present collection could be classified as effects studies.

A

1 Abel, John D. "The Influence of Family Type on the Child's Orientation to Television Viewing." *Dissertation Abstracts International,* 1972, 72, 21: 384.

2 _____ . "Television and Children: A Selective Bibliography of Use and Effects." *Journal of Broadcasting,* 1969, 13, 1: 101-105. Limited to 75 unannotated references.

3 Abelson, H., Cohen, R., Heaton, E., and Suder, C. "National Survey of Public Attitudes Toward and Experience with Erotic Materials." In *Technical Report of the Commission on Obscenity and Pornography: National Survey* (vol. 6). Washington D.C.: Government Printing Office, 1971: 1-138.

4 Abrams, Mark. "Child Audiences for Television in Great Britain." *Journalism Quarterly,* 1956, 33, 1: 35-41.

5 _____ . *The Mass Media and Social Change in Britain.* London: Stresa, 1959.

6 Abruzzini, Pompeo. *Television and the Socialization of Children.* Rome: Radiotelevisione Italiana, 1974.

7 Academy of Television Arts and Sciences. "TV and Politics: A Forum." New York: Academy of Television Arts and Sciences, 1960.

8 *ACT Facts: A History and Chronology of Action for Children's Television.* Newtonville, Mass: Action for Children's Television, 1975.

9 _____ . *The First National Symposium on the Effect of Television Programming and Advertising on Children.* New York: Avon, 1971.

10 _____ . *Second National Symposium on Children and Television Transcript.* Newtonville, Mass: Action for Children's Television, 1971.

11 _____ . "Who is Talking to Our Children?" *Third National Symposium on Children and Television.* Newtonville, Mass.: Action for Children's Television, 1972.

12 Adams, Don P. "Reactions to U.S. Magazines Among Latin American Students." *Journalism Quarterly,* 1969, 46, 1: 142-144.

13 Adams, J. B. Mullen, J. J., and Wilson, H. M. "Diffusion of a Minor Foreign Affairs News Event." *Journalism Quarterly,* 1969, 46: 545-561.

14 Adams, J. Stacy. "Plan 2: A Descriptive and Analytic Study of the Secondary, Remote Effects of Television." In L. Arons, M.A. May (eds.) *Television and Human Behavior: Tomorrow's Research in Mass Communication.* New York: Appleton-Century-Crofts, 1963: 29-30.

15 Addis, Barnett. "Media Credibility: An Experimental Comparison of the Effects of Film, Audio Tape and Written Communications on Beliefs in the Existence of Unusual Phenomena." *Dissertation Abstracts International,* 1970, 31 (5-A): 2491.

16 Adelson, R., Liebert, R. M., Poulos, R. W., and Herskovitz, A. "A Modelling Film to Reduce Children's Fear of Dental Treatment." *International Association of Dental Research Abstracts,* 1972: 114.

17 Adler, R. "Understanding Television: An Overview of the Literature on the Medium as a Social and Cultural Force." In D. Cater (ed.), *Television as a Social Force: New Approaches to TV Criticism.* New York: Praeger, 1975: 23-48.

18 _____ and Cater, D. *Approaches to Television Criticism.* New York: Praeger, 1975.

19 Agne, R. F. "Plan 14: The Principle of Television Orientation." In L. Arons and M. A. May (eds.), *Television and Human Behavior: Tomorrow's Research in Mass Communication.* New York: Appleton-Century-Crofts, 1963: 230-243.

20 Agnir, F. "Testing New Approaches to Agenda-Setting: A Replication and Extension." In M. McCombs and G. Stone (eds.), *Studies in Agenda-Setting.* Syracuse: Newhouse Communications Research Center, Syracuse University, 1975.

21 Agranoff, Robert. *Elections and Electoral Behavior: A Bibliography.* DeKalb, Ill.: Center for Governmental Studies, Northern Illinois University, 1972.

22 Aguilera, J. de. "Características Distintivas del Público de la Televisión" [Distinctive Characteristics of the Television Audience]. *Revista Española de la Opinión Pública,* 1972, 28: 121-129.

23 Aitchison, D. R. "The Measurement of the Television Viewing of Individuals." *Commentary,* 1960, 2, 2: 7-10.

24 Akers, R. L. *Deviant Behavior: A Social Learning Approach.* Belmont, Calif.: Wadsworth, 1973.

25 Akutsu, Y. "An Experimental Study of the Long-time Effects of an Adult Educational Television Program on Attitude Changes." *Kyoiku,* 1962, 17: 188-200.

26 _____. "Opinion Leadership in Children's Television Behavior." In T. Furu (ed.), *The Function of Television for Children and Adolescents.* Tokyo: Sophia University, 1971: 270-281.

27 Alberoni, Francesco. "Society, Culture and Mass Communication Media." *Ikon,* 1966, 19: 29-62.

28 Albert, R. S. "The Role of the Mass Media and the Effect of Aggressive Film Content Upon Children's Aggressive Responses and Identification Choices." *Genetic Psychology Monographs,* 1957, 55: 221-285.

29 _____ and Meline, Harry G. "The Influence of Social Status on the Uses of Television." *Public Opinion Quarterly,* 1958, 22, 2: 145-151.

30 Allen, C. L. "Photographing the T.V. Audience." *Journal of Advertising,* 1965, 5:2-8.

31 Alexander, Herbert E. "Broadcasting and Politics." In M. K. Jennings and L. H. Ziegler (eds.), *The Electoral Process.* Englewood Cliffs, N.J.: Prentice-Hall, 1972.

32 _____. "Communications and Politics: The Media and the Message." *Law & Contemporary Problems,* 1969, 34, 2: 255-277.

33 _____. "Political Broadcasting in 1968." *Television Quarterly,* 1970, 9, 2: 41-50.

34 Alexander, Yonah. *The Role of Communication in the Middle East Conflict: Ideological and Religious Aspects.* New York: Praeger, 1974.

35 Allardt, Erik and Rokkan, Stein. *Mass Politics: Studies in Political Sociology.* New York: Free Press, 1970.

36 Allen, Irving L. "Social Relations and the Two-Step Flow: A Defense of the Tradition." *Journalism Quarterly,* 1969, 46: 492-498.

37 _____ and Colfax, J. David. "The Diffusion of News on LBJ's March 31 Decision." *Journalism Quarterly,* 1968, 45, 2: 321-326.

38 Allen, M. K. and Liebert, R. M. "Effects of Live and Symbolic Deviant Modeling Cues on Adoption of Previous Learned Standard." *Journal of Personality and Social Psychology,* 1969, 11: 253-260.

39 Allen, Thomas H. "Mass Media Use Patterns in a Negro Ghetto." *Journalism Quarterly,* 1968, 45, 3: 525-527.

40 Allouche-Benayoun, B. Joelle. "The Influence of Moving Pictures on Children and Young People: French Research Activities from 1970-1975." In *Television and Socialization Processes in the Family.* Proceedings of the Prix Jeunesse Seminar, 1975: 137-157.

41 Alloway, Lawrence. *Violent America: The Movies 1946-1964.* Distributed by New York Graphics Society, Greenwich, Conn., 1971.

42 Almers, Marie. "Children's Identification with TV-Programs." Stockholm: Sverges Radio, Audience and Programme Research Department, no. 94, 1970.

43 Alper, William S. and Leidy, Thomas R. "The Impact of Information Transmission Through Television." *Public Opinion Quarterly,* 1969, 33, 4: 556-562.

44 Alphandrez, G. and Rousselet, J. "La Television et la Famille" (Television and the Family). *Hygiene Mentale,* 1961, 60: 80-95.

45 AlRoy, Phyllis, et al. "Channeling Children: Sex Stereotyping in Prime-Time TV: An Analysis." Princeton, N.J.: Women on Words and Images, 1975.

46 Aman, Ingrid and Granholm, Birgitta. "Filmvald och Aggressivitet. En Experimentell Studie av Filmpaverkan, TV-bio-vanor och Personlighetsdrag" [Filmed Violence and Aggressiveness: An Experimental Study on Film Impact, TV-movie-going Habits and Personality Traits]. University of Stockholm, Department of Psychology, 1973.

47 The American Institute for Political Communication. *The Credibility Problem.* Washington, D.C.: The American Institute for Political Communication, 1972.

48 _____. *Effects of Local Media Monopoly on the Mass Mind.* Washington, D.C.: The American Insitutue for Political Communication, 1971.

49 _____. *Evolution of Public Attitudes Toward the Mass Media during an Election Year.* Washington, D.C., The American Institute for Political Communication, 1969.

50 _____. *'Liberal Bias' as a Factor in Network Television News Reporting: A Special Report Based on the Monitoring of Three Major Network Evening News Shows During the 1972 Primary Election Campaign Period.* Washington, D.C.: American Institute for Political Communication, 1972.

51 _____. *Media Monopoly and Politics.* Washington, D.C.: American Institute for Political Communication, 1973.

52 _____. *Media. and Non-Media Effects on the Formation of Public Opinion.* Washington, D.C.: American Institute for Political Communication, 1969.

53 _____. *The 1968 Campaign: Anatomy of A Crucial Election.* Washington, D.C.: American Institute for Political Communication, 1970. Assessed attitudes during the 1968 Presidential Campaign in Milwaukee, Wisconsin toward presidential candidates, state-level candidates in the U.S. Congress, and those running for the governorship. Studied the forces that affect attitudes toward candidates and how the campaign issues change over time.

54 _____. *The 1972 Presidential Campaign: Nixon Administration–Mass Media Relationship.* Washington, D.C.: American Institute for Political Communication, 1974.

55 _____. *The 1974 Campaign: Urban and Rural Attitudes Toward the Media, Issues and Candidates.* Washington, D.C.: American Institute for Political Communication, 1975.

56 Ammassari, Elke. "Television Influence and Cultural Innovativeness: A Causal Approach." Doctoral Dissertation, Michigan State University, 1972.

57 Amoroso, D.M., et al. "An Investigation of Behavioral, Psychological, and Physiological Reactions to Pornographic Stimuli." In *Technical Report of The Commission on Obscenity and Pornography: Erotica and Social Behavior* (vol. 8). Washington, D.C.: Government Printing Office, 1971: 1-40.

58 Anast, Philip. "Differential Movie Appeals as Correlates of Attendance." *Journalism Quarterly,* 1967, 44, 1: 86-90.

59 _____. "Personality Determinants of Mass Media Preferences." *Journalism Quarterly,* 1966, 43, 4: 729-732.

60 Ancona, L. "Il Film Come Elemento della Dinamica dell' Aggressivita" [Motion Pictures as Elements in the Dynamics of Aggressivity]. *Contributi dell' Istituto di Psicologia,* 1967, 28: 19-29.

61 _____. and Berkini, M. "Effetto di Scarica dell' Aggressivita per Film a Forte Tensione Emotiva." [The Effect of Aggressivity Discharge Through a Film with Strong Emotional Tension]. *Contributi dell' Istituto di Psicologia,* 1967, 28: 1-18.

62 Andersen, Martin P. "A Mid-Century Survey of Books on Communication." *Journal of Communication,* 1964, 14, 4: 202-214.

63 Anderson, Bo. "Opinion Influentials and Political Opinion Formation in 4 Swedish Communities." *International Social Science Journal,* 1962, 14, 2: 320-337.

64 Anderson, James A. and Meyer, Timothy P. "Functionalism and the Mass Media." *Journal of Broadcasting,* 1975, 19, 1: 11-22.

65 Andreas, Carol R. "War Toys and the Peace Movement." *Journal of Social Issues,* 1969, 25, 1: 83-100.

66 Andrews, Charles R. "The Effect of Short-Term Interruptions Upon Factual Acquisition From Motion Picture Films Among Intermediate Elementary School Pupils." *Dissertation Abstracts International,* 1971, 32(1-A): 109.

67   Antoine, S. and Oulif, J. "La Sociologie Politique et la Television." [Political Sociology and Television]. *Revue Francaise de Science Politique,* 1962, 12: 129-144.

68   Appell, Clara T. "Television's Impact Upon Middle Class Family Life." Doctoral Dissertation, Columbia University, 1959.

69   _____. "Television's Impact Upon Middle Class Family Life." *Teachers College Record,* 1960, 61: 265-274.

70   _____. "Television Viewing and the Preschool Child." *Marriage and Family Living,* 1963, 25, 3: 311-318.

71   Arlen, Michael J. *Living-Room War.* New York: Viking Press, 1969.

72   Arndt, Johan. "A Test of the Two-Step Flow in Diffusion of a New Product." *Journalism Quarterly,* 1968, 45, 3: 457-465.

73   Arnoff, Joel. *Psychological Needs and Cultural Systems: A Case Study.* Princeton, N.J.: Van Nostrand, 1967.

74   Arnold, A. *Violence and Your Child.* New York: Regnery, 1969. Reviews the violence problem including the history of government hearings. Emphasizes the role of the family in combating potential negative effects of television violence.

75   Aronfreed, Justin Manuel. *Conduct and Conscience: The Socialization of Internalized Control Over Behavior.* New York: Academic Press, 1968. Thorough review of the socialization process with a behavioral emphasis.

76   Aronoff, Cliff. "Old Age and Prime Time." *Journal of Communication,* 1974, 24, 4: 86-88.

77   Arons, Leon and May, Mark A., eds. *Television and Human Behavior: Tomorrow's Research in Mass Communication.* New York: Appleton-Century Crofts, 1963. A collection of award winning research proposals stemming from a Television Bureau of Advertising contest. Almost all proposals emphasize media effects.

78   Arora, S. K. and Lasswell, H. D. *Political Communication.* New York: Holt, Rinehart, and Winston, 1969.

79   Associates for Research in Behavior, Inc. "The Effect of Child-Directed Television Advertising on Children: An Analysis of the Charges and a Conceptualization." Washington, D.C. Consumer Research Institute, Inc., 1972.

80   Association for Childhood Education International. *Children and T.V.: Television's Impact on the Child.* Washington, D.C.: ACE, 1966.

81   Astin, Helen S., ed. "Sex Roles: A Research Bibliography." Washington, D.C.: Government Printing Office, 1975.

82   Athanasiou, R. and Shauer, P. "Correlates of Heterosexuals' Reactions to Pornography." *Journal of Sex Research,* 1971, 7, 4: 298.

83   Atkin, Charles K. "Anticipated Communication and Mass Media Information-Seeking." *Public Opinion Quarterly,* 1972, 36, 7: 188-199.

84   _____ . "How Imbalanced Campaign Coverage Affects Audience Exposure Patterns." *Journalism Quarterly,* 1971, 48, 2: 235-244.

85 _____ . "The Impact of Political Poll Reports on Candidate and Issue Preference." *Journalism Quarterly,* 1969, 46, 3: 515-521.

86 _____. "Instrumental Utilities and Information Seeking." In P. Clarke (ed.), *New Models for Mass Communication Research.* Beverly Hills, Sage, 1973: 205-242.

87 _____ . "The Relationship Between Television Violence Viewing Patterns and Aggressive Behavior in Two Samples of Adolescents." *Dissertation Abstracts International,* 1972, 32(12-AO): 7201.

88 Atkin, Charles K. and Greenberg, B. S. "Public Television and Political Socialization." Department of Communication, Michigan State University, March 1974.

89 Atkin, Charles K., Murray, J. P., and Nayman, O. B. "The Surgeon General's Research Program on Television and Social Behavior: A Review of Empirical Findings." *Journal of Broadcasting,* 1972, 16, 1: 21-36.

90 _____ . *Television and Social Behavior; An Annotated Bibliography of Research Focusing on Television's Impact on Children.* Washington, D.C.: Government Printing Office, 1971. A collection of roughly 300 annotated and 250 unannotated references. The search period extends through January 1971.

91 Atkin, Charles K., Bowen, L., Nayman, O.B., and Sheinkopf, K. G. "Quality versus Quantity in Televised Political Ads." *Public Opinion Quarterly,* 1973, 37, 2: 209-224.

92 Atwood, L. Erwin. "Perception of Television Program Preferences Among Teenagers and Their Parents." *Journal of Broadcasting,* 1968, 12, 4: 377-389.

93 _____ and Sanders, K. R. "Perception of Information Sources and Likelihood of Split Ticket Voting." *Journalism Quarterly,* 1975, 52: 421-428.

94 Auerback, E. *Mimesis: The Representation of Reality in Western Literature.* Princeton, N.J.: Princeton University Press, 1953.

95 Augedal, E. "Patterns in Mass Media Use and Other Activities." *Acta Sociologica,* 1972, 15: 145-156.

96 The Australian Royal Commission on Television. "Control of Political Broadcasting in English-Speaking Countries." *Journal of Broadcasting,* 1958, 2, 2: 123-136.

B

97 Back, K. W. Plan 1. Prominence and Audience Structure: The Linkage Between Mass Media and Interpersonal Communication." In L. Arons and M. A. May (eds.), *Television and Human Behavior: Tomorrow's Research in Mass Communication.* New York: Appleton-Century-Crofts, 1968, 14-28.

98 Bagdikian, Ben H. *The Information Machines; Their Impact on Men and the Media.* New York: Harper & Row, 1971.

99 _____ . "TV, the President's Medium." *Columbia Journalism Review,* 1962, 1, 1: 34-38.

100 Bailey, George A. "The Public, the Media, and the Knowledge Gap." *The Journal of Environmental Education,* 1971, 2, 4: 3-8.

101 Bailey, Margaret. "The Women's Magazine Short Story Heroine in 1957 and 1967." *Journalism Quarterly,* 1969, 46, 2: 364-366.

102 Bailyn, Lotte. "Mass Media and Children: A Study of Exposure Habits and Cognitive Effects." *Psychological Monographs: General and Applied,* 1959, 73 1: 1-48.

103 Baird, J. W. *The Mythical World of Nazi War Propaganda, 1939–1945.* Minneapolis: University of Minnesota Press, 1975.

104 Baker, C. *Talking About the Mass Media.* London: Wayland, 1973.

105 Baker, J. W. "The Effects of Four Types of Vicarious Aggression on Physiological and Psychological Arousal." *Dissertation Abstracts,* 1967, 28 (5-BO): 2132-2133.

106 _____ and Schaie, K. W. "Effects of Agressing 'Alone' or 'With Another' on Physiological and Psychological Arousal." *Journal of Personality and Social Psychology,* 1969, 12: 80-86.

107 Baker, R. K. and Ball, S. J. eds. *Mass Media Hearings.* A Report to the National Commission on the Causes and Prevention of Violence (vol. 9A). Washington, D.C.: Government Printing Office, 1969. Presents the testimony of 24 major researchers, policy makers, and network executives concerning media violence.

108 _____ . *Mass Media and Violence.* A Report to the National Commission on the Causes and Prevention of Violence (vol. 9). Washington, D.C.: Government Printing Office, 1969. Contains background summaries of the various aspects of the violence problem, as well as conceptual papers by major researchers covering aspects of effects, functions, and policy.

109 _____ . "The Two Worlds of Violence: Television and Reality." In R. K. Baker and S. J. Ball (eds.) *Violence and the Media.* A staff report to the National Commission on the Causes and Prevention of Violence. Washington, D.C.: Government Printing Office, 1969: 363-369.

110 Baker, S. S. *The Permissible Lie: The Inside Truth about Advertising.* Cleveland: World Publishing, 1968.

111 Baldwin, Thomas and Lewis, Colby. "Violence in Television: The Industry Looks at Itself." In G. A. Comstock and E. A. Rubinstein (eds.), *Television and Social Behavior: Media Content and Control* (vol. 1). Washington, D.C.: Government Printing Office, 1972: 209-373.

112 Baldwin, Thomas and Surlin, Stuart H., "The Contribution of the Visual Element in Television Commercials." *Journalism Quarterly,* 1969, 46, 3: 607-610.

113 Ball, Richard A. and Simoni, Joseph J. "Can We Learn from Medicine Hucksters?" *Journal of Communication,* 1975, 25, 3: 174-181.

114 Ball, S. J. and Bogatz, G. A. "The First Year of Sesame Street: An Evaluation." Princeton, N.J.: Educational Testing Service, 1970.

115 _____ . "Reading with Television: An Evaluation of the Electric Company." Princeton, N.J.: Educational Testing Service, 1973.

116 _____ . "Research on Sesame Street: Some Implications for Compensatory Education." Princeton, N.J.: Educational Testing Service, 1972.

117 _____ . "Sesame Street: A Continuing Evaluation." New York: Teachers College Press, 1972.

118 _____ . "Sesame Street Summative Research: Some Implications." Washington, D.C.: ERIC Document Reproduction Service, 1972.

119 _____ . "Summative Research of Sesame Street: Implications for the Study of Preschool Children." In A. D. Pick (ed), *Minnesota Symposia on Child Psychology* (vol. 6). Minneapolis: University of Minnesota Press, 1972.

120 Ball-Rokeach, S. J. "Values and Violence: A Test of the Subculture of Violence Thesis." *American Sociological Review,* 1973, 38: 736-749.

121 Balogh, J. K. "Attitudinal and Preferential Factors of Selected Male High School Students With Respect To Television Viewing." *Audio-Visual Communication Review,* 1958, 6: 203-206.

122 _____ . "Television Viewing Habits of High School Boys." *Educational Research Bulletin,* 1969, 38: 66-71.

123 Balon, Robert E. and Philport, Joseph C. "Candidate Image in a Broadcast Debate." *Journal of Broadcasting,* 1975, 19, 2: 181-193.

124 Balsley, Daisy. "A Descriptive Study of References Made to Negroes and Occupational Roles Represented by Negroes in Selected Mass Media." Doctoral Dissertation, University of Denver, 1959.

125 Bandura, A. *Aggression: A Social Learning Analysis.* Englewood Cliffs, N.J.: Prentice-Hall. 1973. Covers theories of aggression, origins, instigators, maintaining conditions, and modification and control conditions.

126 _____ . "Imitation of Film-Mediated Aggressive Models." *Journal of Abnormal and Social Psychology,* 1963, 66: 3-11.

127 _____ . "Influence of Model's Reinforcement Contingencies on the Acquisition of Imitative Responses." *Journal of Personality and Social Psychology,* 1965, 1: 589-595.

128 _____ . *Psychological Modeling: Conflicting Theories.* Chicago: Aldine-Atherton, 1971.

129 _____ . *Social Learning Theory.* New York: General Learning Press, 1971.

130 _____ . "Social Learning Theory of Identificatory Processes." In D. A. Goslin (ed.), *Handbook of Socialization Theory and Research.* Chicago: Rand McNally, 1969: 213-262.

131 _____ . "Social Learning Through Imitation." In M. R. Jones (ed.), *Nebraska Symposium on Motivation.* Lincoln: University of Nebraska Press, 1962: 211-274.

132 _____ . "Vicarious Processes: A Case of No-Trial Learning." In L. Berkowitz (ed.), *Advances in Experimental Social Psychology* (vol. 2), New York: Academic Press, 1965: 1-55. Demonstrates that children can learn novel behaviors even if not practiced immediately after exposure and not rewarded.

133 _____ . "Vicarious and Self-Reinforcement Processes." In R. Glaser (ed.), *The Nature of Reinforcement.* New York: Academic Press, 1971: 228-278.

134 Bandura, A. and Huston, A. C. "Identification as a Process of Incidental Learning." *Journal of Abnormal and Social Psychology,* 1961, 63: 311-318.

135 Bandura, A. and Jeffery, R. W. "Role of Symbolic Coding and Rehearsal Processes in Observational Learning." *Journal of Personality and Social Psychology,* 1972, 25: 122-130.

136 Bandura, A. and Kupers, D. J. "Transmission of Patterns of Self-Reward Through Modeling." *Journal of Abnormal and Social Psychology,* 1963, 69: 1-9.

137 Bandura, A. and Menlove, F. "Factors Determining Vicarious Extinction of Avoidance Behavior Through Symbolic Modeling." *Journal of Personality and Social Psychology,* 1968, 8: 99-108.

138 Bandura, A., and Mischel, W. "Modification of Self-Imposed Delay of Reward Through Exposure to Live and Symbolic Models." *Journal of Personality and Social Psychology,* 1965, 2: 698-705.

139 Bandura, A. and Walters, R. H. "Aggression," In H. Stevenson (ed.), *Child Psychology 62nd Yearbook of the National Society for the Study of Education,* (part I). Chicago: University of Chicago Press, 1963: 364-415.

140 _____ . *Social Learning and Personality Development.* New York: Holt, Rinehart and Winston, 1963. Thorough discussion of learning via direct observation vs. film vs. television. Reinforcement, control, and modification strategies are included.

141 Bandura, A., Grusec, J. and Menlove, F. "Observational Learning as a Function of Symbolization and Incentive Set." *Child Development,* 1966, 37: 499-506.

142 _____ . "Vicarious Extinction of Avoidance Behavior." *Journal of Personality and Social Psychology,* 1967, 5: 16-23.

143 Bandura, A., Ross, D., and Ross, S. A. "Imitation of Film-Mediated Aggressive Models." *Journal of Abnormal Social Psychology,* 1963, 66: 3-11.

144 _____ . "Transmission of Aggression Through Imitation of Aggressive Models." *Journal of Abnormal and Social Psychology,* 1961, 63: 575-582.

145 _____ . "Vicarious Reinforcement and Imitative Learning." *Journal of Abnormal and Social Psychology,* 1963, 67: 601-697.

146 Banning, Evelyn I. "Social Influences on Children and Youth." *Review of Educational Research,* 1955, 25: 36-47.

147 Barach, Jeffery A. "Advertising Effectiveness and Risk in the Consumer Decision Process." *Journal of Marketing Research,* 1969, 6, 3: 314-320.

148 Baran, Paul. "On the Impact of the New Communications Media Upon Social Values." *Law & Contemporary Problems,* 1969, 34, 2: 244-254.

149 Baran, S. J. "Prosocial and Antisocial Television Content and Modeling by High and Low Self-Esteem Children." *Journal of Broadcasting,* 1974, 18, 4: 481-495.

150 _____ . "TV and Social Learning in the Institutionalized MR." *Mental Retardation,* 1973, 11: 36-38.
151 Barban, Arnold M. and Cundiff, Edward. "Negro and White Response to Advertising Stimuli," *Journal of Marketing Research,* 1964, 1: 53-56.
152 _____ and Grunbaum, Werner F. "A Factor Analytic Study of Negro and White Responses to Advertising Stimuli," *Journal of Applied Psychology,* 1965, 49, 4: 274-279.
153 Barber, W. H. *The Affective Domain: A Resource Book for Media Specialists.* Washington, D.C.: Gryphon House, 1972.
154 Barclay, W. D., Doub, R. M., and McMurtrey, L. T. "Recall of TV Commercials by Time and Program Slot." *Journal of Advertising Research,* 1965, 5, 2: 41-47.
155 Barcus, F. E. "Communications Content: Analysis of the Research, 1900-1958," Doctoral Dissertation, University of Illinois, 1966.
156 _____ . "Concerned Parents Speak Out on Children's Television." Newtonville, Mass.: Action for Children's Television, 1973.
157 _____ ."A Content Analysis of Trends in Sunday Comics 1900-1959." *Journalism Quarterly,* 1961, 38, 2: 171-180.
158 _____ . "Network Programming and Advertising in the Saturday Children's Hours: A June and November Comparison." Boston: Action for Children's Television, 1972.
159 _____ ."Parental Control of Children's Television Viewing." New York: Office of Social Research, Columbia Broadcasting System, 1968.
160 _____ . "Parental Influence on Children's Television." *Television Quarterly,* 1969, 8: 63-73.
161 _____ . "Romper Room: An Analysis." Newtonville, Mass. Action for Children's Television, 1971.
162 _____ . "Saturday Children's Television: A Report of Television Programming and Advertising on Boston Commercial Television." Action for Children's Television, 1971.
163 _____ . "Saturday's 'Kidvid Ghetto'." *The Progressive,* June 1972: 33-37.
164 _____ . "Television in the Afternoon Hours: A Study of Programming and Advertising for Children on Independent Stations Across the United States." Newtonville, Mass: Action for Children's Television, 1975.
165 _____ . "Weekend Commercial Children's Television – 1975" Newtonville, Mass: Action for Children's Television, 1975.
166 _____ and Levin, J. "Role Distance in Negro and Minority Fiction." *Journalism Quarterly,* 1966, 43, 4: 709-714.
167 Barcus, F.E., Goldstein, J.M. and Pinto, S.K. "Drug Advertising on Television." In National Commission on Marihuana and Drug Abuse, *Drug Use in America: Problem in Perspectives: Social Responses to Drug Use* (vol. 2). Washington, D. C.: Government Printing Office, 1973: 623-668.

168 Bardwick, Judith M. and Schumann, Suzanne I. "Portrait of American Men & Women in TV Commercials." *Psychology,* 1967, 44: 18-23. Reveals dominant themes such as seduction, omnipotent status, unlimited money, acceptance, and admiration.

169 Barger, Harold M. "Images of Political Authority in Four Types of Black Newspapers." *Journalism Quarterly,* 1973, 50, 4: 645-651.

170 Barghouti, Shawki M. "The Role of Communication in Jordan's Rural Development." *Journalism Quarterly,* 1974, 51, 3: 418-424.

171 Barlett, Dorothy L., Drew, Pamela B., Fahle, Eleanor G., and Watts, William A., "Selective Exposure to a Presidential Campaign Appeal." *Public Opinion Quarterly,* 1974, 38, 2: 264-270.

172 Barmash, Isadore. *The World is Full of IT: How We are Oversold, Overinfluenced, and Overwhelmed by the Communications Manipulators.* New York: Delacorte Press, 1974.

173 Barnes, Arthur M. "Research in Radio and Television News–1947-1957." *Journalism Quarterly,* 1957, 34, 3: 323-332.

174 Baron, R. A. "Exposure to an Aggressive Model and Apparent Probability of Retaliation From the Victim as Determinants of Adult Aggressive Behavior." *Journal of Experimental Social Psychology,* 1971, 7:343-355.

175 _____. "Reducing the Influence of an Aggressive Model: The Restraining Effects of Discrepant Modeling Cues." *Journal of Personality and Social Psychology,* 1971, 20: 240-245.

176 Barrow, L. C. "Factors Related to Attention to the First Kennedy-Nixon Debate." *Journal of Broadcasting,* 1961, 5, 3: 229-238.

177 _____ and Westley, B.H. "Exploring the News: An Experiment on the Relative Effectiveness of Radio and TV Versions of a Children's News Programme." In W. Schramm (ed.), *The Impact of Educational Television.* Urbana: University of Illinois Press, 1960: 143-150.

178 _____. "Intelligence and the Effectiveness of Radio and Television." *Audio-Visual Communication Review,* 1975, 7: 293-308.

179 _____. "Television Effects: A Summary of the Literature and Proposed General Theory." Madison: University of Wisconsin Laboratory Bulletin No. 9, 1958.

180 Barry, Jackson G. *Dramatic Structure: The Shaping of Experience.* Berkeley: University of California Press, 1970.

181 Barry, Thomas E. and Hansen, Richard W. "How Race Affects Children's TV Commercials." *Journal of Advertising Research,* 1973, 13, 5: 63-67.

182 Basehart, John R. and Bostrom, Robert N. "Credibility of Source and of Self in Attitude Change." *Journalism Quarterly,* 1972, 49: 742-745.

183 Bassett, H. T., Cowden, J. E., and Cohen, M.F. "The Audiovisual Viewing Habits of Selected Subgroups of Delinquents." *Journal of Genetic Psychology,* 1968, 112: 37-41.

184 Battin, Tom C. "The Use of the Diary and Survey Method Involving the Questionnaire-Interview Technique to Determine the Impact of Television on School Children in Regard to Viewing Habits and Formal and Informal Education." *Dissertation Abstracts,* 1952, 12: 343.

185 Bauer, R. A. "The Audience." In I. Pool, et al. (eds.), *Handbook of Communication.* Chicago: Rand McNally, 1973: 141-152.

186 _____ . "The Initiative of the Audience." *Journal of Advertising Research,* 1963, 3: 2-7.

187 _____ . "The Obstinate Audience: The Influence Process from the Point of View of Social Communication." *American Psychologist,* 1964, 19: 319-328.

188 _____ and Bauer, A. H. "American Mass Society and Mass Media." *Journal of Social Issues,* 1960, 16, 3: 3-66.

189 Bauer, R. A. and Cox, D. F. "Plan 8. Rational versus Emotional Communications: A New Approach." In L. Arons and M. A. May (eds.), *Television and Human Behavior: Tomorrow's Research in Mass Communication.* New York: Appleton-Century-Crofts, 1963: 140-154.

190 Bauer, R. A. and Greyser, Stephen A. "Advertising in America: The Consumer View." Boston: Graduate School of Business Administration, Harvard University, 1968.

191 Bauer, R. A. and Zimmerman, C. "The Effect of an Audience Upon What is Remembered." *Public Opinion Quarterly,* 1956, 20: 238-248.

192 Baxter, Dick H. "Interpersonal Contact and Exposure to Mass Media During a Presidential Campaign." *Dissertation Abstracts,* 1952, 12: 225.

193 Baxter, Leslie A. and Bittner, John R., "High School and College Student Perceptions of Media Credibility." *Journalism Quarterly,* 1974, 51, 3: 517-520.

194 Baxter, William S. "The Mass Communication Behavior of Young People in Grades 5, 7, 9 and 11 in the Des Moines Public Schools in 1958 as Compared with the Mass Communication Behavior of an Equivalent Group in Des Moines before the Advent of Television." Doctoral Dissertation, University of Iowa, 1960.

195 _____ . "The Mass Media and Young People." *Journal of Broadcasting,* 1961, 5, 1: 49-58. Compares the reading, listening, and movie-going behaviors of children before and after the advent of television.

196 Bechtel, Robert B., Achelpohl, Clark, and Akers, Rober. "Correlates Between Observed Behavior and Questionnaire Responses on T.V. Viewing." In E. A. Rubinstein, G. A. Comstock, and J. P. Murray (eds.), *Television and Social Behavior: Television in Day-to-Day Life: Patterns of Use* (vol. 4). Washington, D. C.: Government Printing Office, 1972: 274-344.

197 Becker, G. "Causal Analysis in R-R Studies: Television Violence and Aggression." *American Psychologist,* 1972, 27: 967-969.

198 Becker, Jerome D. and Preston, Ivan L. "Media Usage and Political Activity." *Journalism Quarterly,* 1969, 46, 1: 129-134.

199 Becker, Lee B. and Doolittle, J. C. "How Repetition Affects Evaluations of and Information Seeking about Candidates." *Journalism Quarterly,* 1975, 52: 611-617.

200 Becker, Samuel L. "The Impact of the Mass Media on Society." In R. V. Wiman and W. C. Meierhenry (eds.), *Educational Media: Theory Into Practice.* Columbus, Ohio: Charles E. Merrill, 1969: 27-54.

201 _____ . "Presidential Power: The Influence of Broadcasting." *Quarterly Journal of Speech,* 1961, 47, 1: 10-18.

202 _____ . "Reaction Profiles: Studies of Methodology." *Journal of Broadcasting,* 1960, 4, 3: 253-268.

203 _____ and Wolfe, G. J. "Can Adults Predict Children's Interest in a Televised Programme?" In W. Schramm (ed.), *The Impact of Educational Television.* Urbana: University of Illinois Press, 1960: 195-213.

204 Bedworth, A. E. and D'Elia, J. A. "Multimedia Resources for Drug Education." Journal of Drug Education, 1971, 1, 3: 293-303.

205 Beik, L. L. "Immediate Recall of TV Commercial Elements." *Journal of Advertising Research,* 1962, 2, 3: 13-18.

206 Bell, R. H. "A Study of the American Character as Presented in Selected Network TV Dramas." Doctoral Dissertation, Ohio State University, 1961.

207 Belmans, Jacques. *Cinéma et Violence* [Violence in Moving Pictures]. Paris: La Rennaissance du Livre, 1972.

208 Belson, Jerry J. and Barban, Arnold M. "Riesman's Social Character Theory and Magazine Preference." *Journalism Quarterly,* 1969, 46, 4: 713-720.

209 Belson, William A. "The Effect of Television on Cinema Going." *Audio-Visual Communications Review,* 1958, 6, 2: 131-139.

210 _____ . "The Effects of Television Upon Family Life." *Discovery,* 1960, 10: 1-5. Summarizes the results of a large sample survey conducted for the British Broadcasting Corporation.

211 _____ . "Effects of Television on the Interests and Initiative of Adult Viewers in Greater London." *British Journal of Psychology,* 1959, 50, 2: 145-158.

212 _____ . "The Effects of Television on the Reading and the Buying of Newspapers and Magazines." *Public Opinion Quarterly,* 1961, 25, 3: 366-381.

213 _____ . *The Impact of Television: Methods and Findings in Program Research.* Hamden, Conn.: Archon Books, 1967. Presents sections on (1) studies to aid in program planning, (2) comprehensibility studies, (3) effects of specific information programs, and (4) television's social impact.

214 _____ . "Learning and Attitude Changes Resulting From Viewing a Television Series, 'Bon Voyage.' " *British Journal of Educational Psychology,* 1956, 26: 31-38.

215 _____ . "Measuring the Effects of Television: A Description of Method." *Public Opinion Quarterly,* 1958, 22, 1: 11-18.

216 _____. "Measuring the Influence of Television Programmes and Campaigns." *Advancement of Science,* 1969, 25: 422-429.

217 _____. "Measuring the Influence on Adolescent Boys of Long-Term Exposure to Television Violence." London: London School of Economics, Survey Research Centre, 1970.

218 _____. "New Developments in Audience Research Methods." *American Journal of Sociology,* 1958, 64, 2: 174-179.

219 _____. "Selective Perception in Viewing a TV Broadcast." *Audio-Visual Communication Review,* 1958, 6, 1: 23-32.

220 _____. "A Summary of the Aims and Methods of Research in a Study of the Relationship Between Long-Term Exposure to Television Violence and the Behavior/Attitudes of Adolescent Boys." London: London School of Economics, Survey Research Centre, 1970.

221 _____. *Television and the Family.* London: British Broadcasting Corp., 1959.

222 Benchley N. R. and Hammond, P. G. eds. *The Media and Drug Abuse Messages.* Washington, D. C.: Special Action Office for Drug Abuse Prevention, Monograph Series D, 1, 1974.

223 Benson, Purnell H. "Segmentation Analysis of Media Exposure: Towards a Theory of Learning Opportunity." *Proceedings of the Annual Convention of the American Psychological Association,* 1971, 6(Pt.2): 661-662.

224 Benton, Charles W., et al. *Television in Urban Education: Its Application to Major Educational Problems in Sixteen Cities.* New York: Praeger, 1969.

225 Ben-Veniste, R. "Pornography and Sex Crime: The Danish Experience." In *Technical Report of The Commission on Obscenity and Pornography: Erotica and Antisocial Behavior* (vol. 7). Washington, D. C.: Government Printing Office 1971: 245-262.

226 Ben-Zeev, Saul and White, I. S. "Effects and Implications." In S. Kraus (ed.), *The Great Debates.* Bloomington: Indiana University Press, 1962: 331-337.

227 Berelson, Bernard. "In the Presence of Culture." *Public Opinion Quarterly,* 1964, 28, 1: 1-12.

228 _____. "Plan 3. The Great Experiment in Cultural Democracy." In L. Arons and M. A. May (eds.), *Television and Human Behavior: Tomorrow's Research in Mass Communication.* New York: Appleton-Century-Crofts, 1963: 38-45.

229 _____ and Janowitz, Morris, eds. *Reader in Public Opinion and Communication.* (2nd ed.), New York: Free Press, 1966.

230 Berelson, Bernard and Steiner, Gary A. "Mass Communications." In *Human Behavior: An Inventory of Scientific Findings,* New York: Harcourt, Brace and World, 1964: 527-555.

231 Berelson, Bernard R., Lazarsfeld, Paul F., and McPhee, William N. "Political Processes: The Role of the Mass Media." In W. Schramm and D. F.

Roberts (eds.), *The Process and Effects of Mass Communication* (2nd ed.) Urbana: University of Illinois Press, 1971: 655-677.

232 _____ . *Voting: A Study of Opinion Formation in a Presidential Campaign.* Chicago: University of Chicago Press, 1954. Reports nominal data gathered in Elmira, N.Y. during the 1948 Presidential campaign.

233 Berey, L. A. and Pollay, Richard W. "The Influencing Role of the Child in Family Decision Making." *Journal of Marketing Research,* 1968, 5, 1: 70-72.

234 Berger, Arthur A. "Drug Advertising and the 'Pain, Pill, Pleasure,' Model." *Journal of Drug Issues,* 1974, 4, 3: 208-212.

235 Berger, A. S., Gagnon, J. H., and Simon, W. "Urban Working-Class Adolescents and Sexually Explicit Media." In *Technical Report of the Commission on Obscenity and Pornography: The Consumer and the Community* (vol. 9). Washington, D. C.: Government Printing Office, 1972: 209-272.

236 Berger, R. M. "Promoting the Reading Habit." *Reports and Papers on Mass Communication, No. 72.* Paris: UNESCO (New York: UNIPUB), 1975

237 Berkman, David. "Advertising in *Ebony* and *Life:* Negro Aspirations vs. Reality." *Journalism Quarterly,* 1963, 40, 1: 53-64.

238 Berkowitz, Leonard. *Aggression: A Social-Psychological Analysis.* New York: McGraw-Hill, 1962.

239 _____ . "Aggressive Cues in Aggressive Behavior and the Hostility Catharsis." *Psychological Review,* 1964, 71, 2: 104-122.

240 _____ . "The Contagion of Violence: An S-R Mediational Analysis of Some Effects of Observed Aggression." *Nebraska Symposium on Motivation,* 1970, 18: 95-135.

241 _____ . *The Development of Motives and Values in the Child.* New York: Basic Books, 1964.

242 _____ . "The Effects of Observing Violence." *Scientific American,* 1964, 210, 2: 35-41.

243 _____ . "Experimental Investigations of Hostility Catharsis." *Journal of Consulting and Clinical Psychology,* 1970, 35: 1-7.

244 _____ . "Frustrations, Comparisons, and Other Sources of Emotional Arousal as Contributors to Social Unrest." *Journal of Social Issues,* 1972, 28: 77-91.

245 _____ , ed. *Roots of Aggression: A Re-Examination of the Frustration-Aggression Hypothesis.* New York: Atherton Press, 1969.

246 _____ . "Sex and Violence: We Can't Have It Both Ways." *Psychology Today,* 1971, 5, 7, 14: 18-23.

247 _____ . "Some Aspects of Observed Aggression." *Journal of Personality and Social Psychology,* 1965, 2: 359-369.

248 _____ . "Some Determinants of Impulsive Aggression: Role of Mediated Associations with Reinforcements for Aggression." *Psychological Review,* 1974, 81: 165-176.

249 _____. "Violence in the Mass Media." In L. Berkowitz (ed.), *Aggression: A Social Psychological Analysis.* New York: McGraw Hill, 1962: 229-255.

250 _____. "Words and Symbols as Stimuli to Aggressive Responses." In J. F. Knutson (ed.), *Control of Aggression: Implications From Basic Research.* Chicago: Aldine-Atherton, 1973.

251 _____ and Alioto, J.T. "The Meaning of an Observed Event as a Determinant of its Aggressive Consequences." *Journal of Personality and Social Psychology,* 1973, 28: 206-217.

252 Berkowitz, Leonard and Geen, R. G. "Film Violence and the Cue Properties of Available Targets." *Journal of Personality and Social Psychology,* 1966, 3, 5: 525-530. Demonstrates the subtleties of aggression cues by linking the confederate's name with the name of the victim in the stimulus film.

253 _____. "Stimulus Qualities of the Target of Aggression: A Further Study." *Journal of Personality and Social Psycholgy,* 1967, 5, 3: 364-368.

254 Berkowitz, Leonard, and Macaulay, J. "The Contagion of Criminal Violence." *Sociometry,* 1971, 34: 238-260.

255 Berkowitz, Leonard and Rawlings, E. "Effects of Film Violence on Inhibitions Against Subsequent Aggression." *Journal of Abnormal and Social Psychology,* 1963, 66: 405-412. Links increased aggression to justified vs. unjustified stimulus violence.

256 Berkowitz, Leonard, Corwin, R., and Hieronimous, M. "Film Violence and Subsequent Aggressive Tendencies." *Public Opinion Quarterly,* 1963, 27: 217-229.

257 Berlo, D. K. and Kumata, H. "The Investigator: The Impact of a Satirical Radio Drama." *Journalism Quarterly,* 1956, 33, 3: 287-298.

258 Berlo, David K., Lemert, James B. and Mertz, Robert. "Dimensions for Evaluating the Acceptability of Message Sources." *Public Opinion Quarterly,* 1969-70, 33, 4: 563-576.

259 Berlogea, O., Culea, H., and Tismanaru, M. "Influenta Sociala a Televizionii" [The Social Impact of Television], *Lupta de Clasa,* 1967, 47, 10: 75-83.

260 Bernstein, Carl and Woodward, Bob. *All the President's Men.* New York: Warner Books, 1975.

261 Beuf, Ann. "Doctor, Lawyer, Household Drudge." *Journal of Communication,* 1974, 24, 2: 142-145.

262 Bhoj, A. G. "Into the Wild Blue Yonder: Behavioral Implications of Agenda-Setting for Air Travel." In M. McCombs and G. Stone (eds.), *Studies in Agenda Setting.* Syracuse: Newhouse Communications Research Center, Syracuse University, 1975.

263 Biblow, E. "Imaginative Play and the Control of Aggressive Behavior." In J. L. Singer (ed.), *The Child's World of Make-Believe: Experimental Studies of Imaginative Play.* New York: Academic Press, 1972: 104-128. Links ability and/or opportunity to fantasize with decreased aggressive response to violent stimuli.

264 Biderman, A. D. *Bibliography on Display and Communication: Literature and Films, Selected for their Pertinence to Kinostatistics for Social Indicators.* Washington, D. C.: Bureau of Social Science Research, 1973.

265 Bijou, S. W. "Reinforcement History and Socialization." In R. A. Hoppe, G. A. Milton, and E. C. Simmel (eds.), *Early Experiences and the Processes of Socialization* New York: Academic Press, 1970.

266 Bishop, Michael E. "Media Use and Democratic Political Orientation in Lima, Peru." *Journalism Quarterly,* 1973, 50, 1: 60-67; 101.

267 Bishop, Robert L. "Anxiety and Readership of Health Information." *Journalism Quarterly,* 1974, 51: 40-46.

268 _____. *Public Relations: A Comprehensive Bibliography: Articles and Books on Public Relations, Communication Theory, Public Opinion, and Propaganda, 1964-1972.* Ann Arbor: University of Michigan Press, 1974. Computerized volume of roughly 4000 items.

269 _____, Boersma, Mary, and Williams, John. "Teenagers and News Media: Credibility Canyon." *Journalism Quarterly,* 1969, 46, 3: 597-599.

270 Bither, W. W. "Effects of Distraction and Commitment on the Persuasiveness of Television Advertising." *Journal of Marketing Research,* 1972, 9, 2: 1-5.

271 Bittner, John R., Anatol, Karl W., and Seiler, William J. "College Student Exposure to Mass Media News." *College Student Survey,* 1969, 3, 2: 46-48.

272 Blackwell, Jacqueline and Yawkey, Thomas D. "An Investigation of Advertising for Young Children." *Journal of Instructional Psychology,* 1975, 2, 1: 28-32.

273 Blakely, Robert J. *The Peoples Instrument: A Philosophy of Programming for Public Television.* Washington, D.C.: Public Affairs Press, 1971.

274 Blatt, Spencer and Ward, S. "A Cognitive Developmental Study of Children's Reactions to Television Advertising." In E. A. Rubinstein, G. A. Comstock, and J. P. Murray (eds.) *Television and Social Behavior: Television in Day-to-Day Life: Patterns of Use* (vol. 4). Washington, D. C.: Government Printing Office, 1972: 452-467.

275 Bled, Cynthia E. "Review of Audience Research in Some Developing Countries of Africa." *Journal of Broadcasting,* 1969, 13, 2: 167-180.

276 Blegvad, B. "Newspapers and Rock and Roll Riots in Copenhagen." *Acta Sociologica,* 1964, 7, 3: 151-178.

277 Blizard, J. *Individual Differences and Television Viewing Behavior.* Melbourne: Collins Books, 1972.

278 Block, Carl E. "Communicating with the Urban Poor: An Exploratory Inquiry." *Journalism Quarterly,* 1970, 47, 1: 3-11.

279 _____. "White Backlash to Negro Ads: Fact or Fantasy?" *Journalism Quarterly,* 1972, 49, 2: 258-262.

280 Block, J. "Conceptions of Sex Roles: Some Cross-Cultural and Longitudinal Perspectives." *American Psychologist,* 1973, 28, 6: 512-526.

281 _____ , Block, A., and Van der Lippe, J. "Sex-Role and Socialization Patterns: Some Personality Concomitants and Environmental Antecedents." *Journal of Consulting and Clinical Psychology,* 1973, 4, 3: 321-341.

282 Blood, Robert O., Jr. "Social Class and Family Control of Television Viewing." *Merrill-Palmer Quarterly,* 1961, 7, 3: 205-222.

283 Bloom, M. H. *Public Relations and Presidential Campaigns: A Crisis in Democracy.* New York: Crowell, 1973.

284 Bloom, Samuel William. "A Social Psychological Study of Motion Picture Audience Behavior; A Case Study of the Negro Image in Mass Communication." Doctoral Dissertation, University of Wisconsin, 1956.

285 Bluem, A. W. and Manvell, R. (eds.). *Television: The Creative Experience.* New York: Hastings House, 1967.

286 Bluem, A. W., Cox, J. F., and McPherson, G. *Television in the Public Interest.* New York: Hastings House, 1961.

287 Bluestone, G. "Life, Death and Nature in Children's TV." In P. D. Hazard (ed.), *Art.* Champaign, Ill: National Council of Teachers of English, 1966.

288 Blum, A. F. "Popular Culture and the Image of Gesellschaft." *Studies in Public Communication,* 1961, 3: 145-158.

289 Blum, Eleanor. *Basic Books in the Mass Media: An Annotated Selected Booklist Covering General Communications, Book Publishing, Broadcasting, Film, Magazines, Newspapers, Advertising, Indexes, and Scholarly and Professional Periodicals.* Urbana: University of Illinois Press, 1972.

290 Blumenfeld, W. S. "Some Correlates of TV Medical Drama Viewing." *Psychological Reports,* 1964, 15, 3: 901-902.

291 _____ and Remmers, H. H. "Television Program Preferences and Their Relationship to Self-Reported High School Grades." *Journal of Educational Research,* 1966, 59: 358-359.

292 Blumenthal, M. D. "Conscience Formation and the Mass Media." In R. K. Baker and S. J. Ball (eds.), *Violence and the Media.* A Staff Report to the National Commission on the Causes and Prevention of Violence. Washington, D.C.: Government Printing Office, 1969: 487-492.

293 Blumer, H. "Suggestions for the Study of Mass-Media Effects." In E. Burdick and A. J. Brodbeck (eds.), *American Voting Behavior.* Glencoe, Ill: Free Press, 1959: 197-208.

294 Blumler, Jay G. "The Political Effects of Television." In J. Halloran (ed.), *The Effects of Television.* London: Panther, 1970: 69-104.

295 _____ and Katz, Elihu (eds.). *The Uses of Mass Communications: Current Perspectives on Gratifications Research.* Beverly Hills: Sage, 1974. Fifteen major articles cover the range of uses and gratifications research from media and interpersonal relations through wartime functions, children's uses, the family context, psychological motivations, popular culture, public policy considerations, and methodological notes.

296 Blumler, Jay G. and McLeod, J. M. "Communications and Voter Turnout in Britain." In T. Leggatt (ed.), *Sociological Theory and Survey Research*. Beverly Hills: Sage, 1974: 265-312.

297 Blumler, J. G. and McQuail, D. "The Audience for Election Television." In J. Tunstall (ed.), *Media Sociology: A Reader*. London: Constable, 1970: 452-478.

298 _____ . *Television in Politics: Its Uses and Influence*. Chicago: University of Chicago Press, 1969. Studied the role of television in the British General Election of 1964.

299 Bobrow, Davis B. "Mass Communication and the Political System." *Public Opinion Quarterly*, 1973, 37: 551-568.

300 _____ . "Mass Communication and the Political System." In W. P. Davison and F.T.C. Yu (eds.), *Mass Communication Research: Major Issues and Future Directions*. New York: Praeger, 1974: 93-121.

301 Boffey, Philip M. and Walsh, John. "Study of TV Violence: Seven Top Researchers Blackballed from Panel." *Science*, 1970, May 22: 949-951.

302 Bogardus, Emory. "Sociology of Presidential TV Press Conferences." *Sociology and Social Research*, 1962, 46, 2: 181-185.

303 _____ . "Television and the Political Conventions." *Sociology and Social Research*, 1952, 37: 115-121.

304 Bogart, Leo. "Adult Talk About Newspaper Comics." *American Journal of Sociology*, 1955, 61, 1: 26-30.

305 _____ . *The Age of Television: A Study of Viewing Habits and the Impact of Television on American Life* (3rd. ed.). New York: Frederick Ungar, 1972.

306 _____ . "American Television: A Brief Survey of Research Findings." *Journal of Social Issues*, 1962, 18, 2: 36-42. The survey of findings is limited mainly to usage patterns rather than effects.

307 _____ . "Changing News Interests and the News Media." *Public Opinion Quarterly*, 1968, 32, 4: 560-574.

308 _____ . "The Mass Media and the Blue-Collar Worker." In A. Shostak and W. Gomberg (eds.), *Blue-Collar World: Studies of the American Worker*. Englewood Cliffs, N.J.: Prentice-Hall, 1965: 416-428. Makes a case for the media being powerful forces in the establishment and maintenance of social norms and values.

309 _____ . "Negro and White Media Exposure: New Evidence." *Journalism Quarterly*, 1972, 49, 1: 15-21. Large sample of national data show blacks viewing more than whites and reading less. Women spend more time with TV than do men.

310 _____ , ed. *Psychology in Media Strategy: Proceedings of a Symposium Sponsored by The Media Research Committee of the American Marketing Association*. Chicago: American Marketing Association, 1966.

311 _____ . *Silent Politics: Polls and the Awareness of Public Opinions*. New York: Wiley–Interscience, 1972.

312 _____. *Strategy in Advertising.* New York: Harcourt Brace Jovanovich, 1967.

313 _____. "Warning: The Surgeon General Has Determined That TV Violence is Moderately Dangerous to Your Child's Mental Health." *Public Opinion Quarterly,* 1972, 36, 4: 491-521.

314 _____ and Orenstein, Frank E. "Mass Media and Community Identity in an Interurban Setting." *Journalism Quarterly,* 1965, 42, 2: 179-188.

315 Bogatz, G. A. and Ball, S. J. "The Second Year of Sesame Street: A Continuing Evaluation." (2 vols.). Princeton, N.J.: Educational Testing Service, 1971.

316 Bogle, Donald. *Toms, Coons, Mulattoes, Mammies and Bucks: An Interpretive History of Blacks in American Films.* New York: Bantam Books, 1974.

317 Bokander, Ingran and Lindholm, Kerstin. "The Effects of Aggressive Films on Minors." *Nordisk Psykologi,* 1967, 19, 1.

318 Boorstin, D. J. "From News-Gathering to News-Making: A Flood of Pseudo-Events." In W. Schramm and D. F. Roberts (eds.), *The Process and Effects of Mass Communication* (2nd ed.). Urbana: University of Illinois Press, 1971: 116-150.

319 Booth, Alan. "The Recall of News Items." *Public Opinion Quarterly,* 1970-1971, 34, 4: 604-610.

320 Booth, G. D. "The Comparative Effectiveness of Monochrome and Color Presentations in the Facilitation of Affective Learning." Doctoral Dissertation, University of Southern California, 1971.

321 Borra, Ranjan. "Communication Through Television: UNESCO Adult Education Experiments in France, Japan and India." *Journal of Communication,* 1970, 20, 1: 65-83.

322 Borton, Terry, Belasco, Leonard, and Echewa, Thomas. "Dual Audio TV Instruction: A Mass Broadcast Simulation." *Audio-Visual Communication Review,* 1974, 22, 2: 133-152.

323 Bostian, Lloyd R. "The Two-Step Flow Theory: Cross-Cultural Implications." *Journalism Quarterly,* 1970, 47: 109-117.

324 _____ and Ross, John E. "Functions and Meanings of Mass Media for Wisconsin Farm Women." *Journalism Quarterly,* 1965, 42, 1: 69-76.

325 Boulding, Kenneth E. *The Image.* Ann Arbor: University of Michigan Press, 1956.

326 _____, et al. "Image and Reality in World Politics." New York: School of International Affairs, Columbia University, 1967.

327 Bowen, Lawrence. "Advertising and the Poor; A Comparative Study of Patterns of Response to Television and Magazine Advertising Between Middle-Income and Low-Income Groups." Doctoral Dissertation, University of Wisconsin, 1974.

328 _____ and Chaffee, S. H. "Product Involvement and Pertinent Advertising Appeals." *Journalism Quarterly,* 1974, 4: 613-621.

329 Bowen, Max E. "Responses to Smoking in the Presence of Anxiety-Eliciting Cues." *Dissertation Abstracts International,* 1970, 31 (2-B): 895.

330 Bower, R. T. *Television and the Public.* New York: Holt, Rinehart and Winston, 1973. An extensive survey of audience attitudes toward television, picking up where G. A. Steiner's 1963 report leaves off. The 1970 data are compared with 1960s.

331 Bowers, Thomas A. "The Coverage of Political Advertising by the Prestige Press in 1972." *Mass Comm Review,* 1975, 2, 3: 19-24.

332 _____ . "Issue and Personality Information in Newspaper Political Advertising." *Journalism Quarterly,* 1972, 49, 3: 446-452.

333 _____ . "Newspaper Political Advertising and the Agenda-Setting Function." *Journalism Quarterly,* 1973, 50, 3: 552-556.

334 Boyanowsky, E. O., Newtson, D., and Walster, E. "Film Preferences Following a Murder." *Communication Research,* 1974, 1, 1: 32-43.

335 Boyd, H. W., Ray, M. L., and Strong, E. C. "An Attitudinal Framework for Advertising Strategy." *Journal of Marketing,* 1972, 36, 2: 27-33.

336 Boyenton, William H. "Enter the Ladies–86 Proof: A Study of Advertising Ethics." *Journalism Quarterly,* 1967, 44, 3: 445-453.

337 _____. "The Negro Turns to Advertising." *Journalism Quarterly,* 1965, 42, 2: 227-235.

338 Bramel, D., Taub, B., and Blum, B. "An Observer's Reaction to the Suffering of His Enemy." *Journal of Personality and Social Psychology,* 1968, 8: 384-392.

339 Brandner, Lowell and Sistrunk, Joan. "The Newspaper: Molder or Mirror of Community Values." *Journalism Quarterly,* 1966, 43, 3: 497-504.

340 Brandis, W. and Henderson, D. *Social Class, Language and Communication.* London: Routledge and K. Paul, 1970.

341 Brauer, Ralph and Brauer, Donna. *The Horse, the Gun and the Piece of Property: Changing Images of the TV Western.* Bowling Green, Ohio: Bowling Green University Popular Press, 1975.

342 Braun, Duane D. *Toward a Theory of Popular Culture: The Sociology and History of American Music and Dance, 1920-1968.* Ann Arbor, Mich.: Ann Arbor Publishers, 1969.

343 Braun-Galkowska, M. "The Influence of Television on Children's Personality." *Roczniki Filozoficzne,* 1971, 19.4 : 195-205.

344 Bray, G. C. *The Impact of Mass Media Upon Public Opinion.* Springfield, Va.: National Technical Information Service, 1973.

345 Breed, Warren. "Analyzing News: Some Questions for Research." *Journalism Quarterly,* 1956, 33, 4: 467-477.

346 _____ . "Mass Communication and Social Integration." *Social Forces,* 1958, 37: 109-116.

347 Brennan, L. D. *Modern Communication Effectiveness.* Englewood Cliffs, N.J.: Prentice-Hall, 1963.

348   Brenner, Donald J. and Mauldin, Charles R. "Linking Conversation to Mass Communication: The Calley Case." *Journalism Quarterly*, 1974, 51: 124-129.

349   Briand, Paul L., ed. *Violence and the Media.* A Report of Mass Media Hearings Before the U.S. National Commission on the Causes and Prevention of Violence. Washington, D. C.: Government Printing Office, 1969. See R. K. Baker and S. J. Ball, eds. for the companion volume.

350   Brim, O. G. "Adult Socialization." In J. A. Clausen, ed. *Socialization and Society.* Boston: Little, Brown, 1968: 182-226.

351   _____ and Wheeler, S. *"Socialization After Childhood: Two Essays."* New York: Wiley, 1966.

352   Brink, Edward L. and Kelley, W. T. *The Management of Promotion: Consumer Behavior and Demand Stimulation.* Englewood Cliffs, N.J.: Prentice-Hall, 1963.

353   Brinkman, Del. "Do Editorial Cartoons and Editorials Change Opinion?" *Journalism Quarterly*, 1968, 45, 4: 724-726.

354   Brinton, James E. "Subscriber vs. Non-subscriber Method in Studying Effects." *Journalism Quarterly*, 1957, 34, 1: 92-93.

355   _____ and McKown, Norman L. "Effects of Newspaper Reading on Knowledge and Attitudes." *Journalism Quarterly*, 1961, 38, 2: 187-195.

356   British Broadcasting Corporation. *Children as Viewers and Listeners: A Study by the BBC for its General Advisory Council.* London: BBC, 1974.

357   _____. *Violence on Television: Programme Content and Viewer Perception.* London: Audience Research Department, BBC, 1972.

358   Britt, S. H., Adams, S. C., and Miller, A. "How Many Advertising Exposures Per Day?" *Journal of Advertising Research,* 1973, 12: 3-9.

359   Brock, T. C. "Erotic Materials: A Commodity Theory Analysis of Availability and Desirability." In *Technical Report of the Commission on Obscenity and Pornography: Preliminary Studies* (vol. 1). Washington, D.C.: Government Printing Office, 1971: 131-140.

360   Brodbeck, A. J. "An Exception to the Law of 'Adult Discount': The Need to Take Film Content into Account." *Psychological Reports,* 1961, 8: 59-61.

361   _____ and Jones, D. B. "Plan 7: Television Viewing and the Non-Violating Practices and Perspectives of Adolescents: A Synchronized Depth and Scope Program of Policy Research." In L. Arons and M. A. (eds.), *Television and Human Behavior: Tomorrow's Research in Mass Communication.* New York: Appleton-Century-Crofts, 1963: 98-135.

362   Broddason, Thorbjorn. "Children and Television in Iceland. A Study of Ten to Fourteen Year-Old Children in Three Communities." University of Lund, Department of Sociology, 1970.

363   Brode, John. *The Process of Modernization: An Annotated Bibliography on the Sociocultural Aspects of Development.* Cambridge, Mass.: Harvard University Press, 1969.

364 Broderick, Dorothy M. *Image of the Black in Children's Fiction.* New York: R.R. Bowker, 1973.

365 Brodie, J. F. "Drug Abuse and Television Viewing Patterns." *Psychology,* 1972, 9, 2: 33-36.

366 Brolin, H. "Barns Mottagning av Programstoff i TV: Ett Forsok till Beskrivning av Motivasionsmekanismer Grundad pa SR's Barenkat" [Children's Reception of Radio and Television Programme Content: An Attempt to Describe Motivation Mechanisms on the Basis of SR's Survey of Children]. Stockholm: Sveriges Radio, Audience and Programme Research Department, No. 3, 1964.

367 _____. "Tvs Kvantitativa och Kvalitativa Roll i Tonaringars Massmediautveckling" [The Quantitive and Qualitative Importance of Television for Teenagers' Mass Media Development]. Stockholm: Sveriges Radio Audience and Programme Research Department, No. 3, 1964.

368 Bronfenbrenner, U. "Socialization and Social Class Through Time and Space." In E. E. Maccoby, T. M. Newcomb, and E. L. Hartley (eds.), *Readings in Social Psychology,* New York: Holt, 1958.

369 _____. *Two Worlds of Childhood: U.S. and U.S.S.R.* New York: Russell Sage Foundation, 1970.

370 _____ and Mahoney, Maureen A., eds. *Influences on Human Development* (2nd. ed.). Hinsdale, Ill.: Dryden Press, 1975.

371 Brooks, Harriet. "Motion Pictures, Radio, Newspapers and Comics in Relation to the Attitudes and Conduct of Children and Youth: A Survey of the Literature of the Past Twenty Years." In *Clark University Abstracts of Dissertations (1950),* Worchester, Mass., 1950, 22: 125-127.

372 Brooks, William D. "A Study of the Relationships of Selected Factors to Changes in Voting Attitudes of Audience Listening to Political Speeches of President Johnson and Senator Goldwater." *Dissertation Abstracts,* 1967, 27(12-A): 4337.

373 Brotherus, Greta. *Valdet i Rutan: En Referatsamling med Kommentarer* [Violence on the Screen: A Collection of Abstracts with Commentary]. Ekenas: Soderstrom and Co. Forlags AB, 1974.

374 Brouwer, M. "Mass Communication and the Social Sciences: Some Neglected Areas. In L. A. Dexter and D. M. White (eds.), *People, Society, and Mass Communication.* New York: Free Press, 1964: 547-567.

375 Brown, Charles. "Self-Portrait: The Teen-Type Magazine." *Annals of the American Academy of Political and Social Science,* 1961, 338: 13-21.

376 Brown, D. "Radio and Television: An Annotated Bibliography." *Journalism Quarterly,* 1957, 34: 378-386.

377 _____. "Trust in International Relations: a Mass Media Perspective." *Journalism Quarterly,* 1969, 46: 777-783.

378 Brown, J. R. "Child Socialization: The Family and Television." *Report of the Proceedings of the 9th General Assembly of the International Association for Mass Communication Research.* Leipzig, 1974.

379 _____ . "Children and Television: Interpersonal and Intrapersonal Features of the Effects Process." Leeds, England: University of Leeds, 1973.

380 _____, Cramond, J. K., and Wilde, R. J. "Displacement Effects of Television and the Child's Functional Orientation to Media." In J.G. Blumler and E. Katz (eds.), *The Uses of Mass Communications: Current Perspectives on Gratifications Research.* Beverly Hills: Sage, 1974: 93-112.

381 Brown, R. L. "Television and the Arts." In J. Halloran (ed.), *The Effects of Television.* London: Panther, 1970: 105-137.

382 Brown, William R. "Television and the Democratic National Convention in 1968." *Quarterly Journal of Speech,* 1969, 55, 3: 237-246.

383 Browne, Donald R. "The American Image As Presented Abroad by U.S. Television." *Journalism Quarterly,* 1968, 45, 2: 307-316.

384 _____. "Television and National Stabilization: the Lebanese Experience." *Journalism Quarterly,* 1975, 52: 692-698.

385 Browning, R. P. and Jacob, Herbert. "Power Motivation and the Political Personality." *Public Opinion Quarterly,* 1964, 28, 1: 75-90.

386 Brucker, Herbert. *Communication is Power: Unchanging Values in a Changing Journalism.* New York: Oxford University Press, 1973.

387 Brumbaugh, Florence N., "What Effect Does Television Advertising Have on Children?" *Education Digest,* 1954, 19, 4: 32-33.

388 Bruno, A. V. "The Network Factor in TV Viewing." *Journal of Advertising Research.* 1973, 13, 5: 33-39.

389 _____, Hustad, T. P., and Pessemier, E. A. "Media Approaches to Segmentation." *Journal of Advertising Research,* 1973, 13: 35-42.

390 Bryan, J. H. "Children's Reactions to Helpers: Their Money Isn't Where Their Mouths Are." In J. Macaulay and L. Berkowitz (eds.), *Altruism and Helping Behavior.* New York: Academic Press, 1970: 61-76.

391 _____ . "Model Affect and Children's Imitative Altruism." *Child Development,* 1971, 42: 2061-2065. Children show prosocial effects of observing a model donate to a worthy cause.

392 _____ and Schwartz, T. "Effects of Film Material Upon Children's Behavior." *Psychological Bulletin,* 1971, 75, 1: 50-59.

393 _____ and Walbek, N. H. "The Impact of Words and Deeds Concerning Altruism Upon Children." *Child Development,* 1970, 41: 747-757.

394 Bucci, R. P. "Erroneous Recall of Media." *Journal of Advertising Research,* 1973, 13, 4: 23-27.

395 Buchanan, D. I. "How Interest in the Product Affects Recall: Print Ads vs. Commercials." *Journal of Advertising Research,* 1964, 4, 1: 9-14.

396 _____ . "Product Interest as a Determinant of Differential Levels of Recall Between Magazine Advertisements and Television Commercials." Doctoral Dissertation, Massachusetts Institute of Technology, 1963.

397 Buck, S. F., and West, M. J. "Consistency of Purchasing and Television Viewing Behaviour: Optimum Periods for Study." *Commentary,* 1968, 10: 234-252.

398 Buckle, Gerard F. *The Mind and the Film.* New York: Arno Press, 1970.

399 Budd, Richard, MacLean, Malcolm S., Barnes, Arthur M. "Regularities in the Diffusion of Two Major News Events," *Journalism Quarterly,* 1966, 43, 2: 221-230.

400 Burdick, E. and Brodbeck, A. J. (eds.) *American Voting Behavior.* Glencoe, Ill.: Free Press, 1959.

401 Burnet, M. "The Mass Media in a Violent World." *Reports and Papers on Mass Communication, No. 63.* Paris: UNESCO (New York: UNIPUB), 1971.

402 Burnett, Leo. "Summary of Research on Child Development and the Effects of Mass Media and Television Advertising on Children." Chicago: Leo Burnett Co., 1971.

403 Burton, G. "Sex-Role Stereotyping in Elementary School Primers." Pittsburgh: Know, Inc. 1974.

404 Burton, John W. *Conflict and Communication: The Use of Controlled Communication in International Relations.* New York: Free Press, 1969.

405 Busby, Linda Jean. "Defining the Sex-Role Standard in Network Children's Programs." *Journalism Quarterly,* 1974, 51, 4: 690-696.

406 _____."Sex-role Research on the Mass Media: The Effects of Television on Children and Adolescents." *Journal of Communication,* 1975, 25, 4: 107-131.

407 Bush, George S. "A System of Categories for General News Content." *Journalism Quarterly,* 1960, 37, 2: 206-210.

408 Buss, L. J. "Motivational Variables and Information Seeking in the Mass Media." *Journalism Quarterly,* 1967, 44: 130-133.

409 Butler-Paisley, Matilda, et al. "Image of Women in Advertisements: A Preliminary Study of Avenues for Change." Arlington, Va.: ERIC Document Reproduction Service, n.d.

410 Buzzi, Giancarlo. *Advertising: Its Cultural and Political Effects.* Minneapolis: University of Minnesota Press, 1968.

411 Byrne, D. and Lamberth, J. "The Effect of Erotic Stimuli on Sex Arousal, Evaluative Responses, and Subsequent Behavior." In W. C. Wilson (comp.), *Technical Report of the Commission on Obscenity and Pornography: Erotica and Social Behavior* (vol. 8). Washington, D.C.: Government Printing Office, 1971: 41-67.

412 Byrne, Gary C. "Mass Media and Political Socialization of Children and Pre-Adults." *Journalism Quarterly,* 1969, 46, 1: 140-141.

C

413 Cagley, James W. and Cardozo, Richard N. "White Responses to Integrated Advertising." *Journal of Advertising Research, Special Issue: Research on Negroes,* 1970, 10, 3: 35-40.

414   Cairns, R. B., Paul, J.C.N., and Wishner, J. "Psychological Assumptions in Sex Censorship: An Evaluative Review of Recent Research (1961-1968)." In *Technical Report of the Commission on Obscenity and Pornography: Preliminary Studies* (vol. 1). Washington, D.C.: Government Printing Office, 1971: 5-22.

415   Cameron, P. and Janky, C. "The Effects of TV Violence Upon Children: A Naturalistic Experiment." *Proceedings of the 79th Annual Convention of the American Psychological Association.* Washington, D.C.: American Psychological Association, 1971: 233-234.

416   _____. "The Effects of Viewing 'Violent' TV Upon Children's At-Home and In-School Behavior." University of Louisville and University of California, Berkeley, 1971 (ERIC Document 057388).

417   Campbell, Angus. "Has Television Reshaped Politics?" *Columbia Journalism Review,* Fall 1962: 10-13.

418   _____ and Kahn, R. L. *The People Elect a President.* Ann Arbor: Survey Research Center, University of Michigan, 1952.

419   Campbell, Angus, Gurin, G., and Miller, W. E. "Television and the Election." *Scientific American,* 1953, 188: 46-48.

420   _____. *The Voter Decides.* Evanston, Ill.: Row, Peterson and Co., 1954.

421   Campbell, Angus, Converse, P. E., Miller, W. E. and Stokes, D. E. *The American Voter.* New York, Wiley, 1960.

422   _____. *Election and the Political Order.* New York: Wiley, 1966.

423   Campbell, D. and Clayton, K. "Avoiding Regression Effects in Panel Studies of Communication Impact." *Studies in Public Communication,* 1961, 3: 99-118.

424   Campbell, James H. "A Message System Analysis: Variable Subsystems In Cartoon Humor." *Dissertation Abstracts,* 1968, 28(10-A): 4265-4266.

425   Campbell, W. J. "The Impact of Television on the Primary School Child." In F. M. Katz and R. K. Browne (eds.), *Sociology of Education.* Sydney: Macmillan, 1970, 317-328.

426   _____. *Television and the Australian Adolescent.* Sydney: Angus and Robertson, 1962.

427   Canadian Advertising Advisory Board. "The Child's World and Television Advertising." A report prepared by AIM Limited. Toronto: Canadian Advertising Advisory Board Library, November, 1971.

428   Canadian Council on Children and Youth. *Report of the Consultation on Children's Television.* Scarborough, Ontario: The Guild Inn, 1972.

429   Canadian Radio-Television Commission. *Bibliography: Some Canadian Writings on the Mass Media.* Ottawa: CRTC, 1974. Includes 1075 alphabetical citations with subject index.

430   _____. *Reaching the Retired: A Survey of Media Habits, Preferences and Needs of Senior Citizens in Metropolitan Toronto.* Toronto: Environics Research Group, 1973.

431 Canaris, M. J. "Frustration, Agression and the Instrumental Catharsis of Aggression." Doctoral Dissertation, University of Maryland, 1973.

432 Canavan, K. "Children's Television Viewing Habits and Parental Control." *Education News*, 1974, 14, 11: 12-19.

433 Cannell, Charles and MacDonald, James. "The Impact of Health News on Attitudes and Behavior." *Journalism Quarterly*, 1956, 33, 3: 315-323.

434 Cantor, J.R. and Zillmann, D. "Resentment Toward Victimized Protagonists and Severity of Misfortunes They Suffer as Factors in Humor Appreciation." *Journal of Experimental Research in Personality*, 1973, 6: 321-329.

435 Cantor, J. R., Mody, B., and Zillmann, D. "Residual Emotional Arousal as a Distractor in Persuasion." *Journal of Social Psychology*, 1974, 92: 231-244.

436 Cantor, M. G. *The Hollywood TV Producer.* New York: Basic Books, 1971.

437 _____. "The Role of the Producer in Choosing Children's Television Content." In G. A. Comstock and E. A. Rubinstein (eds.), *Television and Social Behavior: Media Content and Control* (vol. 1). Washington, D.C.: Government Printing Office, 1972: 259-289.

438 Capecchi, V. and Livolsi, M. "The Socialization Process in Pre-Adolescent Children." Rome: Radiotelevisione Italiana Servizio Opinioni, 1973.

439 Carey, James T. "Changing Courtship Patterns in the Popular Song." *American Journal of Sociology*, 1969, 74, 62: 720-731.

440 Carey, J. W. "A Cultural Approach to Communication." *Communication*, 1975, 2, 1: 1-22.

441 _____. "Variations in Negro/White Television Preferences." *Journal of Broadcasting*, 1966, 10, 3: 199-212.

442 _____ and Kreiling, A. L. "Popular Culture and Uses and Gratifications: Notes Toward an Accommodation." In J. G. Blumler and E. Katz (eds.), *The Uses of Mass Communications: Current Perspectives on Gratifications Research.* Beverly Hills: Sage, 1974: 225-248.

443 Carli, Renzo and Ancona, Teresa. "La Dinamica dell'Aggressivita dopo stimolo filmco" [The Dynamics of Aggressiveness Stimulated by Films]. *Contributi dell' Instituto de Psicologia*, 1970, 30: 726-737.

444 Carlson, Earl R. "Psychological Satisfaction and Interest in News." *Journalism Quarterly*, 1960, 37, 4: 547-551.

445 Carlson, Robert O. *Communications and Public Opinion: A Public Opinion Quarterly Reader.* New York: Praeger, 1975.

446 Carlssen, G. "Time and Continuity in Mass Media Attitude Change: The Case of Voting." *Public Opinion Quarterly*, 1965, 29: 133-144.

447 Carmen, I. H. *Movies, Censorship, and the Law.* Ann Arbor: University of Michigan Press, 1966.

448 Carpenter, C. R. "Psychological Research Using Television." *American Psychologist*, 1955, 10: 606-610.

449 Carpentier, Raymond. "Conditionnement et Communication de Masse" [Mass Conditioning and Communication]. *Psychologie Francaise,* 1966, 11, 1: 69-77.

450 Carroll, John B. "The Potentials and Limitations of Print as a Medium Of Instruction." In D. Olson (ed.), *Media and Symbols: The Forms of Expression, Communication, and Education.* Chicago: University of Chicago Press, 1974: 151-179.

451 Carter, Richard F. "Communication and Affective Relations." *Journalism Quarterly,* 1965, 42, 2: 203-312.

452 _____. "On Reactions to Mass Media Content." *AV Communication Review,* 1960, 8: 210-213.

453 _____. "Some Effects of the Debates." In S. Kraus (ed.), *The Great Debates,* Bloomington: Indiana University Press, 1962: 173-223.

454 _____ and Greenberg, Bradley S. "Newspapers or Television: Which Do You Believe?" *Journalism Quarterly,* 1965, 42, 1: 29-34.

455 _____ , Pyska, Ronald H. and Guerrero, Jose L. "Dissonance and Exposure to Aversive Information." *Journalism Quarterly,* 1969, 46, 1: 37-42.

456 Carter, Roy. "Field Research in Journalism: A Tentative Review and Appraisal." *Journal of Marketing,* 1956, 21, 2: 137-148.

457 _____. "Racial Identification Effects Upon the News Story Writer," *Journalism Quarterly,* 1959, 36, 3: 284-290.

458 _____. "Segregation and the News: A Regional Content Study." *Journalism Quarterly,* 1957, 34, 1: 3-18.

459 _____ and Clarke, Peter. "Public Affairs Opinion Leadership Among Educational Television Viewers." *American Sociological Review,* 1962, 27, 6: 792-799.

460 Carter, Roy E. and Sepulveda, Orlando. "Some Patterns of Mass Media Use in Santiago, Chile." *Journalism Quarterly,* 1964,41, 2: 216-224.

461 Cassata, Mary B. "A Study of the Mass Communications Behavior and the Social Disengagement Behavior of 177 Members of the Age Center of New England." *Dissertation Abstracts,* 1968, 28(9-A): 3765-3766.

462 Casty, Alan, ed., *Mass Media and Mass Man* (2nd. ed.). New York: Holt, Rinehart and Winston, 1973.

463 Cater, Douglass. *Television and the Thinking Person.* New York: Praeger, 1975.

464 _____ and Adler, Richard, eds. *Television as a Social Force: New Approaches to T.V. Criticism.* New York, N.Y.: Praeger, 1975.

465 Cater, Douglass, and Strickland, S. *A First Hard Look at the Surgeon General's Report on Television and Violence.* Palo Alto,Calif.: Aspen Program on Communications and Society, 1972.

466 _____ . *TV Violence and The Child: The Evolution and Fate of the Surgeon General's Report.* New York: Russell Sage Foundation, 1975. Covers the origins of advisory committee makeup, major findings, and reactions to the report from researchers, the public, government leaders, and the industry.

467 Catton, W. R. "A Theory of Value." *American Sociological Review,* 1959, 24: 310-317.

468 _____. "Mass Media as Activators of Latent Tendencies." In R.K. Baker and S.J. Ball (eds.), *Mass Media and Violence.* A staff report to the National Commission on the Causes and Prevention of Violence. Washington, D.C.: Government Printing Office, 1969: 301-310.

469 _____. "Mass Media as Producers of Effects: An Overview of Research Trends." in R. K. Baker and S. J. Ball (eds.) *Mass Media and Violence.* A staff report to the National Commission on the Causes and Prevention of Violence. Washington, D.C.: Government Printing Office, 1969: 247-259.

470 _____. "Outline of Research Required on Effects." In R. K. Baker and S. J. Ball (eds.), *Violence and the Media.* A staff report to the National Commission on the Causes and Prevention of Violence. Washington, D.C.: Government Printing Office, 1969: 415-422.

471 _____. "Value Modification by Mass Media." In R. K. Baker and S. J. Ball (eds.), *Mass Media and Violence.* A staff report to the National Commission on the Causes and Prevention of Violence. Washington, D.C.: Government Printing Office, 1969: 285-299.

472 _____. "The Worldview Presented by Mass Media." In R. K. Baker and S. J. Ball (eds.), *Mass Media and Violence.* A staff report to the National Commission on the Causes and Prevention of Violence. Washington, D.C.: Government Printing Office, 1969: 473-486.

473 Cazeneuve, Jean. "Television as a Functional Alternative to Traditional Sources of Need Satisfaction." In J. G. Blumler and E. Katz (eds.), *The Uses of Mass Communications: Current Perspectives on Gratifications Research.* Beverly Hills: Sage, 1974: 213–223.

474 _____. "Television and the Human Condition." *Communication,* 1974, 1, 2: 197-214.

475 Cazeneuve, Jean and Bendano, Paule. "La Television y Los Niños Menores De Cinco Años" [Television and Children Under Five Years Old). *Revista Española de la Opinión Pública,* 1971, 23, Jan.-Mar.: 49-54.

476 Cerha, Jarko. *Selective Mass Communication.* Stockholm: Kungle, 1967.

477 Chaffee, S. H. "Contributions of Wilbur Schramm to Mass Communication Research." *Journalism Monographs,* 36, 1974.

478 _____. "The Interpersonal Context of Mass Communication." In F. G. Kline and P. J. Tichenor (eds.), *Current Perspectives in Mass Communication Research.* Beverly Hills: Sage, 1972: 95-120.

479 _____, ed. *Political Communication: Issues and Strategies for Research.* Beverly Hills, Calif.: Sage, 1975. Fourth in the "Sage Annual Reviews of Communication Research." Contains 10 major chapters by noted scholars dealing with: political cognitions; political behavior and mass society; diffusion; research and analytical frameworks; government and media; and legal research and judicial communication.

480 _____ . "Television and Adolescent Aggressiveness (Overview)." In G. A. Comstock and E. A. Rubinstein (eds.), *Television and Social Behavior: Television and Adolescent Aggressiveness,* (vol. 3). Washington, D.C.: Government Printing Office, 1972: 1-34.

481 Chaffee, S. H. and Izcaray, F. "Mass Communication Functions in a Media-Rich Developing Society." *Communication Research,* 1975, 2, 4: 367-395.

482 Chaffee, S. H. and McLeod, J. M. "Adolescent Television Use in the Family Context." In G. A. Comstock and E. A. Rubinstein (eds.), *Television and Social Behavior, Television and Adolescent Aggressiveness* (vol. 3). Washington, D.C.: Government Printing Office, 1972: 149-172.

483 _____ . "Consumer Decisions and Information Use." In S. Ward and T. Robertson (eds.), *Consumer Behavior: Theoretical Sources.* Englewood Cliffs, N.J.: Prentice-Hall, 1973.

484 _____ . "Individual vs. Social Predictors of Information Seeking." *Journalism Quarterly,* 1973, 50, 2: 237-245.

485 Chaffee, S. H. and Petrick, M. J. *Using the Mass Media: Communication Problems in American Society.* New York: McGraw-Hill, 1975. Conceptualizes media as tools which can be used by society to solve a variety of problems. Major problems are presented and analyzed in this light, including public information relative to the courts, schools, the military, corporate relations, politics, commercial advertising, charity appeals, violence, the environment, sex, radicalism, and diffusion and social change.

486 Chaffee, S. H., McLeod, J. M., and Atkin, C. K. "Parental Influences on Adolescent Media Use." *American Behavioral Scientist,* 1971, 14, 3: 323-340.

487 Chaffee, S. H., McLeod, J. M., and Wackman, D. B. "Family Communication Patterns and Adolescent Political Participation." In J. Dennis (ed.), *Socialization to Politics: A Reader.* New York: Wiley, 1973: 349-364. Adolescents from families emphasizing self-expression over social conformity evidence greater interest, knowledge, and involvement in public affairs and politics.

488 Chaffee, S. H., Ward, S. L., and Tipton, L. P. "Mass Communication and Political Socialization." *Journalism Quarterly,* 1970, 47, 4: 657-659.

489 Chandler, M., Greenspan, S., and Barenboim, C. "Judgments of Intentionality in Response to Videotaped and Verbally Presented Moral Dilemmas: The Medium is the Message." *Child Development,* 1973, 44: 315-320.

490 Chaney, David C. "Involvement, Realism and the Perception of Aggression in Television Programmes." *Human Relations,* 1970, 23, 5: 373-381.

491 _____ . *Processes of Mass Communication.* New York: Herder and Herder, 1972. Assesses the following: the subjective reality of mass communication; audiences; uses and gratifications; production problems; public control; distribution and structure; and analysis of media performance.

492 Chapko, Michael K. and Lewis, Mark H. "Authoritarianism and *All in the Family." Journal of Psychology,* 1975, 90, 2: 245-248.

493   Charren, Peggy and Sarson, Evelyn, eds. *Who is Talking To Our Children?* Newtonville, Mass.: Action for Children's Television, 1972.

494   Charters, W. W. "Motion Pictures and Youth." In B. Berelson and M. Janowitz (eds.), *Reader in Public Opinion and Communication* (2nd ed.). New York: Free Press, 1966: 381-390.

495   Cheles-Miller, Pamela. "Reactions to Marital Roles in Commercials." *Journal of Advertising Research,* 1975, 15, 4: 45-49.

496   Cherry, Colin. *World Communication: Threat or Promise?: A Socio-Technical Approach.* New York: Wiley, 1971. Examines the nature of human communication — ancient and modern, the communication explosion, politics and pleasure, communication and wealth, and social aspects of world communication.

497   Chester, Edward W. *Radio, Television and American Politics.* New York: Sheed and Ward, 1969.

498   Cheydleur, R. and Golter, R. J. "Graduate Theses and Dissertations on Broadcasting: A Topical Index." *Journal of Broadcasting,* 1957, 2: 55-90.

499   Childers, P. R. and Ross, J. "The Relationship Between Viewing Television and Student Achievement." *Journal of Educational Research,* 1972, 66: 317-319.

500   Childers, Thomas and Post, J. A. *The Information Poor in America.* Metuchen, N.J.: Scarecrow Press, 1975. Reviews the literature and provides a bibliography of 725 references.

501   "Children Look at Television." *Educational and Industrial Television,* 1973, 5, 7: 25-28.

502   Chisman, F. P. *The Future Directions of Political Mass Communications Research.* New York: Praeger, 1974.

503   _____ . "Politics and the New Mass Communications." In G. Gerbner, L. Gross, and W. Melody (eds.), *Communications Technology and Social Policy: Understanding the New "Cultural Revolution."* New York: Wiley, 1973: 521-533.

504   Choate, R. B. "The Eleventh Commandment: Thou Shalt Not Covet My Child's Purse." Washington, D.C.: Council on Children, Media, and Merchandising (ERIC Document 071409), 1971.

505   _____ . "Oral Argument in Children's Television Proceeding." Washington, D.C.: Council on Children, Media, and Merchandising, 1973.

506   _____ . "Viewpoint: Pressure on the Airways." *Children Today,* 1973, 2, 1: 10-11.

507   Christenson, R. M. and McWilliams, R. O. (eds.). *Voice of the People: Readings in Public Opinion and Propaganda* (2nd ed.). New York: McGraw-Hill, 1967.

508   Chu, G. C. "Problems of Cross-Cultural Communication Research." *Journalism Quarterly,* 1964, 41, 4: 557-562.

509 Chu, G. C. and Schramm, W. *Learning From Television: What the Research Says.* Washington, D.C.: National Association of Educational Broadcasters, 1967.

510 Cicourel, A. V. *Cognitive Sociology: Language and Meaning in Social Interaction.* New York: Free Press, 1974.

511 Cirino, R. *Don't Blame the People: How the News Media Use Bias Distortion and Censorship to Manipulate Public Opinion.* Los Angeles: Diversity Press, 1971.

512 _____ . *Power to Persuade: Mass Media and the News.* New York: Bantam, 1974.

513 Clancy, K. J. and Kweskin, D. M. "TV Commercial Recall Correlates." *Journal of Advertising Research,* 1971, 11, 2: 18-20.

514 Clark, C. "Race, Identification, and Televised Violence." In G. A. Comstock, E. A. Rubinstein, and J. P. Murray (eds.), *Television and Social Behavior: Television's Effects: Further Explorations* (vol. 5). Washington, D.C.: 1972: 120-184.

515 _____ . "Television and Social Control: Some Observations on the Portrayal of Ethnic Minorities." *Television Quarterly,* 1969, 8: 18-22.

516 Clark, David G. and Blankenburg, William B. "Trends in Violent Content in Selected Mass Media." In G. A. Comstock and E. A. Rubinstein (eds.), *Television and Social Behavior: Media Content and Control* (vol. 1), Washington, D.C.: Government Printing Office, 1972: 188-243.

517 _____ . *You & Media: Mass Communication and Society.* San Francisco, Calif.: Canfield Press, 1973. Emphasizes teaching the consumer how to understand and deal with media. Analyzes broadcasting, advertising, and the creation of mass culture.

518 Clark, R. K. "Misterogers' Neighborhood: An Historical and Descriptive Analysis." Doctoral Dissertation, Athens: Ohio State University, 1971.

519 Clark, Wesley C. "The Impact of Mass Communication in America." *Annals of the American Academy of Political and Social Science,* 1968, 378: 68-74.

520 Clark, W. J. *Of Children and Television.* Cincinnati: Xavier University, 1951.

521 Clarke, Peter. "Children's Responses to Entertainment." *American Behavioral Scientist,* 1971, 14, 3: 353-369.

522 _____ . "Introduction: Some Proposals for Continuing Research on Youth and the Mass Media." *American Behavioral Scientist,* 1971, 14, 3: 313-322.

523 _____ , ed. *New Models for Mass Communication Research,* Beverly Hills: Sage, 1973. A collection of nine articles dealing with signaled stopping techniques, public affairs research, decision making and the media, children's processing of TV ads, marketing communication, coorientation, information seeking strategies, and persuasion.

524 _____ . "Parental Socialization Values and Children's Newspaper Reading." *Journalism Quarterly,* 1965, 42, 4: 539-546.

525 _____ . "Teenager's Co-Orientation and Information-Seeking About Pop Music." *American Behavioral Scientist,* 1973, 16: 551-566.

526 Clarke, Peter and Esposito, Virginia. "A Study of Occupational Advice for Women in Magazines." *Journalism Quarterly,* 1966, 43, 3: 477-485.

527 Clarke, Peter and James, J. "Effects of Situation, Attitude Intensity and Personality on Information Seeking." *Sociometry* 1967, 30: 235-245.

528 Clarke, Peter and Ruggels, L. "Children's Response to Entertainment." *American Behavioral Scientist,* 1971, 14, 3: 353-370.

529 _____ . "Preferences Among Media Coverage of Public Affairs." *Journalism Quarterly,* 1970, 47: 464-471. Reveals that newspapers are preferred over television for public affairs information by adult heads of households.

530 Clausen, John A. "Family Structure, Socialization and Personality." In L. W. Goffman and M. L. Hoffman (eds.), *Review of Child Development Research* (vol. 2). New York: Russell Sage Foundation, 1966: 1-53.

531 _____ , ed. *Socialization and Society.* Boston: Little, Brown, 1968.

532 Clausse, Roger. "The Mass Public at Grips with Mass Communication." *International Social Science Journal,* 1968, 20, 4: 625-643.

533 Clayre, Alasdair. *The Impact of Broadcasting: or Mrs. Buckle's Wall is Singing.* Salisbury, England: Compton Russell, 1973.

534 Cline, Victor B. "Another View: Pornography Effects, the State of the Art." In V. B. Cline (ed.), *Where Do You Draw the Line?: An Exploration into Media Violence, Pornography, and Censorship.* Provo, Utah: Brigham Young University, 1974: 203-244. Presents the summary of and argument for the minority view of the Commission on Obscenity and Pornography—to maintain restrictions on pornographic materials.

535 _____ , ed. *Where Do You Draw the Line?: An Exploration into Media Violence, Pornography, and Censorship.* Provo, Utah: Brigham Young University Press, 1974. The moral, social, and personal aspects of media censorship are examined by twenty contributing scholars—pro and con.

536 Cline, Victor B., Croft, Roger G., and Courrier, Steven. "Desensitization of Children to Television Violence." *Journal of Personality and Social Psychology,* 1973, 27, 3: 360-365. Boys who watch a lot of TV seem to be desensitized to violence in that they showed less arousal to a violent film than did boys of low exposure.

537 Clor, Harry M. *Obscenity and Public Morality: Censorship in a Liberal Society.* Chicago: University of Chicago Press, 1969.

538 Clotfelter, James, ed. *Communication Theory in the Study of Politics: A Review of the Literature.* Chapel Hill: University of North Carolina, School of Journalism (Study No. 7), 1968.

539 Clyde, Robert W. "An Investigation of the Effectiveness of an Intensive Television Information Program Series for Children Aged 7-12 Years." Doctoral Dissertation, University of Iowa, 1964.

540 Clyde, Robert W., Hemmerle, William J., and Bancroft, T. A., "An Application of 'Post Stratification' Technique in Local TV Election Predictions." *Public Opinion Quarterly,* 1963, 27, 3: 467-472.

541 Coelho, George V. *Mental Health and Social Change: an Annotated Bibliography.* Washington, D.C.: Government Printing Office, 1972.

542 Coffin, Thomas E. "Television's Impact on Society." *American Psychologist,* 1955, 10, 10: 630-641. Reviews the effects literature to that date, exonerating the medium.

543 Coffin, Thomas E. and Tuchman, Sam. "A Question of Validity: Some Comments on Apples, Oranges, and the Kitchen Sink." *Journal of Broadcasting,* 1973, 17, 1: 31-33.

544 _____ . "Rating Television Programs For Violence: A Comparison of Five Surveys." *Journal of Broadcasting,* 1973, 17, 1: 3-20.

545 Cohen, Akiba A. "Attention to the Mass Media Among Straight and Split Ticket Voters." *Human Communication Research,* 1975, 2, 4: 75-78.

546 Cohen, A. A., Harrison, R. P., and Wigan, R. T. "Affect and Learning in TV News Viewing by Children." Department of Communication, Michigan State University (Final Report, MH 24496-01), August 1974.

547 Cohen, A. A., Himmelweit, Hilde T., and Bar, Haviva S. "The Effects of 'Contact' on Evaluation: Reactions of the Israeli Public to President Nixon's Visit to Israel, June 1974." *Communication Research,* 1975, 2, 2: 163-172.

548 Cohen, Marcia F. "The Effects of Overt Responding and Cueing in Films Designed for Preschool Children." *Dissertation Abstracts International,* 1971, 32(5-A): 2478-2479.

549 Cohen, Stanley and Young, Jock. *The Manufacture of News.* Beverly Hills: Sage, 1973. A collection of 26 previously published articles dealing with the ways in which the mass media respond to and report deviant behavior and social problems. Reflects the British and European scene as well as the American perspective.

550 Coldevin, G. O. "The Effects of Mass Media Upon the Development of Transnational Orientations." Doctoral Dissertation, University of Washington, 1971.

551 Cole, R. R. "Top Songs In the Sixties: A Content Analysis of Popular Lyrics." *American Behavioral Scientist,* 1971, 14, 3: 389-400.

552 Colfax, J. David. "How Effective is the Protest Advertisement?" *Journalism Quarterly,* 1966, 43: 697-702.

553 Colfax, J., Sternberg, David, and Sternberg, Susan. "The Preparation of Racial Stereotypes: Blacks in Mass Circulation Magazine Advertisements." *Public Opinion Quarterly,* 1972, 36, 1: 8-18.

554 Colldeweth, Jack H. "The Effect of Mass Media Consumption on Accuracy of Beliefs about the Candidates in a Local Congressional Election." Doctoral Dissertation, University of Illinois, 1968.

555 Colle, Royal D. "Negro Image in the Mass Media: A Case Study in Social Change." *Journalism Quarterly,* 1968, 45, 1: 55-60.

556 Collins, W. A. "The Developing Child as Viewer: The Effects of Television on Children and Adolescents." *Journal of Communication,* 1975, 25, 4: 35-44.

557 _____ . "Developmental Aspects of Understanding and Evaluating Television Content." Washington, D.C.: ERIC, 1973.

558 _____ . "Effect of Temporal Separation Between Motivation, Aggression, and Consequences: A Developmental Study." *Developmental Psychology,* 1973, 8: 215-221. Indicates that placing ads between aggressive action and punishment for that action may cause young children to lose the connection between the two and thus evidence more aggressive behavior.

559 _____ . "Effects of Temporal Spacing on Children's Comprehension and Behavior Following Exposure to Media Violence." Doctoral Dissertation, Stanford University, 1971.

560 _____ . "Learning of Media Content: A Developmental Study." *Child Development,* 1970, 41, 4: 1133-1142. Children's learning of essential content (when not given instructions to learn) showed linear relationship with age, while learning of nonessential material was curvilinear.

561 _____ and Zimmerman, S.A. "Convergent and Divergent Social Cues: Effects of Televised Aggression on Children." *Communication Research,* 1975, 2, 4: 331-346.

562 Collins, W. A., Berndt, T. J., and Hess, V. L. "Observational Learning of Motives and Consequences for Television Aggression: A Developmental Study." *Child Development,* 1974, 45: 799-802.

563 Columbia Broadcasting System. "A Study of Messages Received by Children Who Viewed an Episode of Fat Albert and the Cosby Kids." New York: CBS, Office of Social Research, 1974. Demonstrates the absorption of positive, prosocial information for 9 out of 10 of the 7-11-year-olds interviewed in three cities.

564 _____ . "White and Negro Attitudes Toward Race-Related Issues and Activities." Princeton, N.J.: Public Opinion Research Corp., July 9, 1968.

565 Commission on Obscenity and Pornography. *The Report of the Commission on Obscenity and Pornography.* New York: Bantam Books, 1970.

566 Committee on Children and the Cinema. "Report of the Departmental Committee on Children and the Cinema." Presented to the Parliament by the Secretary of State for the Home Department, the Secretary of State for Scotland and the Minister of Education by Command of His Majesty. London: His Majesty's Stationery Office, 1950.

567 Committee on Children's Television. *Children's Television—an Affirmative Program for Community Involvement.* San Francisco: Committee on Children's Television, 1972.

568 _____ . *Television and Children's Needs.* San Francisco: Committee on Children's Television, 1971.

569 Comstock, G. A. "Effects of Television on Children: What is the Evidence?" Santa Monica, Calif.: The Rand Corporation, 1975.

570 _____ . "The Evidence So Far: The Effects of Television on Children and Adolescents." *Journal of Communication,* 1975, 25, 4: 25-34.

571 _____ . "Milgram's Scotch Verdict on TV—A Retrial." Santa Monica, Calif.: The Rand Corporation, 1974.

572 _____ . "New Research on Media Content and Control (Overview)." In G. A. Comstock and E. A. Rubinstein (ed.), *Television and Social Behavior: Media Content and Control* (vol. 1). Washington, D.C.: Government Printing Office, 1972: 1-27.

573 _____ , ed. *Television and Human Behavior: The Key Studies.* Santa Monica, Calif.: The Rand Corporation, 1975. Presents abstracts of key studies selected from the larger bibliography in this three volume set (see Comstock and Fisher, 1975).

574 _____ . "Television and the Young: Setting the Stage For a Research Agenda." Santa Monica, Calif.: The Rand Corporation, 1975.

575 _____ . "Television Violence: Where the Surgeon General's Study Leads." Santa Monica, Calif.: The Rand Corporation, 1972.

576 _____ and Fisher, M., eds. *Television and Human Behavior: A Guide to the Pertinent Scientific Literature.* Santa Monica, Calif.: The Rand Corporation, 1975. Provides a master bibliography of roughly 2300 items—then splits these into content specific smaller bibliographies.

577 Comstock, G. A. and Lindsey, G., eds. *Television and Human Behavior: The Research Horizon, Future and Present.* Santa Monica, Calif.: The Rand Corporation, 1975.

578 Comstock, G.A. and Rubinstein, E. A., eds. *Television and Sociaal Behavior: Media Content and Control* (vol. 1). Washington, D.C.: Government Printing Office, 1972.

579 _____ , eds. *Television and Social Behavior: Television and Adolescent Aggressiveness* (vol. 3). Washington, D.C.: Government Printing Office, 1972.

580 _____ , and Murray, J. P. *Television and Social Behavior: Television's Effects: Further Explorations* (vol. 5). Washington, D.C.: Government Printing Office, 1972.

581 Conference on Behavioral Sciences and the Mass Media, 1966. *Behavioral Sciences and the Mass Media,* Russell Sage Foundation, 1968.

582 Consterdine, G. "Some Recent Evidence on Television Audience Research," *Commentary,* 1968, 10: 38-53.

583 Consumers Union. "Movies for TV: 7393 Ratings; the Results of *Consumer's Reports* Continuing Movie Poll, April 1947–January 1974." Mount Vernon, N.Y.: Consumers Union, 1974.

584 Converse, P. E. "Country Differences in Time Use." In A. Szalai (ed.), *The Use of Time: Daily Activities of Urban and Suburban Populations in Twelve Countries.* The Netherlands: Mouton and Co., 1972: 145-178.

585 ———. "Information Flow and the Stability of Partisan Attitudes." *Public Opinion Quarterly,* 1962, 26: 578-599.

586 ———. "Religion and Politics: The 1960 Election." In A. Campbell (ed.), *Elections and the Political Order.* New York: Wiley, 1966: 96-124.

587 Conway, M. Margaret, Stevens, A. Jay, and Smith, Robert G. "The Relation Between Media Use and Children's Civic Awareness." *Journalism Quarterly,* 1975, 52: 531-538.

588 Cook-Gumperz, J. *Social Control and Socialization: A Study of Class Difference in the Language of Maternal Control.* Boston: Routledge and Kegan Paul, 1973.

589 Cook, R. F. and Fosen, R. H. "Pornography and the Sex Offender: Patterns of Exposure and Immediate Arousal Effects of Pornographic Stimuli." In *Technical Report of the Commission on Obscenity and Pornography: Erotica and Antisocial Behavior* (vol. 7) Washington, D.C.: Government Printing Office, 1971: 149-162.

590 Cott, S. "The Function of Television in the Presidential Election Campaign of 1968." Doctoral Dissertation, Columbia University, 1971.

591 Coughenour, C.M., et al. *Diffusion Research Needs.* University of Missouri Agricultural Experiment Station, Columbus, Missouri, 1968.

592 Counts, T. M., Jr. "Television Use and Word Output." Doctoral Dissertation, University of North Carolina. 1972.

593 Courtney, A. E. and Lockeretz, S. W. "A Woman's Place: An Analysis of the Role Portrayed by Women in Magazine Advertisements." *Journal of Marketing Research,* 1971, 8: 92-95.

594 Courtney, A. E. and Whipple, T. W. "Women in TV Commercials." *Journal of Communication,* 1974, 2: 110-118.

595 Cowan, Peter. "Moving Information Instead of Mass: Transportation vs. Communication." In G. Gerbner, L. Gross and W. Melody (eds.), *Communications Technology and Social Policy: Understanding the New "Cultural Revolution."* New York: Wiley, 1973: 339-352.

596 Cowden, J. E., Bassett, H. T., and Cohen, M. F. "An Analysis of Some Relationships Between Fantasy-Aggressive and Aggressive Behavior Among Institutionalized Delinquents." *Journal of Genetic Psychology,* 1969, 114: 179-183.

597 Cowgill, D. O. and Baulch, N. "The Use of Leisure Time by Older People." *Gerontologist,* 1962, 2: 47-50.

598 Cox, Keith K. "Changes in Stereotyping of Negroes and Whites in Magazine Advertisements." *Public Opinion Quarterly,* 1969, 33, 4: 603-606.

599 Craig, Alec. *The Banned Books of England and Other Countries: A Study of the Conception of Literary Obscenity.* London: Allen & Unwin, 1962.

600 Craig, K. D. and Wood, K. "Autonomic Components of Observers Responses to Pictures of Homicide Victims and Nude Females." *Journal of Experimental Research in Personality,* 1971, 5: 304-309.

601 Crane, E. *Marketing Communications: A Behavioral Approach to Men, Messages and Media.* New York: Wiley, 1965.

602 _____ , Talbott, A., and Hume, R. "Time Use Profiles and Program Strategy." *Journal of Broadcasting,* 1961, 5: 335-343.

603 Cranston, Pat. "Listener Opinion of Radio-TV Advertising Claims." *Journalism Quarterly,* 1958, 35, 3: 285-290.

604 _____ . "Political Convention Broadcasts: Their History and Influence." *Journalism Quarterly,* 1960, 37, 2: 186-194.

605 Crawford, Robert. "Cultural Change and Communications in Morocco." *Human Organization,* 1965, 24, 1: 73-77.

606 Cripps, Thomas R. "The Death of Rastus: Negroes in American Films Since 1945." *Phylon,* 1967, 28, 3: 267-275.

607 Crittenden, John. "Democratic Function of the Open-Mike Radio Forum." *Public Opinion Quarterly,* 1971, 35, 2: 200-210.

608 Croce, M. A. "Condizionamenti Sociali Attraverso Tecniche Cinematografiche: Determinazione dell' Effetto 'Power' di Proiezioni Filmiche" [Social Conditioning through Movies: The Determination of the 'Power' Effect in Movie Projections]. *Contributi dell' Instituto di Psicologia,* 1967, 28: 173-177.

609 Cronen, V. E. "Belief, Salience, Media Exposure, and Summation Theory." *Journal of Communication,* 1973, 23: 86-94.

610 Crossman, R. *The Politics of Television.* London: Panther, 1969.

611 Culbertson, H. M. "Gatekeeper Coorientation—A Viewpoint for Analysis of Popular Culture and Specialized Journalism." *Mass Comm Review,* 1975/76, 3, 1: 3-7.

612 Culkin, John M., ed. "New Directions in Children's Television." *Television Quarterly,* 1970, 9, 3: 5-76.

613 Cunningham and Walsh. *Videotown, 1948-1957.* New York: Cunningham and Walsh Publishers, 1958.

614 Curran, J. "The Impact of TV on the Audience for National Newspapers, 1945-68." In J. Tunstall (ed.), *Media Sociology: A Reader.* London: Constable, 1970: 104-131.

615 Cushing, William G. and Lemert, James B. "Has TV Altered Students' News Media Preferences?" *Journalism Quarterly,* 1973, 50, 1: 138-141.

616 Cutler, N. E., Tedesco, A. S., and Frank, R. S. *The Differential Encoding of Political Images: A Content Analysis of Network Television News.* Philadelphia: Foreign Policy Research Institute, 1972.

D

617 Dahlgren, Peter. "Television in the Socialization Process: Structures and Programming of the Swedish Broadcasting Corporation." In G. A Comstock, and E. A. Rubinstein, *Television and Social Behavior: Media Content and Control* (vol. 1). Washington, D.C.: Government Printing Office, 1972: 533-546.

618 Dajani, Nabil H. "Media Exposure and Mobility in Lebanon." *Journalism Quarterly,* 1973, 50: 297-305.

619 Daly, C. V., ed. *The Media and the Cities.* Chicago, University of Chicago Press, 1968.

620 Danielson, W. A. "Eisenhower's February Decision: A Study of News Impact." *Journalism Quarterly,* 1956, 33: 433-441.

621 _____ and Wilhoit, G. C. *A Computerized Bibliography of Mass Communication Research, 1944-64.* New York: Magazine Publisher's Association, Inc., 1967.

622 Danish, Ray. "The American Family and Mass Communications." *Marriage and Family Living,* 1963, 25, 3: 305-310.

623 Danziger, Kurt, ed. *Readings in Child Socialization.* New York: Pergamon Press, 1970.

624 Dator, James Allen. "Non-Verbal, Non-Numerical Models and Media in Political Science." *American Behavioral Scientist,* 1968, 11, 5: 9-11.

625 Davis, D. K. "The Process of Defining Reality and Television Use." Doctoral Dissertation, University of Minnesota, 1973.

626 Davis, K. E. and Braucht, G. N. "Exposure to Pornography, Character, and Sexual Deviance: A Retrospective Survey." In *Technical Report of the Commission on Obscenity and Pornography: Erotica and Antisocial Behavior* (vol. 7). Washington, D.C.: Government Printing Office, 1971: 245-262.

627 _____ . "Reactions to Viewing Films of Erotically Realistic Heterosexual Behavior." In *Technical Report of the Commission on Obscenity and Pornography: Erotica and Social Behavior* (vol. 8). Washington, D.C.: Government Printing Office, 1971: 68-96.

628 Davis, Richard H. "A Descriptive Study of Television in the Lives of an Elderly Population." Doctoral Dissertation, University of Southern California, 1972.

629 _____ . "The Mass Media and Its Potential for Information Dissemination." In L. Gelwicks (ed.), *Report on Older Population Needs, Resources and Services,* Los Angeles: Model Neighborhood Program, Department of Housing and Urban Development, 1971.

630 _____ . "Television Communication and the Elderly." In D. S. Woodruff and J. E. Birren (eds.), *Aging: Scientific Perspective and Social Issues.* New York: Van Nostrand, 1975.

631 _____ . "Television and the Older Adult." *Journal of Broadcasting,* 1971, 15: 153-159. Documents older adults' preference for news and public affairs programs, with television as the overall preferred news source. The images of old people in commercials, media violence, sex, and commercials in general were found to be objectionable.

632 Davis, Richard H. and Edwards, A. E. *Television: A Therapeutic Tool for the Aged.* Los Angeles: Ethel Percy Andrus Gerontology Center, University of Southern Calif., 1975. Reports on viewing behaviors, information utilization and the development of systems to improve use by the aged.

633 Davison, W. Phillips. "On the Effects of Communication." *Public Opinion Quarterly,* 1959, 23: 343-360.

634 _____ . "Functions of Mass Communication for the Collectivity." In W. P. Davison and F. T. C. Yu (eds.), *Mass Communication Research: Major Issues and Future Directions.* New York: Praeger, 1974: 66-82.

635 _____ . *International Political Communication.* New York: Praeger, 1965.

636 _____ . *Mass Communication and Conflict Resolution: The Role of the Information Media in the Advancement of International Understanding.* New York: Praeger, 1974. Assesses the potential influence of the media on decision makers and on those who influence the decision makers. Analyzes the Middle East situation as a case in point.

637 Davison, W. Phillips and Yu, F. T. C., eds. *Mass Communication Research: Major Issues and Future Directions.* New York: Praeger, 1974. A collection of 10 summary papers by major scholars covering uses, functions, socialization, politics, development, organizational structures, new technology, and priorities for future research.

638 _____ . "Some Priority Areas for Future Research." In W. P. Davison and F. T. C. Yu (eds.), *Mass Communication Research: Major Issues and Future Directions.* New York: Praeger, 1974: 184-196.

639 Dawson, R. E. and Prewitt, L. *Political Socialization.* Boston: Little, Brown, and Co., 1969.

640 Day, A. "Child and Adult TV Fiction in New Zealand." *Delta,* 1972, 11: 12-25.

641 Day, George S. "Attitude Change, Media and Word of Mouth." *Journal of Advertising Research,* 1971, 11, 6: 31-40.

642 _____ . *Buyer Attitudes and Brand Choice Behavior.* New York: Free Press, 1970.

643 DeCrow, Karen. *The Young Woman's Guide to Liberation: Alternatives to a Half-Life While the Choice is Still Yours.* Indianapolis: Bobbs-Merrill, 1971. An anthology of writings about women's roles, economic comparisons, youth images, sexism on television, and women's magazines.

644 DeCurtins, L. "Film und Jugendkriminalitaet" [Motion Pictures and Juvenile Delinquency]. *Kriminalistik,* 1969, 21, 7: 349-355.

645   DeDomenico, Francesco. "RAI Audience Research Study Programme on Television, Family and Children Socialization." In *Television and Socialization Processes in the Family.* Proceedings of the Prix Jeunesse Seminar, 1975: 100-116.

646   DeFleur, Melvin L. "Children's Knowledge of Occupational Roles and Prestige: Preliminary Report." *Psychological Reports,* 1963, 13, 3: 760.

647   _____ . "Mass Communication and Social Change." *Social Forces,* 1966, 44, 3: 314-326.

648   _____ . "Mass Communication and the Study of Rumor." *Sociological Inquiry,* 1962, 32, 1: 51-70.

649   _____ . "Mass Media as Social Systems." In W. Schramm and D. F. Roberts (eds.), *The Process and Effects of Mass Communication* (2nd ed.). Urbana: University of Illinois Press, 1971: 63-83.

650   _____ . "Occupational Roles as Portrayed on Television." *Public Opinion Quarterly,* 1964, 28, 1: 57-74. A content analysis showing little relationship between the proportional occurrence of particular roles in the media and their occurrence in real life.

651   DeFleur, Melvin L. and Ball-Rokeach, S. *Theories of Mass Communication* (3rd. ed.). New York: McKay, 1975.

652   DeFleur, Melvin L., and DeFleur, L. B. "The Relative Contribution of Television as a Learning Source for Children's Occupational Knowledge." *American Sociological Review,* 1967, 32: 777-789.

653   DeFleur, Melvin L., and Larsen, O.N. *The Flow of Information: An Experiment in Mass Communication.* New York: Harper, 1958.

654   DeFleur, Melvin L. and Petranoff, Robert M. "A Televised Test of Subliminal Persuasion." *Public Opinion Quarterly,* 1959, 23, 2: 168-180.

655   De Grazia, S. *Of Time, Work, and Leisure.* Garden City, N.Y.: Anchor Books, 1964.

656   _____ . "The Uses of Time." In R. W. Kleemeier (ed.) *Aging and Leisure.* New York: Oxford University Press, 1961: 113-154.

657   Demant, U. A. "The Unintentional Influences of Television." *Cross Currents,* 1955, 5, 3: 220-225.

658   Dembo, Richard. "Aggression and Media Use Among English Working-Class Youths." Leicester, England: Centre for Mass Communication Research, University of Leicester, 1972.

659   _____ . "Gratifications Found in Media by British Teenage Boys." *Journalism Quarterly,* 1973, 50, 3: 517-526.

660   _____ . "Life Style and Media Use Among English Working-Class Youths." *Gazette,* 1972, 18: 24-36.

661   Denis, Michel. "La Memoire d'un Message Filmique Comparee a celle d'un Message Verbal Chez des Enfants d'Age Scolaire" [A Comparison of the Memory for a Filmed Message in Children of School Age]. *Journal de Psychologie Normale et Pathologique,* 1971, 68, 1: 69-87.

662 Denney, D. R. "Modeling Effects Upon Conceptual Style and Cognitive Tempo." *Child Development,* 1972, 43: 105-119.

663 _____. "Modeling and Eliciting Effects Upon Conceptual Strategies." *Child Development,* 1972, 43: 810-823.

664 Dennis, Jack and Jennings, M. K. *Comparative Political Socialization.* Beverly Hills: Sage, 1973.

665 _____ and Webster, C. "Changes in Children's Images of the President and of Government Between 1962 and 1974." *American Politics Quarterly,* October, 1975.

666 DeRita, Lidia. *I Contadini e la Televisione* [Peasants and Television]. Bologna, Societa editrice il Mulino, 1964.

667 Dervin, Brenda. "Communication Behaviors as Related to Information Control Behavior of Black Low-Income Adults." Doctoral Dissertation, Michigan State University, 1971.

668 _____. "The Everyday Information Needs of the Average American Citizen: A Taxonomy for Analysis." In M. Kocher and J. Donahue (eds.), *Information for the Community.* Chicago: American Library Association, 1975: Chapter 2.

669 _____ and Greenberg, B. S. "The Communication Environment of the Urban Poor." In F. G. Kline and P. J. Tichenor (eds.), *Current Perspectives in Mass Communication Research.* Beverly Hills: Sage, 1972: 195-233.

670 Deutschmann, Paul J. "The Mass Media in an Underdeveloped Village." *Journalism Quarterly,* 1963, 40, 1: 27-35.

671 _____. "Viewing, Conversation and Voting Intentions." In S. Kraus (ed.), *The Great Debates.* Bloomington: Indiana University Press, 1962: 232-252.

672 Deutschmann, Paul J. and Danielson, W. A. "Diffusion of Knowledge of the Major News Story." *Journalism Quarterly,* 1960, 37, 3: 345-355.

673 Deutschmann, Paul J., Ellingsworth, H., and McNelly, J.T. *Communication and Social Change in Latin America: Introducing New Technology.* New York: Praeger, 1968.

674 Deutschmann, Paul J., McNelly, John, and Ellingsworth, Huber. Mass Media Use by Sub-Elite in 11 Latin American Countries." *Journalism Quarterly,* 1961, 38, 4: 460-472.

675 Devlin, L. Patrick. "Contrasts in Presidential Campaign Commercials of 1972." *Journal of Broadcasting,* 1974, 18, 1: 17-26.

676 Devol, K. S., ed. *Mass Media and the Supreme Court.* New York: Hastings House, 1971.

677 DeVries, W. and Tarrance, L., Jr. *The Ticket Splitter: A New Force in American Politics.* Grand Rapids, Mich.: Eerdmans Publishing, 1972.

678 Dexter, Lewis A. "Opportunities for Further Research in Mass Communications." In L. A. Dexter and D. M. White (eds.), *People, Society, and Mass Communications.* Glencoe, Ill.: Free Press, 1964: 568-579.

679 _____ and White, David Manning, eds. *People, Society and Mass Communications.* New York: Free Press, 1964.

680 Diab, Lutfy, N. "Studies in Social Attitudes: II. Selectivity in Mass-Communication Media as a Function of Attitude-Medium Discrepancy." *Journal of Social Psychology,* 1965, 67, 2: 297-302.

681 Dick, Donald. "Religious Broadcasting: 1920-1965, A Bibliography." *Journal of Broadcasting,* 1965, 3: 249-279.

682 _____. Religious Broadcasting: 1920-1965, Part Two of a Bibliography." *Journal of Broadcasting,* 1966, 10, 2: 163-180.

683 _____. "Religious Broadcasting: 1920-1965, Part Three of a Bibliography." *Journal of Broadcasting,* 1966, 10, 3: 257-276.

684 Dickens, Milton and Williams, Frederick. "Mass Communication." *Review of Educational Research,* 1964, 34, 2: 211-221.

685 Dillon, J. "TV Drinking: Do Networks Follow Own Code?" *Christian Science Monitor,* July 1, 1975.

686 _____. "TV Drinking Does Not Mirror U.S." *Christian Science Monitor,* July 11, 1975.

687 _____. "TV Drinking: How Networks Pour Liquor into Your Living Room." *Christian Science Monitor,* June 30, 1975.

688 Dimas, Chris. "The Effect of Motion Pictures Portraying Black Models on the Self-Concept of Black Elementary School Children." *Dissertation Abstracts International,* 1970, 31(6-A): 2609-2610.

689 Di Palma, G. *Apathy and Participation: Mass Politics in Western Societies.* New York: Free Press, 1970.

690 Dittes, James E. "On the Need for Control in Persuasive Scientific Communications." *Psychological Reports,* 1970, 27, 2: 672.

691 Dixon, N. F. *Subliminal Perception: The Nature of a Controversy.* New York: McGraw-Hill, 1971. Covers the concept of subliminal perception, research problems, opposing views, and concludes with the present status of the scientific research.

692 Dizard, Wilson P. "The Political Impact of Television Abroad." *Journal of Broadcasting,* 1965, 9, 3: 195-214.

693 _____. *Television: A World View.* Syracuse, N.Y.: Syracuse University Press, 1966.

694 Dohrmann, Rita. "A Gender Profile of Children's Educational TV: The Effects of Television on Children and Adolescents." *Journal of Communication,* 1975, 25, 4: 56-65.

695 Dominick, Joseph R. "Children's Viewing of Crime Shows and Attitudes on Law Enforcement." *Journalism Quarterly,* 1974, 51, 1: 5-12. Relates attitudes to use and suggests a possible dysfunction of violent content for those who accept the "efficiency" of media police may be a decreased likelihood of reporting a witnessed crime.

696 _____ . "Crime and Law Enforcement on Prime-Time Television." *Public Opinion Quarterly,* 1973, 37, 2: 241-250. Found that 64 percent of the shows analyzed portrayed at least one crime, with 42 percent showing more than one. The overall message, however, is that crime does not pay—with 88 percent of the crimes being solved. Other comparisons are made to real world statistics.

697 _____ . "The Influence of Social Class, the Family, and Exposure to Television Violence on the Socialization of Aggression." *Dissertation Abstracts International,* 1971, 31(12-A): 6641.

698 _____ . "The Portable Friend: Peer Group Membership and Radio Usage." *Journal of Broadcasting,* 1974, 18, 2: 161-170.

699 _____ . "Television and Political Socialization." *Educational Broadcasting Review,* 1972, 6, 1: 48-55.

700 Dominick, Joseph R. and Greenberg, Bradley, S. "Attitudes Toward Violence: The Interaction of Television Exposure, Family Attitudes, and Social Class." In G. A. Comstock and E. A. Rubinstein (eds.), *Television and Social Behavior: Television and Adolescent Aggressiveness* (vol. 3), Washington, D.C.: Government Printing Office, 1972: 314-335.

701 _____ . "Mass Media Functions Among Low-Income Adolescents." In B. S. Greenberg and B. Dervin (eds.), *Uses of the Mass Media by the Urban Poor.* New York: Praeger, 1970: 31-49.

702 _____ . "Three Seasons of Blacks on Television." *Journal of Advertising Research,* 1970, 10, 2: 21-28.

703 Dominick, Joseph R. and Rauch, Gail E. "Image of Women in Network TV Commercials." *Journal of Broadcasting,* 1972, 16, 3: 259-266.

704 Dominick, Joseph R., Wurtzel, Alan and Lometti, Guy. "Television Journalism vs. Show Business: A Content Analysis of Eyewitness News." *Journalism Quarterly,* 1975, 52: 213-218.

705 Donagher, Patricia C., Poulas, Rita W., Leibert, Robert M., and Davidson, Emily S. "Race, Sex and Social Example: An Analysis of Character Portrayals on Inter-Racial Television Entertainment." *Psychological Reports,* 1975, 37, 3 Pt. 2: 1023-1034.

706 Donner, S. T. (ed.) *The Meaning of Commercial Television.* Austin: University of Texas Press, 1966.

707 Donnerstein, E., Lipton, S., and Evans, R. "Erotic Stimuli and Aggression: Facilitation or Inhibition." Evanston: Southern Illinois University, 1974.

708 Donohew, Lewis. "Communication and Readiness for Change in Appalachia." *Journalism Quarterly,* 1967, 44: 679-687.

709 _____ . "Decoder Behavior on Incongruent Political Material: A Pilot Study." *Journal of Communication,* 1966, 16: 133-142.

710 Donohew, Lewis and Palmgreen, Philip. "An Investigation of 'Mechanisms' of Information Selection." *Journalism Quarterly,* 1971, 48: 627-639, 666.

711 _____ . "A Reappraisal of Dissonance and the Selective Exposure Hypothesis." *Journalism Quarterly,* 1971, 48, 3: 412-420.

712 Donohew, Lewis and Singh, B. Krishna. "Communication and Life Styles in Appalachia." *Journal of Communication,* 1969, 19, 3: 202-216.

713 _____ . "Modernization of Life Styles. An Appraisal of the 'War on Poverty' in a Rural Setting of Southeastern Kentucky." Lexington: University of Kentucky, 1968.

714 Donohew, Lewis and Thorp, Robert. "An Approach to the Study of Mass Communications Within a State." *Journalism Quarterly,* 1966, 43, 2: 264-268.

715 Donohew, Lewis and Tipton Leonard P. "A Conceptual Model of Information Seeking, Avoiding and Processing." In P. Clarke (ed.), *New Models for Mass Communication Research.* Beverly Hills: Sage, 1973: 243-268.

716 Donohew, Lewis, Parker, J. M. and McDermott, V. "Psychophysiological Measurement of Information Selection: Two Studies." *Journal of Communication,* 1972, 22: 54-63.

717 Donohue, G. A., Tichenor, P. J., and Olien, C. N. "Gatekeeping: Mass Media Systems and Information Control." In F. G. Kline and P. J. Tichenor (eds.), *Current Perspectives in Mass Communication Research.* Beverly Hills: Sage, 1972: 41-70.

718 _____ . "Mass Media Functions, Knowledge and Social Control." *Journalism Quarterly,* 1973, 50, 4: 652-659.

719 _____ . "Mass Media and the Knowledge Gap: A Hypothesis Reconsidered." *Communication Research,* 1975, 2, 1: 3-23.

720 Donohue, John E. "Sources of Sexuality Concept Formation Among High School Students." *Dissertation Abstracts International,* 1971, 32(1-A): 159-160.

721 Donohue, Thomas R., "Black Children's Perceptions of Favorite TV Characters as Models of Antisocial Behavior." *Journal of Broadcasting,* 1975, 19, 2: 153-166.

722 _____ . "Effects of Commercials on Black Children." *Journal of Advertising Research,* 1975, 15, 6: 41-47.

723 _____ . "Impact of Viewer Predisposition on Political TV Commercials." *Journal of Broadcasting,* 1974, 18, 1: 3-16.

724 _____ . "Viewer Perceptions of Color and Black-and-White Paid Political Advertising." *Journalism Quarterly,* 1973, 50, 4: 660-665.

725 Doob, Anthony N. "Some Determinants of Aggression." Doctoral Dissertation, Stanford University, 1967.

726 _____ and Climie, Robert J. "Delay of Measurement and the Effects of Film Violence." *Journal of Experimental and Social Psychology,* 1972, 8, 2: 136-142.

727 Doob, Anthony N. and Kirshenbaum, H. M. "The Effects on Arousal of Frustration and Aggressive Films." *Journal of Experimental Social Psychology,* 1973, 9: 57-64.

728 Doolittle, John and Pepper, Robert. "Children's TV Ad Content: 1974." *Journal of Broadcasting,* 1975, 19, 2: 131-142.

729 Douglas, D. F., Westley, B. H., and Chaffee, S. H. "An Information Campaign that Changed Community Attitudes." *Journalism Quarterly,* 1970, 47: 487-492.

730 Downing, Mildred. "Heroine of the Daytime Serial." *Journal of Communication,* 1974, 24, 2: 130-137. A content analytic comparison which indicates that the heroines in daytime television are more representative than those in prime-time.

731 _____ . "The World of Daytime Television Serial Drama," Doctoral Dissertation, University of Pennsylvania, 1974.

732 Drabman, R. S. and Thomas, M. H. "Does Media Violence Increase Children's Toleration of Real-Life Aggression?" *Developmental Psychology,* 1974, 10: 418-421. The findings of this experimental study indicate that the answer to the question posed is yes.

733 _____ . "Does TV Violence Breed Indifference?; The Effects of Television on Children and Adolescents." *Journal of Communication,* 1975, 25, 4: 86-89.

734 Dreyer, Edward C. "Media Use and Electoral Choices: Some Political Consequences of Information Exposure." *Public Opinion Quarterly,* 1971, 35, 4: 544-553.

735 _____ and Rosenbaum, Walter A., eds. *Political Opinion and Electoral Behavior: Essays and Studies.* Belmont, Calif.: Wadsworth, 1970.

736 Dubanoski, R. A. and Parton, D. A. "Imitative Aggression in Children as a Function of Observing a Human Model." *Developmental Psychology,* 1971, 4: 489.

737 Dubas, Orest and Martel, Lisa. *Media Impact: Science, Mass Media and the Public—A Research Study on Science Communication.* Ottawa: Information Canada, 1975.

738 Duberman, L. *Gender and Sex in Society.* New York: Praeger, 1975.

739 Duck, S. W. and Baggaley, J. "Audience Reaction and its Effect on Perceived Expertise." *Communication Research,* 1975, 2, 1: 79-85. An experimental television manipulation of positive vs. negative audience reaction shots, showing significantly different effects on evaluation of the speaker.

740 Dunham, F. "Effect of Television on School Achievement of Children." *School Life,* 1952, 34: 88-89.

741 _____ . *What Do They Learn? Criteria Are Needed for Gauging TV Programs.* Washington, D.C.: Office of Education, 1957.

742 Durgnat, R. *Films and Feelings.* Cambridge, Mass.: M.I.T. Press, 1967.

743 Dussich, J.P.J. "Violence and the Media." *Criminology,* 1970, 8, 1: 80-94.

744 Dyoniziak, Ryszard. "Recent Sociological Research on the Mass Media in Poland." *Journalism Quarterly,* 1962, 39, 2: 210-212.

745 Dye, R. P. "Video Violence." *Journal of Broadcasting,* 1966, 10: 97-102.

E

746 Easton, D. and Dennis, J. *Children in the Political System: Origins of Political Legitimacy.* New York: McGraw-Hill, 1969.

747 Edelman, Murray. *Politics as Symbolic Action: Mass Arousal and Quiescence.* Chicago: Markham, 1971. From the Institute for Research on Poverty Monograph Series. Assesses political psychology, including violence.

748 _____. *The Symbolic Uses of Politics.* Urbana: University of Illinois Press, 1964.

749 Edelstein, Alex S. "An Alternative Approach to the Study of Source Effects in Mass Communication." *Studies of Broadcasting,* 1973, 9: 6-29.

750 _____. "Decision-Making and Mass Communication: A Conceptual and Methodological Approach to Public Opinion." In P. Clarke (ed.), *New Models for Mass Communication Research,* Beverly Hills: Sage, 1973: 81-118.

751 _____. *Perspectives in Mass Communications.* Copenhagen: Einar Harcks Forlag, 1966.

752 _____. *The Uses of Communication in Decision-Making: A Comparative Study of Yugoslavia and the United States.* New York: Praeger, 1974. Focuses on the individual's use of communication for day-to-day decisions, as opposed to governmental or agency decision makers. Also offers a refined methodology for survey research.

753 _____ and Nelson, J.L. "Violence in the Comic Cartoon." *Journalism Quarterly,* 1969, 45, 2: 355-358.

754 Edelstein, Alex S. and Tefft, D. P. "Media Credibility and Respondent Credulity with Respect to Watergate." *Communication Research,* 1974, 1, 4: 426-439.

755 Edgar, Patricia M. *Sex Type Socialization and Television Family Comedy Programmes* (Technical report no. 2). Bundoora, Victoria, Australia: The Centre for the Study of Educational Communication and Media, 1972.

756 _____. "Social and Personality Factors Influencing Learning from Film and Television." Washington, D.C.: ERIC, 1973.

757 _____ and Edgar, Donald E. "Television Violence and Socialization Theory." *Public Opinion Quarterly,* 1971-1972, 35, 4: 608-612.

758 Edge, David, ed. *The Formative Years: How Children Become Members of Their Society.* New York: Schocken, 1970.

759 Edmondson, M. and Rounds, D. *The Soaps: Daytime Serials of Radio and TV.* New York: Stein and Day, 1973.

760 Efron, E. and Hickey, N. *TV and Your Child: In Search of an Answer.* New York: Triangle Publications, 1969.

761 Ehrenberg, A.S.C. "A Comparison of TV Audience Measures." *Journal of Advertising Research,* 1964, 4, 4: 11-16.

762 _____. "A Review of 7-day Recall." *Commentary,* 1963, 12: 3-18.

763 _____ . "How Reliable is Aided Recall of TV Viewing?" *Journal of Advertising Research,* 1961, 1, 4: 29-31.

764 _____ . "Repetitive Advertising and the Consumer." *Journal of Advertising Research,* 1974, 14, 2: 25-34.

765 _____ . "Towards an Integrated Theory of Consumer Behavior." *Journal of the Market Research Society,* 1969, 11, 4: 305-337.

766 Ehrenberg, A.S.C. and Goodhardt, G. J. "Duplication of Viewing Between and Within Channels." *Journal of Advertising Research,* 1969, 6: 169-178.

767 _____ . "Practical Applications of the Duplication of Viewing Law." *Journal of the Market Research Society,* 1969, 11: 6-24.

768 Ehrle, R. A. and Johnson, B. G. "Psychologists and Cartoons." *American Psychologist,* 1961, 16: 693-698.

769 Eifler, Deborah, Hokoda, Elizabeth, Ross, Catherine, and Weitzman, Lenore J. "Sex-role Socialization in Picture Books for Preschool Children." *American Journal of Sociology,* 1972, 77: 1125-1150.

770 Eiler, S. W. and Scheer, C. J. "A Comparison of Canadian and American Network Television News." *Journal of Broadcasting,* 1972, 16: 159-164.

771 Einhorn, Hillel J., Komorita, S. S., and Rosen, Benson. "Multidimensional Models for the Evaluation of Political Candidates." *Journal of Experimental Social Psychology,* 1972, 8, 1: 58-73.

772 Eiselein, E. B. "Television and the Mexican-American." *Public Telecommunications Review,* 1974, 2: 13-18.

773 _____ and Marshall, W. " 'Fiesta'—An Experiment in Minority Audience Research and Programming." *Educational Television,* 1971, 2: 11-15.

774 Eisenberg, Jeanne G., Gersten, Joanne C., Langner, Thomas S., McCarthy, Elizabeth D, and Orzeck, Linda. "Violence and Behavior Disorders: The Effects of Television on Children and Adolescents." *Journal of Communication,* 1975, 25, 4: 71-85.

775 Ekman, P. and Friesen, W. V. "A Tool for the Analysis of Motion Picture Film or Videotape." *American Psychologist,* 1969, 24: 240-243.

776 _____ and Taussig, T. G. "VID-R and SCAN: Tools and Methods for the Automated Analysis of Visual Records." In G. Gerbner, O. Holsti, K. Krippendorff , W. Paisley, and P. Stone (eds.), *The Analysis of Communication Content.* New York: Wiley, 1969: 297-312.

777 Ekman, P., Liebert, R. M., Friesen, W. V., Harrison, R. P., Zlatchin, C., Malmstrom, E. J., and Baron, R. A. "Facial Expressions of Emotion While Watching Televised Violence as Predictors of Subsequent Aggression." In G. A. Comstock, E. A. Rubinstein, and J. P. Murray (eds.), *Television and Social Behavior: Television's Effects: Further Explorations* (vol. 5). Washington, D.C.: Government Printing Office, 1972: 22-58.

778 El-Assal, Mohamed M. "An Experimental Study of Opinion Leadership: Theoretical Formulation and Test of Selected Variables." *Dissertation Abstracts,* 1968, 28(9-A): 3766-3767.

779 Elder, G. H. *Adolescent Socialization and Personality Development.* Chicago: Rand McNally, 1968.

780 Eleey, Michael F., Gerbner, George, and Tedesco, Nancy. "Apples, Oranges and the Kitchen Sink: An Analysis and Guide to the Comparison of 'Violence Ratings.' " *Journal of Broadcasting,* 1973, 17, 1: 21-31.

781 _____. "Validity Indeed!" *Journal of Broadcasting,* 1973, 17, 1: 34-35.

782 Elfin, M. and Zweig, Leonard. "The Battle of Political Symbols." *Public Opinion Quarterly,* 1954, 18, 2: 205-210.

783 Elias, M. "How to Win Friends and Influence Kids on Television." *Human Behavior,* 1974, 3, 4: 16-23.

784 Elkin, Frederick. *The Child and Society: The Process of Socialization* (2nd ed.). New York, Random House, 1972.

785 _____. "The Psychological Appeal of the Hollywood Western." *Journal of Educational Sociology,* 1950, 24: 72-86.

786 Elliott, P. *The Making of a Television Series: A Case Study in the Sociology of Culture.* New York: Hastings House, 1973.

787 _____. "Uses and Gratifications Research: A Critique and a Sociological Alternative." In J. G. Blumler and E. Katz (eds.), *The Uses of Mass Communications: Current Perspectives on Gratifications Research.* Beverly Hills: Sage, 1974: 249-268.

788 Elliott, W. Y., ed. *Television's Impact on American Culture.* East Lansing: Michigan State University Press, 1956.

789 Elliott, P. and Chaney, D. "A Sociological Framework for the Study of Television Production." *Sociological Review,* 1969, 17: 355-376.

790 Elliott, P. and Golding, P. "Mass Communication and Social Change." In E. DeKadt and G. Williams (eds.), *Sociology and Development.* London: Tavistock, 1974: 229-254.

791 Ellis, G. T. "The Effect of Aggressive Cartoons on Children's Behavior." Doctoral Dissertation, Mississippi State University, 1971.

792 _____ and Sekyra, F. "The Effect of Aggressive Cartoons on the Behavior of First Grade Children." *Journal of Psychology,* 1972, 81: 37-43.

793 Elthammar, Olof. *Emotionella reaktioner infor Film hos 11-18 Arsgrupper* [Emotional Reactions to Films Seen by 11-18-year-olds]. Stockholm: Almquist and Wiksell, 1967.

794 Emery, F. E. "Psychological Effects of the Western Film: A Study in Television Viewing. I. The Theoretical Study: Working Hypotheses on the Psychology of Television." *Human Relations,* 1959, 12, 3: 195-213.

795 _____. "Psychological Effects of the Western Film: A Study in Television Viewing. II. The Experimental Study." *Human Relations,* 1959, 12, 3: 215-232.

796 Emmett, B. P. "The Design of Investigations into the Effects of Radio and Television Programmes and Other Mass Communications." *Journal of the Royal Statistical Society,* 1966, 129: 26-60.

797 _____ . "A New Role for Research in Broadcasting." *Public Opinion Quarterly,* 1968, 32, 4: 654-665.

798 _____ . "Television and Violence—Two Years and a Million Dollars Later." *EBU Review,* 1972, 23, 5: 19-22.

799 Emrich, E. *Young People and Television: An International Study of Juries, Producers and Their Young Audiences Based on the Prize-Winning Programmes of Prix Jeunesse 1970: "Man in Metropolis" and "Baff."* Munich: International Central Institute for Youth and Educational Television, 1972.

800 Endleman, S., ed. *Violence in the Streets.* Chicago: Quadrangle Books, 1968.

801 Engel, James F., Kollat, David T., and Blackwell, Roger D. *Consumer Behavior.* New York: Holt, Rinehart & Winston, 1968.

802 Epstein, E. J. *News From Nowhere: Television and the News.* New York: Random House, 1973.

803 Erickson, Erik H. *Childhood and Society* (2nd ed.). New York: Norton, 1964.

804 Ernst, Morris L. and Schwartz, Alan U. *Censorship: The Search for the Obscene.* New York: Macmillan, 1964.

805 Eron, L. D. "Relationship of TV Viewing Habits and Aggressive Behavior in Children." *Journal of Abnormal Social Psychology,* 1963, 67, 2: 193-196.

806 Eron, L. D., Walder, L. O., and Lefkowitz, M. M. *Learning of Aggression in Children.* Boston: Little, Brown, 1971.

807 Eron, L. D., Huesmann, L. R., Lefkowitz, M. M., and Walder, L. O. "Does Television Violence Cause Aggression?" *American Psychologist,* 1972, 27: 253-263.

808 Eron, L. D., Lefkowitz, M. M., Walder, L. O., and Huesmann, L. R. "Relation of Learning in Childhood to Psychopathology in Aggression in Young Adulthood." In A. Davids (eds.) *Child Personality and Psychopathology: Current Topics* (vol. 1). New York: Wiley, 1974.

809 Erskine, Hazel. "The Polls: Opinion of the News Media." *Public Opinion Quarterly,* 1970, 32, 4: 630-643.

810 Evry, Hal. *The Selling of A Candidate: The Winning Formula.* Los Angeles: Western Opinion Research Center, 1971.

811 _____ . "TV Murder Causes Bad Dreams." *Film World,* 1952, 8: 247.

812 Evans, C. C. "Television For The Pre-School Child." *Elementary English,* 1955, 32: 541-542.

813 Evarts, Dru and Stempel, G. H. "Coverage of the 1972 Campaign by TV, News Magazines and Major Newspapers." *Journalism Quarterly,* 1974, 51, 4: 645-648; 676.

814 Eyre-Brook, E. "The Role of the Mass Media in Political Socialization." Leicester, England: University of Leicester, 1973.

815 _____ . "The Role of the Mass Media in the Political Socialization of English Adolescents." Leipzig: *Report of the Proceedings of the 9th General*

Assembly of the International Association for Mass Communication Research, 1974.

816 Ezratty, S. "Television and Society." *Impact of Science on Society,* 1965, 15, 3: 149-172.

F

817 Fagen, R. R. "Mass Media Growth: a Comparison of Communist and Other Countries." *Journalism Quarterly,* 1964, 41, 4: 563-567, 572.

818 _____. *Politics and Communication: An Analytic Study.* Boston: Little, Brown & Co., 1966.

819 Fane, X. F. "Television Image of the Father: A Comparison of the Father Image Held by Home Economics Teachers With the Image Perceived by High School Students on Commercial Television." Doctoral Dissertation, New York University, 1965.

820 Farace, Vincent. "A Study of Mass Communication and National Development." *Journalism Quarterly,* 1966, 43, 2: 305-313.

821 _____ and Donohew, Lewis. "Mass Communication in National Social Systems: A Study of 43 Variables in 115 Countries." *Journalism Quarterly,* 1965, 42, 2: 253-261.

822 Farley, Frank H. and Grant, A. D. "Arousal and Reminiscence in Learning from Color and Black/White Visual Presentations." Washington, D.C.: Educational Resources Information Center, 1973.

823 Fathi, Asghar and Heath, Carole L. "Group Influence, Mass Media and Musical Taste Among Canadian Students." *Journalism Quarterly,* 1974, 51, 4: 705-709.

824 Fearing, F. "Influence of the Movies on Attitudes and Behavior." *Annals of the American Academy of Political and Social Science,* 1947. 254: 70-80.

825 _____. "Social Impact of the Mass Media of Communication." In N. B. Henry (ed.), *Mass Media and Education.* Chicago: University of Chicago Press, 1954.

826 Fechter, John V. "Modeling and Environmental Generalization by Mentally Retarded Subjects of Televised Aggressive or Friendly Behavior." *American Journal of Mental Deficiency,* 1971, 76, 2: 266-267.

827 Fedler, Fred. "The Mass Media and Minority Groups." *Journalism Quarterly,* 1973, 50, 1: 109-117.

828 von Feilitzen, Cecilia. "Findings of Scandinavian Research on Child and Television in the Process of Socialization." In *Television and Socialization Processes in the Family.* Proceedings of the Prix Jeunesse Seminar, 1975: 54-84.

829 _____. "Om Etermediernas Funktioner" [On the Functions of Broadcast Media]. In *Radio Och TV Moter Publiken.* Stockholm: Sveriges Radio Forlag. 1972: 291-322.

830 von Feilitzen, Cecilia and Linne, O. "Children and Identification in the Mass Communication Process," Stockholm: Sveriges Radio Audience and Programme Research Department, 146, 1973.

831 _____ . "Identifying With Television Characters: The Effects of Television on Children and Adolescents." *Journal of Communication,* 1975, 25, 4: 51-55.

832 _____ . "Living Habits and Broadcast Media Behavior of 3–6-year-olds." Stockholm: Sveriges Radio Audience and Programme Research Department, 7, 1968.

833 Feinstein, P. *All about Sesame Street.* New York: Tower, 1971.

834 Fejer, Dianne, Smart, Reginald G., Whitehead, Paul C., and La Forest, Lucien. "Sources of Information About Drugs Among High School Students." *Public Opinion Quarterly,* 1971, 35, 2: 235-241.

835 Feldman, S. and Wolf, A. "What's Wrong with Children's Commercials?" *Journal of Advertising Research,* 1974, 14, 1: 39-43.

836 Ferber, Robert and Wales, Hugh G. "Advertising Recall in Relation to Type of Recall." *Public Opinion Quarterly,* 1958, 22, 4: 529-536.

837 Ferguson, Richard D. and Gitter, George A. "Blacks in Magazine and Television Advertising." *CRC Report,* No. 56. Communication Research Center, Boston Univ., 1971.

838 Ferracuti, Franco and Lazzari, Renato. "Indagine Sperimentale sugli Effetti Immediati della Presentazione di Scene di Violenza Filmata" [An Experimental Research on the Immediate Effects of the Presentation of Scenes of Violence in Motion Pictures]. *Bollettino di Psicologia Applicata,* 1970, 100-102: 87-153.

839 _____ . "La Violenza nei Mezzi di Communicationi di Massa" [Violence in the Mass Media]. Toririno, Italy: *Quarderni del Servizio Opinioni,* Special Series No. 1, 1968.

840 Feshbach, N. D. "The Effects of Violence in Childhood." *Journal of Clinical Child Psychology,* 1973, 2, 2: 28-31.

841 _____ and Feshbach, S. "Children's Aggression." In W. Hartup (ed.), *The Young Child* (vol. 2). Washington, D.C.: National Association for the Education of Young Children, 1972: 234-302.

842 Feshbach, S. "Aggression." In P. H. Mussen (ed.), *Carmichael's Manual of Child Psychology* (3rd ed., vol. 2). New York: Wiley, 1970: 159-250.

843 _____ . "The Catharsis Effect: Research and Another View." In R. K. Baker and S. J. Ball (eds.), *Mass Media and Violence.* A staff report to the National Commission on the Causes and Prevention of Violence. Washington, D.C.: Government Printing Office, 1969: 461-472.

844 _____ . "The Catharsis Hypothesis and Some Consequences of Interaction With Aggressive and Neutral Play Objects." *Journal of Personality,* 1956, 24: 449-462.

845 _____ . "The Drive-Reducing Function of Fantasy Behavior." *Journal of Abnormal and Social Psychology,* 1955, 50: 3-11. Engaging in fantasy behavior by way of making up stories from pictures reduced the subsequent aggressiveness of undergraduates who had been insulted. No reduction was evident for the control group who performed a skill task rather than the fantasy task.

846 _____ . "Effects of Exposure to Aggressive Content in Television Upon Aggression in Boys." Copenhagen: *Proceedings of the XVI International Congress of Applied Psychology,* 1968: 669-672.

847 _____ . "Fantasy and the Regulation of Aggression." In P. J. Elich (ed.), *Social Learning. Fourth Western Symposium on Learning.* Bellingham: Western Washington State College, 1973: 5-23.

848 _____ . "The Function of Aggression and the Regulation of Aggressive Drive." *Psychological Review,* 1964, 71: 257-272.

849 _____ . "Plan 6: The Effects of Aggressive Content in Television Upon the Aggressive Behavior of the Audience." In L. Arons and M. A. May (eds.), *Television and Human Behavior: Tomorrow's Research in Mass Communication.* New York: Appleton-Century-Crofts, 1963: 83-97.

850 _____ . "Reality and Fantasy in Filmed Violence." In J. P. Murray, E. A. Rubinstein, and G. A. Comstock (eds.), *Television and Social Behavior: Television and Social Learning* (vol. 2). Washington, D.C.: Government Printing Office, 1972: 318-345. A stimulus film, when labeled as news coverage of an actual event produced more aggressive response than when it was labeled as a fictional Hollywood film.

851 _____ . "The Stimulating versus Cathartic Effects of a Vicarious Aggressive Activity." *Journal of Abnormal and Social Psychology,* 1961. 63: 381-385.

852 Feshbach, S. and Singer, R. D. "Catharsis of Aggression Among Institutionalized Boys: Further Discussion." In G. A. Comstock, E. A. Rubinstein, and J. P. Murray (eds.), *Television and Social Behavior: Television's Effects: Further Explorations* (vol. 5). Washington, D.C.: Government Printing Office, 1972: 359-365.

853 _____ . *Television and Aggression: An Experimental Field Study.* San Francisco: Jossey-Bass, 1971. Details the controversial six-week field experiment, conducted with institutionalized boys, which appears to support the catharsis hypothesis. See vol. 5 of the *Television and Social Behavior* series (Liebert, Sobol, Davidson) for a sequence of exchanges and critiques.

854 _____ . "Television and Aggression: Some reactions to the Leibert, Davidson, and Sobol Review and Response." In G. A. Comstock, E. A. Rubinstein, and J. P. Murray (eds.), *Television and Social Behavior: Further Explorations* (vol. 5). Washington, D.C.: Government Printing Office, 1972: 373-375.

855 Fike, David F. "Mass Media and Social Work Practice; an Experimental Research Design to Test Attitude-Changing Effectiveness of a Planned Parenthood Advertising Campaign." Doctoral Dissertation, West Texas State College, 1972.

856 Filep, R., Millar, G. R., and Gillette, P. T. *The Sesame Street Mother Project: Final Report.* El Segundo, Calif.: Institute for Educational Development, 1971.

857 Findahl, Olle. "The Effect of Visual Illustrations Upon Perception and Retention of News Programmes." Stockholm: Sveriges Radio, Audience and Programme Research Department, 1971.

858 _____ and Hoijer, Birgitta. "Effect of Additional Verbal Information on Retention of a Radio News Program." *Journalism Quarterly,* 1975, 52: 493-498.

859 Fine, Gary A. "Recall of Information about Diffusion of Major News Event." *Journalism Quarterly,* 1975, 52: 751-755.

860 Finney, Robert J. "Television News Messages and Their Perceived Effects In a Congressional Election Campaign." Doctoral Dissertation, Ohio State University, 1971.

861 Fischer, Heinz D., and Merrill, J. C., eds. *International Communication: Media, Channels, Functions.* New York: Hastings House, 1970.

862 Fisher, Paul L. and Lowenstein, Ralph L., eds. *Race and the News Media.* New York: Praeger, 1967.

863 Fisk, George. "Media Influence Reconsidered." *Public Opinion Quarterly,* 1959, 23, 1: 83-91.

864 Fitch, Robert E. "The Impact of Violence and Pornography on the Arts and Morality." In V. B. Cline (ed.), *Where Do You Draw the Line?: An Exploration into Media Violence, Pornography, and Censorship.* Provo, Utah: Brigham Young University, 1974: 15-24.

365 Fitzsimmons, Stephen J. and Osborn, Hobart G. "The Impact of Social Issues and Public Affairs Television Documentaries." *Public Opinion Quarterly,* 1968, 32, 3: 379-397.

866 Fixx, James F., ed. *The Mass Media and Politics.* New York: Arno Press, 1972.

867 Flanders, James P. "A Review of Research on Imitative Behavior. *Psychological Bulletin,* 1968, 69, 5: 316-337. Reviews the evidence on live vs. mediated models and imitative behavior.

868 Flapan, D. *Children's Understanding of Social Interaction.* New York: Teachers College Press, 1968.

869 Flavell, J. H. *The Development of Role Taking and Communication Skills in Children.* New York: Wiley, 1968.

870 Fleiss, D. and Ambrosino, L. "An International Comparison of Children's Television Programming." Washington, D.C.: National Citizens Committee for Broadcasting, 1971.

871 Fletcher, Alan D. "Negro and White Children's Television Program Preferences." *Journal of Broadcasting,* 1969, 13, 4: 359-366.

872 _____ . "Television Viewing Behavior of Negro and White Children in Athens, Georgia." Doctoral Dissertation, University of Illinois, 1969.

873 _____ and Winn, Paul R. "An Intermagazine Analysis of Factors in Advertisement Readership." *Journalism Quarterly,* 1974, 51, 3: 425-430: 489.

874 Foley, J. M. "A Functional Analysis of Television Viewing." Doctoral Dissertation, University of Iowa, 1968.

875 Foote, Cone and Belding, Inc. "The Public's Reaction to Political Advertising." New York: A Report Prepared by the Research Department. Foote, Cone and Belding, Jan. 1971.

876 Ford, G. H. *Protest, Violence and Conflict: Some Observations on the Role of Television.* London: Seaford House Papers, Royal College of Defence Studies, 1972.

877 Ford, Joseph B. "The Primary Group in Mass Communication." *Sociology and Social Research,* 1955, 38, 3: 152-158.

878 Fore, W. F. *Image and Impact: How Man Comes Through in the Mass Media.* New York: Friendship Press, 1970.

879 Forer, R. "The Impact of a Radio Program on Adolescents." *Public Opinion Quarterly,* 1955, 19, 2: 184-194.

880 Forsey, S. D. "Plan 5. The Influence of Family Structures Upon the Patterns and Effects of Family Viewing." In L. Arons and M. A. May (eds.), *Television and Human Behavior: Tomorrow's Research in Mass Communication.* New York: Appleton-Century-Crofts, 1963: 64-80.

881 Foster, June E. "Father Images: Television and Ideal." *Journal of Marriage and the Family,* 1965, 26, 3: 353-355.

882 Foulkes, D. and Rechtschaffen, A. "Presleep Determinants of Dream Content: Effects of Two Films." *Perceptual and Motor Skills,* 1964, 19: 983-1005.

883 Foulkes, D., Belvedere, E., and Brubaker, T. "Televised Violence and Dream Content." In G. A. Comstock, E. A. Rubinstein, and J. P. Murray (eds.), *Television and Social Behavior: Television's Effects: Further Explorations* (vol. 5). Washington, D.C.: Government Printing Office, 1972: 59-119.

884 Foundation for Character Education. *Television for Children.* Boston: Foundation for Character Education, 1958.

885 Fowles, Barbara R. and Voyat, Gilbert. "Piaget Meets Big Bird: Is TV a Passive Teacher?" *Urban Review,* 1974, 7, 1: 69-80.

886 Fox, Peter D. "Non Cooperation Bias in Television Ratings." *Public Opinion Quarterly,* 1963, 27, 2: 312-314.

887 Fox, William S. and Williams, James D. "Political Orientation and Music Preferences Among College Students." *Public Opinion Quarterly,* 1974, 38, 3: 352-371.

888 Fougeyrollas, P. "Television and the Social Education of Women." *Reports and Papers on Mass Communication, No. 50.* Paris: UNESCO (New York: UNIPUB), 1967.

889 Fraiberg, S. H. "The Mass Media." *Child Study,* 1960, 37: 3-12.

890 Francher, Scott J. "It's the Pepsi Generation . . . Accelerated Aging and the Television Commercial." *International Journal of Aging and Human Development,* 1973, 4, 3: 245-254.

891 Frank, J. *Television: How to Use it Wisely With Children* (rev. ed.). New York: Child Study Association of America, 1969.

892 Frank, R.S. "The 'Grammar of Film' in Television News." *Journalism Quarterly,* 1974, 51: 245-250.

893 _____. "Home-School Differences in Political Learning: Television's Impact on School Children's Perception of National Needs." Washington, D.C.: National Institute of Education, 1974.

894 _____. *Message Dimensions of Television News.* Cambridge, Mass.: Lexington Books, 1973.

895 Franzwa, Helen H. "Working Women in Fact and Fiction." *Journal of Communication,* 1974, 24, 2: 104-109.

896 Freedman, L. A. "Daydream in a Vacuum Tube: A Psychiatrist's Comments on the Effects of Television." In W. Schramm, J. Lyle, and E. Parker (eds.), *Television in the Lives of Our Children.* Stanford, Calif.: Stanford University Press, 1961: 189-194.

897 Freidson, E. "Communications Research and the Concept of Mass." *American Sociological Review,* 1954, 18: 313-317.

898 _____. "The Relation of the Social Situation of Contact to the Media in Mass Communication." *Public Opinion Quarterly,* 1953, 17: 230-238.

899 Frey, F. W. *Survey Research on Comparative Social Change: A Bibliography.* Cambridge, Mass.: MIT Press, 1969.

900 Frideres, J. S. "Advertising, Buying Patterns and Children." *Journal of Advertising Research,* 1973, 13: 34-36.

901 Friedman, Herbert and Johnson, Raymond L. "Mass Media Use and Aggression: A Pilot Study." In G. A. Comstock and E. A. Rubinstein (eds.), *Television and Social Behavior: Television and Adolescents' Aggressiveness* (vol. 3). Washington, D.C.: Government Printing Office, 1972: 336-360.

902 Friedman, M. "Television Program Preference and Televiewing Habits of Children as Related to Their Socioeconomic Status." Doctoral Dissertation, Yeshiva University, 1957.

903 Friedrich, L. K. and Stein, A. H. "Aggressive and Prosocial Television Programmes and the Natural Behavior of Pre-School Children." *Monographs of the Society for Research in Child Development,* 1973, 151.

904 _____. "Prosocial Television and Young Children: The Effects of Verbal Labeling and Role Playing on Learning and Behavior." *Child Development,* 1975, 46: 27-38.

905 Friel, Charlotte. "The Influence of Television in the Political Career of Richard Nixon, 1946-1962." Doctoral Dissertation, New York University, 1968.

906 Frueh, T. and McGhee, P. E. "Traditional Sex Role Development and Amount of Time Spent Watching Television." *Developmental Psychology,* 1975, 11: 109.

907 Frye, K. H. "Television's 'Sesame Street': An Experiment in Early Education." Los Angeles: Afro-American Studies, University of California, 1972.

908 Fuchs, Douglas A. "Does TV Election News Influence Voters?" *Columbia Journalism Review*, 1965, 4, 3: 39-41.

909 ———. "Election Day Newscasts and Their Effects on Western Voter Turnout." *Journalism Quarterly*, 1965, 42, 1: 22-28.

910 ———. "Election Day Radio-Television and Western Voting." *Public Opinion Quarterly*, 1966, 30, 2: 226-236.

911 ——— and Lyle, J. "Mass Media Portrayal – Sex and Violence." In F. G. Kline and P. J. Tichenor (eds.), *Current Perspectives in Mass Communication Research.* Beverly Hills: Sage, 1972: 235-264.

912 Fujiwara, N. "Televiewing of Japanese People." In H. Takashima and H. Ichinohe (eds.), *Studies of Broadcasting.* Tokyo: Radio and Television Culture Research Institute, Nippon Hoso Kyokai, 1969: 55-104.

913 Funkhouser, G. Ray. "The Issues of the Sixties: An Exploratory Study in the Dynamics of Public Opinion." *Public Opinion Quarterly*, 1973, 37, 1: 62-75.

914 ———. "A Probabilistic Model for Predicting News Diffusion." *Journalism Quarterly*, 1970, 47:41-45.

915 ———. "Trends in Media Coverage of the Issues of the 60s." *Journalism Quarterly*, 1973, 50, 3: 533-338.

916 ——— and Maccoby, N. "An Experimental Study on Communicating Specialized Science Information to a Lay Audience." *Communication Research*, 1974, 1, 1: 110-128.

917 Funkhouser, G.R. and McCombs, M.E. "The Rise and Fall of News Diffusion." *Public Opinion Quarterly*, 1971, 35: 107-113.

918 Furhammar, Leif, *Filmpaverkan* [The Influence of Film]. Stockholm: P. A. Norstedts and Soners Forlag, 1965.

919 ——— and Isaksson, F. *Politics and Film.* New York: Praeger, 1971.

920 Furu, T. "The Function of Television for Children and Adolescents." Tokyo: Sophia University, 1971.

921 ———. "The Functions of TV for Children: A Cross-Cultural Study." In *Studies of Broadcasting* (no. 5). Tokyo: Radio and Television Culture Research Institute, Nippon Hoso Kyokai, 1967, 5-48.

922 ———. "Research on 'Television and the Child' in Japan." In *Studies in Broadcasting: Radio and Television*, (no. 3). Tokyo: Radio and Television Culture Research Institute, Nippon Hoso Kyokai, 1965: 51-81.

923 ———. "A Survey of Broadcasting Research in Japan." *AV Communication Review*, 1964, 12: 440-457.

924 ———. *Television and Children's Life: A Before-After Study.* Tokyo: Radio and Television Culture Research Institute, 1962.

G

925 Gadberry, S. "Television as Baby-Sitter: A Field Comparison of Pre-schoolers' Behavior During Playtime and During Television Viewing." *Child Development*, 1974, 45: 1132-1136.

926 Gans, H. J. "The Creator-Audience Relationship in the Mass Media: An Analysis of Movie-Making." In B. Rosenberg and D. M. White (eds.), *Mass Culture.* New York: Free Press, 1957: 315-324.

927 _____. "The Mass Media as an Educational Institution." *Television Quarterly,* 1967, 6, 2: 20-37.

928 _____. *Popular Culture and High Culture: An Analysis and Evaluation of Taste.* New York: Basic Books, 1974.

929 _____. "The Sociologist and the Television Journalist:Observations on Studying Television News." In J. Halloran and M. Gurevitch (eds.), *Broadcaster/Researcher Cooperation in Mass Communication Research.* Leicester, England: University of Leicester, Center for Mass Communication Research, 1971.

930 _____. "The Uses of Television and Their Educational Implications." New York: Center for Urban Education, 1968.

931 Gardner, Leroy W. "A Content Analysis of Japanese and American Television," *Journal of Broadcasting,* 1962, 6, 1: 45-52.

932 Garnham, N. *Structures of Television.* London: British Film Institute, 1973.

933 Garrison, Lee C. "The Composition, Attendance Behavior and Needs of Motion Picture Audiences: A Review of the Literature." Los Angeles: University of California, Management in the Arts Research Program, 1971.

934 Garry, R., comp. *Findings and Cognition on the Television Perception of Children and Young People Based on the Prize-Winning Programe of Prix Jeunesse 1968: "The Scarecrow."* Munich: International Central Institute for Youth and Educational Television, 1970.

935 _____. *The Social Influence of Television.* New York: Alfred P. Sloan Foundation (Sloan Commission on Cable Communications), 1971.

936 _____. "Television for Children." *Journal of Education,* 1967, 150, 1:1-46.

937 _____. "Television's Impact on the Child." In *Children and TV: Television's Impact on the Child.* Washington, D.C.: Association for Childhood Education International, Bull. 31-A, 1967: 7-13.

938 _____, Rainsberry, F. B., and Winick, C., eds. *For the Young Viewer: Television Programming For Children . . . At the Local Level.* New York: McGraw-Hill, 1962.

939 Gasca, G. "On the Subject of Criminogenic Action of Cinematographic Presentation of Violence, I: Short- and Long-Term Effects of the Symbolic Satisfaction of Aggressive Impulses on Antisocial Behavior, Catharsis and Formation of Plans for Response." *Minerva Medicolegale,* 1968, 88: 187-192.

940 Gattegno, Caleb. *Towards a Visual Culture: Educating Through Television.* New York: Avon Books, 1969.

941 Gecy, S. K. "Some Current Methodologies for StudyingAggression and Their Status in the Field of Media Research." Institute of Child Development, University of Minnesota, 1974.

942 Geen, R. G. "Effects of Frustration, Attack, and Prior Training in Aggressiveness Upon Aggressive Behavior." *Journal of Personality and Social Psychology,* 1968, 9: 316-321.

943 Geen, R. G. and Berkowitz, L. "Name-Mediated Aggressive Cue Properties." *Journal of Personality,* 1966, 34, 37: 456-465.

944 _____ . "Some Conditions Facilitating the Occurrence of Aggression After the Observation of Violence." *Journal of Personality,* 1967, 35: 666-676. The facilitating conditions are frustration, and identification of the confederate with the film victim.

945 Geen, R. G. and O'Neal, E. "Activation of Cue-Elicited Aggression by General Arousal." *Journal of Personality & Social Psychology,* 1969, 11, 3: 289-292.

946 Geen, R. G. and Stonner, D. "Context Effects in Observed Violence." *Journal of Personality & Social Psychology,* 1972, 25: 145-150. A vengeful context produced more aggressive reactions than did the cool professional context.

947 Geen, R. G., Stonner, D., and Kelley, D. R. "Aggression Anxiety and Cognitive Appraisal of Aggression-Threat Stimuli." *Journal of Personality and Social Psychology,* 1974, 29: 196-200.

948 Geiger, Kent and Sokol, Robert. "Social Norms in Television-Watching." *American Journal of Sociology,* 1959, 64, 2: 174-181.

949 Geiger, Theodore. "A Radio Test of Musical Taste." *Public Opinion Quarterly,* 1950, 14, 3: 453-460.

950 Gensch, D. H. "Media Factors: A Review Article." *Journal of Marketing Research,* 1970, 7: 216-225.

951 Gentile, Frank, and Miller, S. M. "Television and Social Class." *Sociology and Social Research,* 1961, 45, 3: 259-264.

952 George, F. B. "A Study of the Attitudes of Selected Officers of the 'California Congress of Parents and Teachers' Toward the Relation of Motion Pictures and Television to Children." Doctoral Dissertation, University of Southern California, 1965.

953 Gerber, Albert B. *Sex, Pornography, and Justice.* New York: Stuart, 1965.

954 Gerbner, George. "Comments on 'Measuring Violence on Television: The Gerbner Index,' by Bruce M. Owen (Staff Research Paper, Office of Telecommunications Policy)." Annenberg School of Communications, University of Pennsylvania, 1972.

955 _____ . "Communication and Social Environment." *Scientific American,* 1972, 227: 152-162.

956 _____ . "Communication: Society is the Message." *Communication,* 1974, 1, 1: 57-66.

957 _____ . "Cultural Indicators: The Case of Violence in Television Drama." *The Annals of the American Academy,* 1970, 388: 69-81.

958 _____ . "Cultural Indicators: The Third Voice." In S. Gerbner, L. Gross, and W. Melody (eds.), *Communications Technology and Social Policy: Understanding the New "Cultural Revolution."* New York: Wiley, 1973: 555-573.

959 _____ . "Education and the Challenge of Mass Culture." *Audio-Visual Communication Review,* 1959, 7, 4: 264-278.

960 _____ . "The Film Hero: A Cross-Cultural Study." *Journalism Monographs,* 13, 1969.

961 _____ . "Ideological Perspectives and Political Tendencies in News Reporting." *Journalism Quarterly,* 1964, 41, 4: 495-508.

962 _____ . "Images Across Cultures: Teachers in Mass Media Fiction and Drama." *Scholastic Review,* 1966, 74: 212-230.

963 _____ . "An Institutional Approach to Mass Communications Research." In L. Thayer (ed.), *Communication: Theory and Research.* Springfield, Ill.: Charles C. Thomas, 1967: 429-451.

964 _____ . Institutional Pressures Upon Mass Communicators." In P. Halmos (ed.), *the Sociology of Mass Media Communicators.* University of Keele, England: The Sociological Review Monograph, 13, 1969: 205-248.

965 _____ . "Mass Media and Human Communication Theory." In F. Dance (ed.), *Human Communication Theory: Original Essays.* New York: Holt, Rinehart and Winston, 1967: 40-60.

966 _____ . "Mental Illness on Television: A Study of Censorship," *Journal of Broadcasting,* 1959, 3, 4: 293-303.

967 _____ . "On Content Analysis and Critical Research in Mass Communication." *Audio-Visual Communication Review,* 1958, 6, 2: 85-108.

968 _____ . "Scenario for Violence." *Human Behavior,* October, 1975: 64-69.

969 _____ . "The Social Anatomy of the Romance-Confession Cover Girl," *Journalism Quarterly,* 1958, 35, 3: 299-306.

970 _____ . "The Social Role of the Confession Magazine." *Social Problems,* 1958, 6, 1: 29-40.

971 _____ . "The Structure and Process of Television Program Content Regulation in the United States." In G. A. Comstock and E. A. Rubinstein (eds.), *Television and Social Behavior: Media Content and Control* (vol. 1). Washington, D.C.: Government Printing Office, 1972: 386-414.

972 _____ . "Symbolic Functions of Drug Abuse: A Mass Communication Approach." *Studies in the Anthropology of Visual Communication.* 1974, 1, 1: 27-34.

973 _____ . "Teacher Image In Mass Culture: Symbolic Functions of the 'Hidden Curriculum'." In D. Olson (ed.), *Media and Symbols: The Forms of Expression, Communication, and Education.* Chicago: University of Chicago Press, 1974: 470-497.

974 _____ . "Violence in Television Drama: Trends and Symbolic Functions." In G. A. Comstock and E. A. Rubinstein (eds.), *Television and Social Behavior:*

Media Content and Control (vol. 1), Washington, D.C.: Government Printing Office, 1972: 28-187.

975 _____ and Gross, Larry P. "Violence Profile No. 6: Trends in Network Television Drama and Viewer Conceptions of Social Reality: 1967-1973." Philadelphia: University of Pennsylvania, Annenberg School of Communications, 1973.

976 Gerbner, George and Tannenbaum, P. H. "Regulation of Mental Illness Content in Motion Pictures and Television." *Gazette,* 1961, 6: 365-385.

977 Gerbner, George, Gross, L. P., and Melody, W. H., eds. *Communications Technology and Social Policy: Understanding the New "Cultural Revolution."* New York: Wiley, 1973.

978 Gerson, Walter M. "Mass Media Socialization Behavior: Negro-White Defferences." *Social Forces,* 1966, 45, 1: 40-50. Suggests that black adolescents use the media more for dating related information than do whites.

979 _____ . "Social Structure and Mass Media Socialization." Doctoral Dissertation, University of Washington, 1963.

980 Gersoni-Staun, D. *Sexism and Youth.* New York: R.R. Bowker, 1974.

981 Gewirtz, J. L. "The Roles of Overt Responding and Extrinsic Reinforcement in 'Self-' and 'Vicarious-Reinforcement' Phenomena and in 'Observational Learning' and Imitation." In R. Glaser (ed.), *The Nature of Reinforcement.* New York: Academic Press, 1971: 279-309.

982 Gibson, R. L. "Some Preferences of Television Audiences." *Journal of Marketing,* 1946, 10: 289-290.

983 Gibbon, S. Y. *Symposium Paper on Children and Television.* Ann Arbor: Conference on Creative Activities for Young Children, University of Michigan, 1973.

984 Gieber, W. "The 'Lovelorn' Columnist and Her Social Role." *Journalism Quarterly,* 1960, 37, 4: 499-514.

985 Gilbert, Robert E. "The Influence of Television on American Politics." Doctoral Dissertation, State University of Iowa, 1951.

986 _____ . *Television and Presidential Politics.* North Quincy, Mass.: Christopher Publishing House, 1972. Considers effects of TV on politics in general, campaign expenses, and major campaigns from 1952-1968.

987 Gilkison, P. "What Influences the Buying Decisions of Teenagers." *Journal of Retailing,* 1965, 41: 33-41, 48.

988 Girodo, M. "Film-Induced Arousal, Information Search, and the Attribution Process." *Journal of Personality and Social Psychology,* 1973, 25: 357-360.

989 Gist, Noel P. "Mate Selection and Mass Communication in India," *Public Opinion Quarterly,* 1953, 17, 4: 481-495.

990 Gitter, A. George, O'Connell, Stephen M., and Mostofsky, David. "Trends in Appearance of Models in *Ebony* Ads over 17 Years." *Journalism Quarterly,* 1972, 38, 3: 547-550.

991   Glaser, William A. "Television and Voting Turnout." *Public Opinion Quarterly,* 1965, 29, 1: 71-86.

992   Glass, David C. and Mayhew, Patricia. "The Effects of Cognitive Processes on Skin Conductance Reactivity to an Aversive Film." *Psychonomic Science,* 1969, 16, 2: 72-74.

993   Glass, D. C., Gordon A., and Henchy, T. "The Effects of Social Stimuli on Psychophysiological Reactivity to an Averse Film." *Psychonomic Science,* 1970, 20: 255-256.

994   Glick, Ira O. and Levy, Sidney J. *Living with Television.* Chicago: Aldine, 1962.

995   Glucksman, Andre. *Violence on the Screen.* London: The British Film Institute Education Department, 1971. Translated from the French, provides a European perspective on the violence problem. Includes survey of opinions, the effects research, psychological determinants, and a cultural perspective to the problem.

996   Glynn, E. D. "Television and the American Character—A Psychiatrist Looks at Television." In W. Y. Elliott (ed.), *Television's Impact on American Culture.* Lansing: Michigan State University Press, 1956: 175-182.

997   Goldberg, A. L. "The Effects of Two Types of Sound Motion Pictures on the Attitudes of Adults Toward Minorities." *Journal of Educational Sociology,* 1956, 29: 386-391.

998   Goldberg, Marvin E. and Gorn, Gerald J. "Children's Reactions to Television Advertising: An Experimental Approach." *Journal of Consumer Research,* 1974, 1, 2: 69-75.

999   Goldberg, Toby. "A Selective Bibliography of the Writings of and About Marshall McLuhan," *Journal of Broadcasting,* 1968, 12, 2: 179-182.

1000   Goldhamer, Herbert, ed. "The Social Effects of Communication Technology." Santa Monica, Calif.: Rand, 1970.

1001   Golding, Peter. "Media Role in National Development: Critique of Theoretical Orthodoxy." *Journal of Communication,* 1974, 24, 3: 39-53.

1002   Goldsen, R. K. "NBC's Make-Believe Research on TV Violence." *Transaction,* 1971, 8, 12: 28-35.

1003   Goldstein, Bernard. "New Bases for Library and Information Services in Metropolitan Areas: Information Usage; Beliefs, Attitudes, and Exposure to the Mass Media." New Brunswick, N.J.: Rutgers University Urban Studies Center, 1972.

1004   Goldstein, Bernice and Perrucci, Robert. "The TV Western and Modern American Spirit." *Southwestern Social Science Quarterly,* 1963, 34, 4: 357-366.

1005   Goldstein, H. K. "Guidelines for Drug Education Through Electronic Media." *Journal of Drug Education,* 1974, 4, 1: 105-110.

1006   Goldstein, M. J. "Exposure to Erotic Stimuli and Sexual Deviance." *Journal of Social Issues,* 1973, 29, 3: 197-220.

1007 _____ and Kant, H. S. *Pornography and Sexual Deviance*. Berkeley: University of California Press, 1973.

1008 Goldstein, M. J. et al. "Exposure to Pornography and Sexual Behavior in Deviant and Normal Groups." In *Technical Report of the Commission on Obscenity and Pornography: Erotica and Antisocial Behavior* (vol. 7). Washington, D.C.: Government Printing Office, 1971: 1-90.

1009 Goldstein, N. S. "The Effect of Animated Cartoons on Hostility in Children." *Dissertation Abstracts,* 1957, 17: 1125.

1010 Gollob, H. F. "More Comment on Need for Control in Studies of Persuasibility." *Psychological Reports,* 1970, 27, 2: 678.

1011 _____ and Levine, J. "Distraction as a Factor in the Enjoyment of Aggression." *Journal of Personality and Social Psychology,* 1967, 5: 368-372.

1012 Goodhardt, G. J. "The Constant in Duplicated Television Viewing." *Nature,* 1966, 212, 5070: 1616.

1013 _____ , Ehrenberg, A.S.C., and Collins, M. A. *The Television Audience: Patterns of Viewing*. Lexington, Mass.: Lexington Books, 1975.

1014 Goodman, Mary Ellen. *The Culture of Childhood: Child's- Eye View of Society and Culture*. New York: Teachers College Press, 1970.

1015 Goodrich, H. "Man and Society in Mass Media Fiction: The Pattern of Life in the Mass Medias Revealed by Content-Analysis Studies." Doctoral Dissertation, University of Illinois, 1964.

1016 Goodwin, Michael and Marcus, Griel. *Double Feature: Movies and Politics*. New York: Outerbirdge and Lazard, 1972.

1017 Goranson, R. E. "The Catharsis Effect: Two Opposing Views." In R. K. Baker and S. J. Ball (eds.), *Violence and the Media*. A Staff Report to the National Commission on the Causes and Prevention of Violence. Washington, D.C.: Government Printing Office, 1969: 453-459. Reviews the relevant catharsis related literature and finds little support for the proposition that viewing violence drains aggressive energies.

1018 _____ . "Media Violence and Aggressive Behavior: A Review of Experimental Research." In L. Berkowitz (ed.), *Advances in Experimental Social Psychology* (vol. 5). New York: Academic Press, 1970: 1-31.

1019 _____ . "Observed Violence and Aggressive Behavior: The Effects of Negative Outcomes to the Observed Violence." *Dissertation Abstracts International,* 1970, 31(1-B): 381.

1020 _____ . "A Review of Recent Literature on Psychological Effects of Media Portrayals of Violence." In R. K. Baker and S. J. Ball (eds). *Violence and the Media*. A Staff Report to the National Commission on the Causes and Prevention of Violence. Washington, D.C.: Government Printing Office, 1969: 395-413.

1021 Gordon, George N., ed. *Communications and Media: Constructing a Cross-Discipline*. New York: Hastings House, 1975.

1022 Gordon, J. E. and Cohn, R. "Effect of Fantasy Arousal of Affiliative Drive on Doll Play Aggression." *Journal of Abnormal and Social Psychology,* 1963, 66: 301-307.

1023 Gordon, Thomas A. "Political Socialization of Black Youth: An Exploratory Study." *Dissertation Abstracts International,* 1972, 32(7-B): 4183-4184.

1024 Gordon, Thomas F. "The Effect of Viewing Physical Consequences of Violence on Perceptions and Aggressiveness." Doctoral Dissertation, Michigan State University, 1973.

1025 _____ . "The Effects of Time Context on Children's Perceptions of Aggressive Television Content." Philadelphia: School of Communications and Theater, Temple University, 1973.

1026 _____ . "An Exploration into Television Violence." *Educational Broadcasting Review,* 1969, 3, 6: 44-48.

1027 _____ . "Mass Media and Socialization: Theoretic Approaches." Philadelphia: School of Communications and Theater, Temple University, 1974.

1028 _____ and Verna, Mary Ellen. "Mass Media and Socialization: A Selected Bibliography." Philadelphia: School of Communications and Theater, Temple University, 1973. A collection of 760 references.

1029 Gornick, Vivian and Moran, Barbara. *Woman in Sexist Society.* New York: Basic Books, 1971.

1030 Goslin, David A., ed. *Handbook of Socialization Theory and Research.* Chicago: Rand McNally, 1969.

1031 Gotz, Ignacio L. "On Children and Television." *Elementary School Journal,* 1975, 75, 7: 415-488.

1032 Gould, John W., Sigban, Norman B., and Zoerner, C. E. "Black Consumer Reactions to 'Integrated' Advertising: An Exploratory Study." *Journal of Marketing,* 1970, 34: 20-26.

1033 Grace, H. A. "The Effects of Different Degrees of Knowledge About an Audience on the Content of Communication: The Male Audience." *Journal of Social Psychology,* 1952, 36: 83-88.

1034 _____ . "The Effects of Different Degrees of Knowledge About an Audience on the Content of Communication: The Comparison of Male and Female Audiences." *Journal of Social Psychology,* 1952, 36: 89-96.

1035 _____ . "A Taxonomy of American Crime Film Themes." *Journal of Social Psychology,* 1955, 42: 129-136.

1036 Graham, Saxon. "Cultural Compatibility in the Adoption of Television." *Social Forces,* 1954, 33: 166-170.

1037 Grambs, J. D. and Waetjen, W. B. *Sex, Does it Make a Difference?: Sex Roles in the Modern World.* Scituate, Mass.: Duxbury Press, 1975.

1038 Granberg, D. "Selectivity in Exposure and the Effect of Attitudes on Judgments of the Mass Media Coverage of the King Assassination." *Journal of Social Psychology,* 1971, 85: 147-148.

1039 Graney, Marshall J. "Communication Uses and the Social Activity Constant." *Communication Research,* 1975, 2, 4: 347-366.

1040 _____ . "Media Use as a Substitute Activity in Old Age." *Journal of Gerontology,* 1974, 29, 3: 322-324.

1041 _____ and Graney, Edith E. "Communications Activity Substitutions in Aging." *Journal of Communication,* 1974, 24, 4: 88-96.

1042 Grass, Robert C. and Wallace, Wallace H. "Advertising Communications: Print vs. TV." *Journal of Advertising Research,* 1974, 14, 5: 19-23.

1043 _____ . "Satiation Effects of TV Commercials." *Journal of Advertising Research,* 1969, 9, 3: 3-8.

1044 Grass, Robert C., Winters, Lewis C., and Wallace, Wallace H. "Communication Effectiveness of Advertising: A Method of Pretesting." *Proceedings of the Annual Convention of the American Psychological Association,* 1971, 6: 659-660.

1045 Gratiot-Alphandery, H. "L'Enfant et la Television" [The Child and Television]. *L'Ecole des Parents,* 1962, 4: 14-21.

1046 _____ and Rousselet, J. "La Television et la Famille" [Television and the Family]. *L'Ecole des Parents,* 1961, 3: 24-37.

1047 Gray, B. "The Social Effects of the Film." *Sociological Review,* 1950, 42, 7: 12.

1048 Greb, G. "Analysis of Broadcast Literature: The Journalism Quarterly, 1948-1958." *Journal of Broadcasting,* 1959, 3: 244-251.

1049 Green, M. "Television and Violence: Who's Doing What to Whom?" *Human Behavior,* 1972, 1: 73-78.

1050 Green, P. E., Carmone, F. J., and Fox, L. B. "Television Program Similarities: An Application of Subjective Clustering." *Journal of the Market Research Society,* 1969, 11: 70-90.

1051 Green, T. *The Universal Eye: World Television in the Seventies.* London: Bodley Head, 1972.

1052 Greenberg, A. and Suttoni, C. "Television Commercial Wearout." *Journal of Advertising Research,* 1973, 13: 47-54.

1053 Greenberg, Bradley S. "British Children and Televised Violence." *Public Opinion Quarterly,* 1974, 38, 4: 531-547.

1054 _____ . "Children's Reactions to T.V. Blacks." *Journalism Quarterly,* 1972, 49, 1: 5-14.

1055 _____ . "The Content and Context of Violence in the Mass Media." In R. K. Baker and S. J. Ball (eds.), *Mass Media and Violence.* A staff report to the National Commission on the Causes and Prevention of Violence. Washington, D.C.: Government Printing Office, 1969: 423-452.

1056 _____ . "Diffusion of News of the Kennedy Assassination." *Public Opinion Quarterly,* 1964, 28, 2: 225-232.

1057 _____ . "Dimensions of Information Communication." In W. A. Danielson (ed.), *Paul J. Deutschmann Memorial Papers in Mass Communications Research.* Cincinnati: Scripps-Howard Research, 1963: 35-43.

1058 _____ . "The Effects of Communicator Incompatibility on Children's Judgements of Television Programs." *Journal of Broadcasting,* 1964, 8, 2: 157-172.

1059 _____ . "Gratifications of Television Viewing and Their Correlates for British Children." In J. G. Blumler and E. Katz (eds.), *The Uses of Mass Communications.* Beverly Hills: Sage, 1974: 71-92. A factor analytic study of children's reasons for viewing television.

1060 _____ . "Mass Communication and Social Behavior." In G. Hanneman and W. McEwen (eds.), *Communication and Behavior.* Reading, Mass.: Addison-Wesley, 1975: 268-284.

1061 _____ . "Media Use and Believability: Some Multiple Correlates." *Journalism Quarterly,* 1966, 43, 4: 665-670.

1062 _____ . "On Relating Attitude Change and Information Gain." *Journal of Communication,* 1964, 14: 157-171.

1063 _____ . "Person-to-Person Communication in the Diffusion of News Events." *Journalism Quarterly,* 1965, 41, 4: 489-494.

1064 _____ . "Televised Violence: Further Explorations (Overview)." In G. A. Comstock, E. A. Rubinstein, and J. P. Murray (eds.), *Television and Social Behavior: Television's Effects: Further Explorations* (vol. 5). Washington, D.C.: Government Printing Office, 1972: 1-21.

1065 _____ . "Television for Children: Dimensions of Communicator and Audience Perceptions." *Audio-Visual Communication Review,* 1965, 13, 4: 385-396.

1066 _____ . "Viewing and Listening Parameters Among British Youngsters." *Journal of Broadcasting,* 1973, 17, 2: 173-188.

1067 _____ . "Voting Intentions, Election Expectations and Exposure to Campaign Information." *Journal of Communications,* 1965, 15, 3: 149-160.

1068 _____ and Dervin, Brenda. "Mass Communication Among the Urban Poor." *Public Opinion Quarterly,* 1970, 34, 2: 224-235.

1069 Greenberg, Bradley S. and Dominick, Joseph R. "Racial and Social Class Differences in Teen-Agers' Use of Television." *Journal of Broadcasting,* 1969, 13, 4: 331-334. Documents that low-income teens, especially blacks, spend more time with television, see it as more like real life, use it for information about life, and use it more often for thrills and excitement than do other teenagers.

1070 Greenberg, Bradley S. and Gordon, Thomas F. "Children's Perceptions and Televised Violence: A Replication" In G. A. Comstock, E. A. Rubinstein, and J. P. Murray (eds.), *Television and Social Behavior: Television's Effects: Further Explorations* (vol. 5). Washington, D.C.: Government Printing Office, 1972: 211-230.

1071 _____ . "Critics' and Public Perceptions of Violence in TV Programs." *Journal of Broadcasting,* 1970-1971, 15, 1: 29-49.

1072 _____ . "Perceptions of Violence in Television Programs: Critics and the Public." In G. A. Comstock, E. A. Rubinstein (eds.), *Television and Social*

Behavior: Media Content and Control (vol. 1). Washington, D.C.: Government Printing Office, 1972: 244-258.

1073 _____ . "Social Class and Racial Differences in Children's Perceptions of Television Violence." In G. A. Comstock, E. A. Rubinstein, and J. P. Murray (eds.), *Television and Social Behavior: Television's Effects: Further Explorations* (vol. 5). Washington, D.C.: Government Printing Office, 1972: 185-210.

1074 Greenberg, Bradley S. and Hanneman, Gerhard J. "Racial Attitudes and the Impact of T.V. Blacks." *Educational Broadcasting Review,* 1970, 4, 2: 27-34.

1075 Greenberg, Bradley S. and Kahn, Sandra. "Blacks in Playboy Cartoons." *Journalism Quarterly,* 1970, 47, 3: 557-560.

1076 Greenberg, Bradley S. and Kumata, Hiderya. "National Sample Predictors of Mass Media Use." *Journalism Quarterly,* 1968, 45, 4: 651-646.

1077 Greenberg, Bradley S. and Parker, Edwin B., (eds.) *The Kennedy Assassination and the American Public: Social Communication in Crisis.* Stanford, Calif.: Stanford University Press, 1965.

1078 _____ . "Social Research on the Kennedy Assassination." In B. S. Greenberg and E. B. Parker (eds.), *The Kennedy Assassination and the American Public.* Stanford, Calif.: Stanford University Press, 1965: 361-382.

1079 Greenberg, Bradley S. and Razinsky, Edward. "Some Effects of Variations in Message Quality." *Journalism Quarterly,* 1966, 43, 3: 386-492.

1080 Greenberg, B. S. and Roloff, M. E. *Mass Media Credibility: Research Results and Critical Issues.* Washington, D.C.: American Newspaper Publishers Association, News Research Bulletin No. 6, 1974.

1081 Greenberg, Bradley S. and Tannenbaum, Percy H. "The Effects of Bylines on Attitude Change," *Journalism Quarterly,* 1961, 38, 4: 535-537.

1082 Greenberg, Bradley S. and Wotring, C. Edward. "Television Violence and Its Potential for Aggressive Driving Behavior." *Journal of Broadcasting,* 1974, 18, 4: 453-480.

1083 Greenberg, Bradley S., Dervin, Brenda, and Dominick, Joseph. "Do People Watch 'Television' or 'Programs'?" *Journal of Broadcasting,* 1968, 12, 4: 367-377.

1084 Greenberg, Bradley S., Ericson, Philip M., and Vlahos, Mantha. "Children's Television Behaviors as Perceived by Mother and Child." In E. A. Rubinstein, G. A. Comstock, and J. P. Murray (eds.), *Television and Social Behavior: Television in Day-to-Day Life: Patterns of Use* (vol. 4). Washington, D.C.: Government Printing Office, 1972: 395-409.

1085 Greenberg, Bradley S., Dervin, Brenda, Dominick, Joseph R., and Bowes, John. *Use of the Mass Media by the Urban Poor: Findings of Three Research Projects, with an Annotated Bibliography.* New York: Praeger, 1970.

1086 Greenberg, D. A. "Television—Its Critics and Criticism: A Survey and Analysis." Doctoral Dissertation, Wayne State University, 1965.

1087   Greenberg, E. and Barnett, H. J. "TV Program Diversity—New Evidence and Old Theories." *American Economic Review,* 1971, 61: 89-100.

1088   Greenberg, H. R. "Television Induced Psychosis." *New York State Journal of Medicine,* 1967, 67: 1188.

1089   Greenstein, J. "Effects of Television Upon Elementary School Grades." *Journal of Educational Research,* 1954, 48: 161-176.

1090   Gregg, James E. "Newspaper Editorial Endorsements and California Elections, 1948-62," *Journalism Quarterly,* 1965, 42, 4: 532-38.

1091   Grewe-Partsch, Marianne. "Report on Some Research Activities in Israel and Japan on Socialization Processes in the Family by Television." In *Television and Socialization Processes in the Family.* Proceedings of the Prix Jeunesse Seminar. 1975: 132-136.

1092   Grey, David L. "Use of Ideal Types in Newsman Studies, *Journalism Quarterly,* 1967, 44: 13-16.

1093   Greyser, Stephen A. and Bauer, Raymond A. "Americans and Advertising: Thirty Years of Public Opinion." *Public Opinion Quarterly,* 1966, 30, 1: 69-78.

1094   Griebel, F. and Burger, A. eds. *"Patrik and Putrik" and "Clown Ferdl": Findings and Cognition on the Television Perception of Children and Young People Based on the Prize-Winning Programmes of Prix Jeunessee 1966.* Munich: International Central Institute for Youth and Educational Television, 1969.

1095   Groombridge, Brian. *Television and the People.* London: Penguin, 1972.

1096   Grotjahn, M. "Some Psychodynamics of Unconscious and Symbolic Communication in Present-Day Television." *Psychological Reports,* 1963, 13: 886.

1097   Gruber, Frederick. "Radio and Television and Ethical Standards," *Annals of the American Academy of Political and Social Science,* 1952, 280: 116-124.

1098   Grunig, J. E. "Communication in Community Decisions on the Problems of the Poor." *Journal of Communication,* 1972, 22: 5-25.

1099   Grupp, Fred W. "The Magazine Reading Habits of Political Activists." *Public Opinion Quarterly,* 1969, 33: 103-106.

1100   Grusec, J. E. "Effects of Co-observer Evaluations on Imitation: A Developmental Study." *Developmental Psychology,* 1973, 8: 141.

1101   Gryspeerdt, A. "Directions Pour l'investigation en Sociologie de la Television: Theories Problematiques et Techniques [Directions for Investigation in the Sociology of Television: Theories, Problems and Techniques]. *Recherches Sociologiques,* 1971, 2: 214-225.

1102   Guba, E., Wolf, W., de Groot, S., Knemeyer, M., Van Atta, R., and Light, L. "Eye Movements and TV Viewing in Children." *Audiovisual Communication Review,* 1964, 12: 386-401.

1103   Guest, Lester. "How Negro Models Affect Company Image." *Journal of Advertising Research,* Special Issue: Research on Negroes, 1970, 10, 2: 29-33.

1104   Gumpert, P., Hornstein, H. A., Lasky E., and Lewicki, R. J. "Modeling as a Factor in the Internalization of Social Standards." *Perceptual and Motor Skills,* 1968, 27, 2: 555-563.

1105   Gurevitch, Michael. "The Structure and Content of Television Broadcasting in Four Countries: An Overview." In G. A. Comstock and E. A. Rubinstein (eds.), *Television and Social Behavior: Media Content and Control* (vol. 1). Washington, D.C.: Government Printing Office, 1972: 374-385.

1106   _____ and Loevy, Z. "The Diffusion of Television as an Innovation: The Case of the Kibbutz." *Human Relations,* 1972, 25: 181-197.

1107   Guthrie, G., Becker, S., and Siegel, S. "Preferences and Differences in Preference for Political Candidates." *Journal of Social Psychology,* 1961, 53: 25-32.

1108   Gutman, Jonathan. "Self-Concepts and Television Viewing Among Women." *Public Opinion Quarterly,* 1973, 37, 3: 388-397. Heavy viewers, as opposed to light viewers, see themselves as less active, more sociable, and higher in self-respect. On ideal self, heavy viewers stress assertiveness and leadership, while light viewers emphasize self-confidence.

H

1109   Haag, E. "Democracy and Pornography." In V. B. Cline (ed.), *Where Do You Draw the Line?: An Exploration into Media Violence, Pornography, and Censorship.* Provo, Utah: Brigham Young University, 1974: 257-270.

1110   Haber, Ralph Norman. "Public Attitudes Regarding Subliminal Advertising." *Public Opinion Quarterly,* 1959, 23, 2: 291-293.

1111   Hadwiger, Ken. "Some Effects of Voice Quality on Retention." *Journal of Broadcasting,* 1970, 14, 3: 317-324.

1112   Haefner, J. E. and Permut, S. E. "Perceived Deception in Television Advertising: A Factor-Analytic Approach." *Proceedings of the 81st annual convention of the American Psychological Association.* Washington, D.C.: American Psychological Association, 1973: 817-818.

1113   Haight, Anne L. *Banned Books: Informal Notes on Some Books Banned for Various Reasons at Various Times in Various Places.* New York: R. R. Bowker, 1955.

1114   Haines, W. H. "Juvenile Delinquency and Television." *Journal of Social Therapy,* 1955, 1: 192-198.

1115   Haldane, I. R. "The Pattern of Television Viewing." *Commentary,* 1969, 11, 1: 1-5.

1116   Hale, G. A., Miller, L. K., and Stevenson, H. W. "Incidental Learning of Film Content: A Developmental Study." *Child Development,* 1968, 39: 69-77.

1117   Hale, Julian. *Radio Power: Propaganda and International Broadcasting.* Philadelphia: Temple University Press, 1975. Fifteen chapters examine major propaganda efforts from the Nazi and Communist models thru the Voice of America, BBC, Middle East, Africa, Latin America and clandestine approaches.

1118 Haley, Russell L. and Gatty, Ronald. "Measuring Effectiveness of Television Exposure by Computer." *Journal of Advertising Research,* 1969, 9, 3: 9-12.

1119 Halloran, James D. *The Effects of Mass Communication; with Special Reference to Television: A Survey.* New York: Humanities Press, 1965.

1120 _____. "The Effects of the Media Portrayal of Violence and Aggression." In J. Tunstall (ed.), *Media Sociology.* London: Constable, 1970: 314-321.

1121 _____, ed. *The Effects of Television.* London: Panther, 1970. A collection of five major articles dealing with social effects, political effects, television and the arts, TV's effects on other media, and television and education.

1122 _____. "Introduction: The Communicator in Mass Communication Research." *Sociological Review: Monograph No. 13,* 1969: 5-22.

1123 _____. "Mass Media and Socialization." In *Report of the Proceedings of the 9th General Assembly of the International Association for Mass Communication Research.* Leipzig, 1974.

1124 _____. "On the Research Approaches for Studying Socialization in the Family: An Outline from Great Britain." In *Television and Socialization Processes in the Family.* Proceedings of the Prix Jeunesse Seminar, 1975: 15-25.

1125 _____. "The Social Effects of Television." In J. Halloran (ed.) *The Effects of Television.* London: Panther, 1970: 24-68.

1126 "Television and Violence." In O. Larsen (ed.), *Violence and the Mass Media.* New York: Harper and Row, 1968: 139-151.

1127 _____ and Croll, Paul. "Television Programs in Great Britain: Content and Control (A Pilot Study)." In G. A. Comstock and E. A. Rubinstein (eds.), *Television and Social Behavior: Media Content and Control* (vol. 1). Washington, D.C.: Government Printing Office, 1972: 415-492.

1128 Halloran, James D. and Elliot, P.R.C. *Television for Children and Young People.* Geneva: European Broadcasting Union, 1970.

1129 Halloran, James D. and Eyre-Brook, E. "Children's News — Danish Project," Leicester, England: University of Leicester, 1971.

1130 Halloran, James D., Brown, R. L., and Chaney, D. C. *Television and Delinquency.* Leicester, England: Leicester University Press, 1970. Reports on research which examines, for British delinquents, viewing patterns; excitement and masculinity; information and education; conversation and cognitive poverty; and media identifications and pop music.

1131 Halmos, Paul, ed. "The Sociology of Mass Media Communicators." *The Sociological Review* (Monograph no. 13.). Keele, Staffordshire, England: University of Keele, 1969.

1132 Halpern, Werner I. "Turned-on Toddlers: The Effects of Television on Children and Adolescents." *Journal of Communication,* 1975, 25, 4: 66-70.

1133 Hamill, P. B. *Radio and Television: A Selected Bibliography.* Washington, D.C.: U.S. Department of Health, Education and Welfare, Office of Education, 1960.

1134 Hamilton, Robert V. and Lawless, Richard H. "Television Within the Social Matrix." *Public Opinion Quarterly,* 1956, 20, 2: 393-403.

1135 Hanneman, Gerhard J. "Communicating Drug Abuse Information Among College Students." *Public Opinion Quarterly,* 1973, 37, 2: 171-191.

1136 _____. "Communications, Mass Media and Drug Abuse—the Issues and Research Findings." In N. R. Benchley and P. G. Hammond (eds.), *The Media and Drug Abuse Messages.* Washington, D.C.: Special Action Office for Drug Abuse Prevention, Monograph Series D, no. 1, 1974: 1-11.

1137 _____. "Televised Drug Abuse Appeals: A Content Analysis." *Journalism Quarterly,* 1973, 50, 2: 329-333.

1138 _____ and Greenberg, Bradley S. "Relevance and Diffusion of News of Major and Minor Events." *Journalism Quarterly,* 1973, 50: 433-437.

1139 Hanneman, Gerhard J. and McEwen, W. J., eds. *Communication and Behavior.* Reading, Mass.: Addison-Wesley, 1975.

1140 Hanneman, Gerhard J., McEwen, W. J., and Coyne, S. A. "Public Service Advertising on Television." *Journal of Broadcasting,* 1973, 17: 387-404.

1141 Hanratty, Margaret A. "Imitation of a Filmed Aggressive Model as a Function of Frustration and Age." *Dissertation Abstracts International,* 1972, 32(7-B): 4249.

1142 _____ , O'Neal, E., and Sulzer, J. L. "Effects of Frustration Upon Imitation of Aggression." *Journal of Personality and Social Psychology,* 1972, 21: 30-34.

1143 Hanratty, Margaret A., Liebert, R. M., Morris, L. W., and Fernandez, L. E. "Imitation of Film-Mediated Aggression Against Live and Inanimate Victims." *Proceedings of the 77th Annual Convention of the American Psychological Association,* 1969, 4: 457-458.

1144 Hansen, Donald A. and Parson, J. Herschel, eds. *Mass Communication: A Research Bibliography.* Santa Barbara, Calif.: Glendessary Press, 1968.

1145 Hapkiewicz, W. G. and Roden, Aubrey H. "The Effect of Aggressive Cartoons on Children's Interpersonal Play." *Child Development,* 1971, 42, 5: 1583-1585.

1146 Hapkiewicz, W. G. and Stone, R. D. "The Effect of Realistic Versus Imaginary Aggressive Models on Children's Interpersonal Play." *Child Study Journal,* 1974, 4, 2: 47-58.

1147 Harper, D., Munro, J., and Himmelweit, H. T. "Social and Personality Factors Associated with Children's Taste in Television Viewing." In *Second Progress Report and Recommendations,* Television Research Committee, Leicester, England: Leicester University Press, 1969.

1148 Harris, Dale B. "Children and Television: An Annotated Bibliography." Urbana, Illinois: National Association of Educational Broadcasters, 1959.

1149 Harris, J. and McCombs, M. E. "The Interpersonal/Mass Communication Interface Among Church Leaders." *Journal of Communication,* 1972, 22: 257-262.

1150   Louis Harris and Associates, Inc. *The Viewing of Public Television—1971.* Washington, D.C.: Corporation for Public Broadcasting, 1971.

1151   Harrison, A., Jr. and Scriven, E. G. "TV and Youth: Literature and Research Reviewed." *Clearing House,* 1969, 44, 2: 82-90.

1152   Harrison, M. "Television and Radio." In D. E. Butler and A. King (eds), *The British General Election of 1964.* New York: Macmillan, 1965.

1153   Harrison, R. P. and Ekman, P. "Television in South Africa: The Research Paradox, Problem and Potential." Michigan State University and University of California, San Francisco, 1973.

1154   Hart, Lance R. "Immediate Effects of Exposure to Filmed Cartoon Aggression on Boys." *Dissertation Abstracts International,* 1972, 32 (11-B): 6648-6649.

1155   Hartley, R. E. "The Impact of Viewing Aggression: Studies and Problems of Extrapolation." New York: Office of Social Research, C.B.S., Inc., 1964.

1156   _____ . "A Review and Evaluation of Recent Studies on the Impact of Violence." New York: Office of Social Research, C.B.S., Inc., 1964.

1157   Hartman, Frank R. "A Behavioristic Approach to Communication: A Selective Review of Learning Theory and a Derivation of Postulates." *Audio-Visual Communication Review,* 1963, 11, 5: 155-190.

1158   Hartmann, Donald P. "Influence of Symbolically Modeled Instrumental Aggression and Pain Cues on Aggressive Behavior." *Journal of Personality and Social Psychology,* 1969, 11, 3: 280-288.

1159   Hartmann, P. and Husband, C. "The Mass Media and Racial Conflict." *Race,* 1971: 12, 3.

1160   _____ . *Racism and the Mass Media.* Totowa, N.J.: Rowman and Littlefield, 1974. Content analyses and audience survey data are used to examine the role of the media in the formation of white beliefs and attitudes toward blacks in Britain.

1161   Hartnagel, Timothy F., Teevan, James J., and McIntyre, Jennie J. "Television Violence and Violent Behavior." *Social Forces,* 1975, 54, 2: 341-351.

1162   Hartup, W. W. and Coates, B. "The Role of Imitation in Childhood Socialization." In R. Hoppe, E. Simmel, and G. A. Milton (eds.), *Early Experience and the Processes of Socialization.* New York: Academic Press, 1970.

1163   Harwood, K. "A World Bibliography of Selected Periodicals on Broadcasting (rev.)." *Journal of Broadcasting,* 1972, 16: 131-146.

1164   Haselden, K. *Morality and the Mass Media.* Nashville: Boardman Press, 1968.

1165   Haskins, Jack B. "The Effects of Violence in the Printed Media." In R. K. Baker and S. J. Ball (eds.), *Mass Media and Violence.* A Staff Report to the National Commission on the Causes and Prevention of Violence. Washington, D.C.: Government Printing Office, 1969: 493-502.

1166 _____ . "How to Evaluate Mass Communications: The Controlled Field Experiment." New York: Advertising Research Foundation, 1968.

1167 Havighurst, R. J. "Leisure and Aging." In A. M. Hoffman (ed.), *The Daily Needs and Interests of Older People.* Springfield, Ill.: Charles C. Thomas, 1970.

1168 _____ and Albrecht, R. *Older People.* New York: Longmans, Green, 1953.

1169 Hawell, W. "Untersuchung Sweier Verschiedener Filmdarbietungen Als Psychologische Ursache Fur Emotionalen Stress" [Investigation of Two Different Film Presentations as the Psychological Cause of Emotional Stress]. *Psychologie und Praxis,* 1970, 14, 3: 125-133.

1170 Hawkins, R. P. "Learning of Peripheral Content in Films: A Developmental Study." *Child Development,* 1973, 44: 214-217.

1171 _____ , Lingree, S., and Roberts, D. F. "Political Socialization of Children: Two Studies of Responses to Watergate." Institute for Communication Research, Stanford University, 1973.

1172 Hayakawa, S. I. "Popular Songs vs. The Facts of Life." In Berelson and White (eds.), *Mass Culture.* New York: Free Press, 1957.

1173 Hazard, Patrick D. "The Entertainer as Hero: A Problem of the Mass Media." *Journalism Quarterly,* 1962, 39, 4: 436-444.

1174 Hazard, William R. "Anxiety and Preference for Television Fantasy." *Journalism Quarterly,* 1967, 44, 3: 461-469. High anxiety subjects, especially low status individuals, showed greater preference for fantasy television content and less "cultural participation."

1175 _____ . "On the Impact of Television's Pictured News." *Journal of Broadcasting,* 1963, 7, 1: 43-51.

1176 _____ . "Responses to News Pictures: A Study in Perceptual Unity." *Journalism Quarterly,* 1960, 37, 4: 514-524.

1177 _____ . "Some Personal and Social Influences on Telecast Viewing." *Public Opinion Quarterly,* 1962, 26, 3: 429-434.

1178 _____ . "A Specification of Eight Television Appeals." *Journal of Broadcasting,* 1966, 10: 45:54.

1179 _____ . "Tension and Television Tendency." Doctoral Dissertation, State University of Iowa, 1965.

1180 _____ , Moriaty, J. David, and Timmons, Victoria C. "A Nontopical System of TV Program Categories." *Audio-Visual Communication Review,* 1964, 12, 2: 146-163.

1181 Head, Sydney. "Content Analysis of Television Drama Programs." *Quarterly of Film, Radio and Television,* 1954, 9: 175-194. An early look at dramatic content which analyzed more than 200 network shows.

1182 _____ . "Television and Social Norms: An Analysis of the Social Content of a Sample of Television Dramas." Doctoral Dissertation, New York University, 1953.

1183 _____ and Beck, Lois. "The Bibliography of African Broadcasting: An Annotated Guide." Philadelphia: School of Communications and Theater, Temple University, 1974. A collection of 458 references listed alphabetically with a topic index.

1184 Heeler, R. M. "The Effects of Mixed Media, Multiple Copy, Repetition, and Competition in Advertising: A Laboratory Investigation." Doctoral Dissertation, Graduate School of Business, Stanford University, 1972.

1185 Heffner, Richard and Associates, Inc. "Over the Counter Drug Commercials: Network Television, Spring, 1971." In National Commission on Marihuana and Drug Abuse, *Drug Use in America: Problem in Perspective: Social Responses to Drug Use* (vol. 2). Washington, D.C.: Government Printing Office, 1973: 669-697.

1186 Heinrich, K. *Filmerleben, Filmwirkung, Filmerziehung: Der Einfluss des Films auf die Aggressivitaet bei Jugendlichen: Experimentelle Untersuchungen und ihre lernpsychologischen Konsequenzen* [Film Experience, Film Effects, Film Education: The Influence of Films on Aggressiveness of Youth: Experiments and Consequences for the Psychology of Learning]. Berlin: Hannover, Darmstadt, H. Schroedel, 1961.

1187 Heller, M. S. and Polsky, S. "A Pilot Search for Susceptible Children, and Pro-Social Factors and Cognitive Controls." In *Studies of Children and Television: Years III and IV.* New York: American Broadcasting Co., Inc., 1974.

1188 _____ . "Project I: Responses of Emotionally Vulnerable Children to Televised Violence." In *Studies in Violence and Television: Years I and II.* New York: American Broadcasting Co., Inc., 1972.

1189 _____ . "Project II. A Comparison of Effects of Cartoon and Human Portrayed Violence on Emotionally 'Vulnerable' Children." In *Studies in Violence and Television: Years I and II.* New York: American Broadcasting Co., Inc., 1972.

1190 _____ . "Project III. Television Studies With Young Adult Offenders." In *Studies in Violence and Television: Years I and II.* New York: American Broadcasting Co., Inc., 1972.

1191 _____ . "Pro-Social Behavior, Violence, and Television Viewing Habits: A Comparative Study." In *Studies of Children and Television: Years III and IV.* New York: American Broadcasting Co., Inc., 1974.

1192 _____ . "Television Violence: Guidelines for Evaluation." *Archives of General Psychiatry,* 1971, 24, 3: 279-285.

1193 Henderson, R. W., Zimmerman, B. J., Swanson, R., and Bergan, J. R. "Televised Cognitive Skill Instruction for Papago Native American Children." Tucson: Arizona Center for Educational Research and Development, University of Arizona, 1974.

1194 Henningsson, R. and Filipson, L. *3-8 Aringars TV-tittande* [Television Viewing of 3-8-year-olds]. Stockholm: Sveriges Radio Audience and Programme Research Dept., 1975.

1195   Hermann, R. O. *The Consumer Behavior of Children and Teenagers: An Annotated Bibliography.* Chicago: American Marketing Association, 1969.

1196   Herschensohn, Bruce. *The Gods of Antenna.* New Rochelle, N.Y.: Arlington House, 1975. A critical analysis of what the media 'did to' Richard Nixon. The author, a former White House aide, analyzes numerous examples of media bias and their effects on the public and the politician.

1197   Hess, Beth B. "Stereotypes of the Aged." *Journal of Communication,* 1974, 24, 4: 76-85.

1198   Hess, Daniel, J. "The Religious Journal's Image of the Mass Media." *Journalism Quarterly,* 1964, 41, 1: 106-108.

1199   Hess, R. D. "Social Class and Ethnic Differences in Socialization." In P. H. Mussen (ed.), *Carmichael's Manual of Child Psychology.* New York: John Wiley, 1970.

1200   _____ and Goldman, Harriet. "Parents' Views of the Effect of Television on Their Children." *Child Development,* 1962, 33, 2: 411-426.

1201   Hess, R. D. and Torney, J. V. *the Development of Political Attitudes in Children.* Chicago: Aldine, 1967.

1202   Hetherington, E. Mavis and Carlson, Mary. "Effects of Candidate Support and Election Results Upon Attitudes to the Presidency." *Journal of Social Psychology,* 1964, 64: 333-338.

1203   Heucki, Almut. "Zur Gefuhlsansprechlarkeit Von Verwahrlosten Weiblichen Jugendlichen: Eine Studie Auf Grund Von Filmgesprachen in einem Madchenheim" [Emotional Sensitivity of Neglected Female Adolescents: A Study Based on Talks about Movies in a Girl's Home]. *Praxis der Kinderpsychologie und Kinderpsychiatrie,* 1971, 20, 2: 67-71.

1204   Heyman, Doris S. "The Effect of Film-Mediated Aggression on Subsequent Aggressive Behavior." *Dissertation Abstracts International,* 1970, 30 (7-B): 3386.

1205   Hickey, Neil. "What America Thinks of TV's Political Coverage." *TV Guide,* April 8, 1972: 6-11.

1206   Hicks, D. J. "Effects of Co-Observer's Sanctions and Adult Presence on Imitative Aggression." *Child Development,* 1968, 38: 303-309. Adult sanctions, positive or negative, affected children's aggressive reactions to a film accordingly—but only when the adult remained with children in the post-viewing situation.

1207   _____ . "Imitation and Retention of Film-Mediated Aggressive Peer and Adult Models." *Journal of Personality and Social Psychology,* 1965, 2: 97-100. Peer models produced more imitative behavior than did adult models.

1208   _____ . "Short- and Long-Term Retention of Affectively Varied Modeled Behavior." *Psychonomic Science,* 1968, 11: 369-370.

1209   Hiebert, Ray, Jones, Robert, Lotito, Ernest, and Lorenz, John. *The Political Image Merchants: Strategies in the New Politics.* Washington, D.C.: Acropolis Books, 1971. One of the eight major sections contains articles on television and image making, including advertising hints and how to handle candidates on television.

1210 Hiett, Robert, et al. "A Study of the Effectiveness of Gun Control Advertising." *Journalism Quarterly,* 1969, 46, 3: 592-594.

1211 Hileman, Donald G. "The Young Radio Audience: A Study of Listening Habits." *Journalism Quarterly,* 1953, 1: 37-43.

1212 Hill, J. H., Liebert, R. M., and Mott, D. E. W. "Vicarious Extinction of Avoidance Behavior Through Films: An Initial Test." *Psychological Reports,* 1968, 22: 192.

1213 Hill, R. B. "Political Uses of Broadcasting in the United States in the Context of Public Opinion and the Political Process, 1920–1960." Doctoral Dissertation, Northwestern University, 1964.

1214 Hill, Richard J. and Bonjean, Charles. "News Diffusion: A Test of the Regularity Hypothesis." *Journalism Quarterly,* 1964, 41, 3: 336-342.

1215 Himmelweit, H. T. "Plan 4: An Experimental Study of Taste Development in Children." In L. Arons and M. May (eds.), *Television and Human Behavior: Tomorrow's Research in Mass Communication.* New York: Appleton-Century-Crofts, 1963: 46-63. A research proposal from the Television Bureau of Advertising contest.

1216 ———. "A Theoretical Framework for the Consideration of the Effects of Television: A British Report." *Journal of Social Issues,* 1962, 18: 16-28.

1217 ———, Openheim, A. N., and Vince, P. *Television and the Child: An Empirical Study of the Effect of Television on the Young.* London: Oxford University Press, 1958. This classic before-and-after study of the effects of introducing television into a community assessed both content introduced and its relationship to attitudes and values.

1218 Hindman, A. P. "The Interaction of Political Values and Viewing Aggression on Anger and Aggression." Doctoral Dissertation, University of Massachusetts, 1973.

1219 Hines, B. W. *Children's Reactions to Types of Television.* Charleston, W. Va.: Appalachian Regional Laboratory, 1973.

1220 Hinton, James L., Seggar, John F., Northcott, Herbert C., and Fontes, Brian F. "Tokenism and Improving Imagery of Blacks in TV Drama and Comedy: 1973." *Journal of Broadcasting,* 1974, 18, 4: 423-432.

1221 Hirsch, K. W. "Children's Discrimination Between and Reaction to Actuality and Make-Believe in Violent Television/Film Messages." Doctoral Dissertation, University of Oregon, 1969.

1222 ———. "TV Program Selection as a Function of Prestige." *AV Communication Review,* 1960, 8: 284-285.

1223 Hirsch, Paul M. "An Analysis of *Ebony:* The Magazine and its Readers." *Journalism Quarterly,* 1968, 45, 2: 261-270.

1224 ———. "Sociological Approaches to the Pop Music Phenomenon." *American Behavioral Scientist,* 1971, 14, 3: 371-388.

1225 Hoar, J. R. "Reading, Listening and Viewing Behavior of the Aged: An Inventory of the Mass Communication Habits and Preferences of 200 Aged Persons in Oxford, Mississippi." Doctoral Dissertation, State University of Iowa, 1960.

1226 Hoffman, M., and Hoffman, L. W., eds. *Review of Child Development Research* (vol. 1). New York: Russell Sage Foundation, 1964.

1227 Hoggart, Richard. *On Culture and Communication.* New York: Oxford University Press, 1972.

1228 _____. *The Uses of Literacy: Aspects of Workingclass Life with Special Reference to Publications and Entertainment.* London: Oxford University Press, 1970.

1229 Hokansen, Jack, E. "Psychophysiological Evaluation of the Catharsis Hypotheses." In E. I. Megargee and Jack E. Hokanson (eds.), *The Dynamics of Aggression: Individual, Group and International Analysis.* New York: Harper & Row, 1970.

1230 Holden, C. "TV Violence: Government Study Yields More Evidence, No Verdict." *Science,* Feb. 11, 1972, 175: 608-611.

1231 Holland, N. N. "Pornography and the Mechanisms of Defense." In *Technical Report of the Commission on Obscenity and Pornography: Preliminary Studies* (vol. 1). Washington, D.C.: Government Printing Office, 1971: 115-130.

1232 Hollander, Gayle D. *Soviet Political Indoctrination: Developments in Mass Media and Propaganda Since Stalin.* New York: Praeger, 1972.

1233 Hollander, Neil. "Adolescents and the War: The Sources of Socialization." *Journalism Quarterly,* 1971, 48, 3: 472-479. Television proved to be the primary source for information about the Vietnam War, more important than friends, family, school, or church.

1234 Hollander, S. W. and Jacoby, J. "Recall of Crazy, Mixed-Up TV Commercials." *Journal of Advertising Research,* 1973, 13, 3: 39-40.

1235 Holm, J., Kraus, S., and Bochner, A. P. "Communication and Opinion Formation: Issues Generated by the Watergate Hearings." *Communication Research,* 1974, 1, 4: 368-390.

1236 Holmes, John H. "Dogmatism as a Predictor of Communication Behavior in the Diffusion of Consumer Innovations." *Dissertation Abstracts,* 1968, 28 (10-A): 4270-4271.

1237 Holper, Laurie J., Goldstein, Jeffrey H., and Snyderman, Paul. "The Placement of Neutral Stimulus Material in Reducing the Effects of Mass Media Violence on Aggression." *Representative Research in Social Psychology,* 1973, 4, 2: 28-35.

1238 Holz, R. "Television Violence: A Paper Tiger?" *CRC Report,* 1971, no. 57.

1239 Homans, P. "Puritanism Revisited: An Analysis of the Contemporary Screen-Image Western." *Studies in Public Communication,* 1961, 3: 73-84.

1240 Hoppe, Ronald A., Milton, G. A., and Simmel, E. C. *Early Experiences and the Process of Socialization.* New York: Academic Press, 1970.

1241 Horikawa, N. "Television in Everyday Life." *Japanese Journalism Review,* 1960, 10: 148-160.

1242 Horner, Vivian M. and Fowles, Barbara R. "A Suggested Research Strategy: The Effects of Television on Children and Adolescents." *Journal of Communication,* 1975, 25, 4: 98-101.

1243 Horton, Donald. "The Dialogue of Courtship in Popular Songs." *American Journal of Sociology,* 1957, 62, 6: 569-578.

1244 _____ and Strauss, Anselm. "Interaction in Audience-Participation Shows." *American Journal of Sociology,* 1957, 62, 6: 579-587.

1245 _____ and Wohl, R. "Mass Communication and Para-Social Interaction." *Psychiatry,* 1956, 19: 215-229.

1246 Hoshino, K. "Mass Communication and Delinquency." *Journal of Educational Sociology,* 1970, 25: 89-104.

1247 Houn, Franklin W. "Radio Broadcasting and Propaganda in Communist China." *Journalism Quarterly,* 1957, 34, 3: 366-377.

1248 Hoving, T. *Television and the Kept Society.* New York: McGraw-Hill, 1970.

1249 Hovland, C. I. "Effects of the Mass Media of Communication." In G. Lindzey (ed.), *Handbook of Social Psychology* (vol. 2). Cambridge, Mass.: Addison-Wesley, 1954: 1062-1103. One of the first major reviews of the effects literature.

1250 _____ , Lumsdaine, A. A., and Sheffield, F. D. "Short-Time and Long-Time Effects of An Orientation Film." In B. Berelson and M. Janowitz (eds.), *Reader in Public Opinion and Communication* (2nd ed.). New York: Free Press, 1966: 391-401.

1251 Howard, J. A. and Hulbert, J. M. *Advertising and the Public Interest.* Chicago: Crain Communications, 1973.

1252 _____ , Hulbert J. M., and Lehmann, D. R. "An Exploratory Analysis of the Effect of Television Advertising on Children." *Proceedings of the American Marketing Association.* Washington, D.C.: American Marketing Association, 1973.

1253 Howard, J. L., Liptzin, Myron B., and Reifler, Clifford B. "Is Pornography a Problem?" *Journal of Social Issues,* 1973, 29, 3: 133-146.

1254 _____ . "Effects of Exposure to Pornography." In *Technical Report of The Commission on Obscenity and Pornography: Erotica and Social Behavior* (vol. 8). Washington, D.C.: Government Printing Office, 1971: 97-132.

1255 Howitt, D. "Attitudes Towards Violence and Mass Media Exposure." *Gazette,* 1972, 18: 208-234.

1256 _____ . "Comment on Leo Bogart's 'Warning . . .' " *Public Opinion Quarterly,* 1973-1974, 37, 4: 645-646.

1257 _____ . "Television and Aggression: A Counterargument." *American Psychologist,* 1972, 27: 969-970.

1258 Howitt, D. and Cumberbatch, G. "Affective Feeling for a Film Character and Evaluation of an Anti-Social Act." *British Journal of Social and Clinical Psychology,* 1972, 2: 102-108. Found that liking a media character is not related to a more positive evaluation of antisocial acts by the character.

1259 _____. "Audience Perceptions of Violent Television Content." *Communication Research,* 1974, 1, 2: 204-223.

1260 _____. "Children's Moral Judgements of Aggressive Behavior Set in Different Program Contents." Leicester, England: University of Leicester, 1971.

1261 _____. *Mass Media Violence and Society.* New York: Halsted Press, 1975. Reviews the violence research but takes the position that mass media have no significant effect on the level of violence in society.

1262 _____. "The Parameters of Attraction to Mass Media Figures." *Moral Education,* 1973, 2, 3: 269-281.

1263 Howitt, D. and Dembo, Richard. "A Sub-cultural Account of Media Effects." *Human Relations,* 1974, 27, 1: 25-41.

1264 Hoyt, James L. "Effect of Media Violence 'Justification' of Aggression." *Journal of Broadcasting,* 1970, 14, 4: 455-464.

1265 _____. "Source-Message Orientation, Communication Media and Attitude Change." Doctoral Dissertation, University of Wisconsin, 1970.

1266 Hsia, H. J. "Audience Recall as Tolerance Toward Television Commercial Breaks." *Journalism Quarterly,* 1974, 51, 1: 96-101.

1267 Hubbell, Anne Boyer. "Social Origins of Control of Aggression." *Dissertation Abstracts,* 1963, 23, 9: 3526.

1268 Huesmann, L. R., Eron, D. D., Lefkowitz, M. M., and Walder, L. O. "Television Violence and Aggression: The Causal Effect Remains." *American Psychologist,* 1973, 28: 617-620.

1269 Huggins and Entwisle, D. R. *Iconic Communication; An Annotated Bibliography.* Baltimore: John Hopkins University Press, 1974.

1270 Hughes, G. D. and Ray, M. L., eds. *Buyer/Consumer Information Processing.* Chapel Hill: University of North Carolina Press, 1974.

1271 Hulteng, John L. and Nelson, R. P. *The Fourth Estate: An Informal Appraisal of the News and Opinion Media.* New York: Harper & Row, 1971.

1272 Huntley, Stirling. "Color as an Emotional Factor in Television," *Journal of Broadcasting,* 1948, 2, 3: 259-262.

1273 Hurley, Neil. "Chilean Television: A Case Study of Political Communication." *Journalism Quarterly,* 1974, 51: 683-689, 725.

1274 _____. "Using Motion Pictures to Aid Intercultural Communication." *Journal of Communication,* 1968, 18, 2: 97-108.

1275 Hutchison, Bruce D. "Comic Strip Violence, 1911–1966." *Journalism Quarterly,* 1969, 46: 358-362.

1276 Hwang, John C. "Information Seeking and Opinion Leadership Among Older Americans." Doctoral Dissertation, University of Oregon, 1971.

1277   Hyman, Herbert H. "Mass Communication and Socialization." *Public Opinion Quarterly,* 1973, 37, 4: 524-540. A discussion of the potential prosocial effects of the media on sympathy responses and concern for the suffering of others.

1278 _____ . "Mass Communication and Socialization." In W. P. Davison and F.T.C. Yu (eds.), *Mass Communication Research: Major Issues and Future Directions.* New York: Praeger, 1974: 36-65.

1279 _____ . "Mass Media and Political Socialization: The Role of Patterns of Communication." In Lucien W. Pye (ed.), *Communications and Political Development: Studies in Political Development.* Princeton, N.J.: Princeton University Press, 1963: 128-148.

1280 _____ . *Political Socialization.* Glencoe, Ill.: Free Press, 1969.

1281 _____ and Sheatsley, P. B. "Some Reasons Why Information Campaigns Fail." In E. E. Maccoby, T. M. Newcomb, and E. L. Hartley (eds.), *Readings in Social Psychology.* New York: Holt, Rinehart and Winston, 1958: 164-173. Discusses five psychological barriers to effective communication.

I

1282   Ide, T. R. "The Potentials and Limitations of Television as an Educational Medium." In D. Olson (ed.), *Media and Symbols: The Forms of Expression, Communication, and Education.* Chicago: University of Chicago Press, 1974: 330-356.

1283   Inglis, Fred. *The Imagery of Power: A Critique of Advertising.* London: Heinemann, 1972.

1284   Innis, Harold A. *Empire and Communications* (2nd ed.). Toronto, Canada: University of Toronto Press, 1972. A revision, by Mary Q. Innis, of the original 1950 publication in which Innis develops his theory that the history of empires is determined largely by their means of communication.

1285   Instituto de la Opinión Pública. "Encuestas Sobre Medios de Comunicación de Masas Infantiles" [Surveys on Juvenile Mass Communications Media]. *Revista Española de la Opinión Pública,* 1966, 3, Jan.-Mar.: 247-266.

1286   "Is Multi-Set Ownership Changing TV Viewing Patterns?" *Media/scope,* 1966, 10: 113.

1287   Israel, Harold and Robinson, John P. "Demographic Characteristics of Viewers of Television Violence and News Programs." In E. A. Rubinstein, G. A. Comstock, and J. P. Murray (eds.), *Television and Social Behavior: Television and Day-to-Day Life: Patterns of Use* (vol. 4). Washington, D.C.: Government Printing Office, 1972: 87-128.

1288   International Organization of Journalists Developing World and Mass Media. *Mass Media and Developing Nations: A Global Perspective of the Present State of Mass Communications and Its Research.* Prague, 1975.

J

1289 Jacobson, Gary Charles. "The Impact of Radio and Television on American Election Campaigns." Doctoral Dissertation, Yale University, 1972.

1290 Jacobson, Harvey. "The Credibility of Three Mass Media as Information Sources." *Dissertation Abstracts,* 1968, 28 (8-A): 3132.

1291 _____. "Mass Media Believability: A Study of Receiver Judgements." *Journalism Quarterly,* 1969, 46, 1: 20-28.

1292 Jakab, Zoltan. "Hungarian Studies on Socialization of Children and Young People for Television." In *Television and Socialization Processes in the Family.* Proceedings of the Prix Jeunesse Seminar, 1975: 117-131.

1293 Jakobovits, L. A. "Studies of Fads: The Hit Parade." *Psychological Reports,* 1966, 18, 2: 443-450.

1294 _____ and Lambert, W. E. "Plan 10. The Effects of Repetition in Communication on Meanings and Attitudes." In L. Arons and M. A. May (eds.), *Television and Human Behavior: Tomorrow's Research in Mass Communication.* New York: Appleton-Century-Crofts, 1963: 168-176.

1295 James, L. "Youth, Media and Advertising." Austin: University of Texas Bureau of Business Research, 1971.

1296 Janis, I. L., and Feshbach, S. "Effects of Fear-Arousing Communications." *Journal of Abnormal and Social Psychology,* 1953, 48: 78-92.

1297 Janowitz, M. "The Study of Mass Communication." In *International Encyclopedia of the Social Sciences* (vol. 3). New York: Macmillan and Free Press, 1968: 41-53.

1298 Jaros, Dean. *Socialization to Politics.* New York: Praeger, 1973.

1299 Jarvie, I. C. "Film and the Communication of Values." *Archives Europeenes de Sociologie,* 1969, 10, 2: 205-219.

1300 _____. *Movies and Society.* New York: Basic Books, 1970.

1301 Jeffres, Leo W. "Functions of Media Behaviors." *Communication Research,* 1975, 2, 2: 137-161.

1302 Jennings, M. K. and Niemi, R. "The Transmission of Political Values From Parent to Child." *American Political Science Review,* 1968, 62: 169-184.

1303 Jennings, Ralph M. "Dramatic License in Political Broadcasts." *Journal of Broadcasting,* 1968, 23, 3: 229-246.

1304 _____. *Programming and Advertising Practices Directed to Children.* Newton Centre, Mass.: Action for Children's Television, 1970.

1305 _____ and Jennings, C. J. *Programming and Advertising Practices in Television Directed to Children: Another Look.* Newton Centre, Mass.: Action for Children's Television, 1971.

1306 Jervis, Robert. *The Logic of Images in International Relations.* Princeton, N.J.: Princeton University Press, 1970.

1307   Jobes, Patrick. "An Empirical Study of Short-Term Mass Communication Saturation and Perception of Population Problems." *Journal of Sex Research,* 1973, 9, 4: 342-352.

1308   Johnson, Dorothy R. "Television in Appalachia: A Comparison of Appalachian and Non-Appalachian Perception of Various Concepts and the Influence of Television Viewing Upon Such Perceptions." Doctoral Dissertation, Ohio State University, 1972.

1309   Johnson, Norris R. "Television and Politicization: A Test of Competing Models." *Journalism Quarterly,* 1973, 50, 3: 447-455, 474.

1310   Johnson, N. "Television and Violence: Perspective and Proposals." In B. Rosenberg and D. M. White (eds.), *Mass Culture Revisited.* New York: Van Nostrand Reinhold, 1971: 169-195.

1311   Johnson, R. A. E. "The Relationship Between Reading Ability and the Use of Communication Media by Adolescents." Doctoral Dissertation, University of Wisconsin, 1954.

1312   Johnson, Raymond L., Friedman, Herbert, L., and Bross, Herbert S., "Four Masculine Styles in Television Programming: A Study of the Viewing Preferences of Adolescent Males." In G. A. Comstock and E. A. Rubinstein (eds.) *Television and Social Behavior: Television and Adolescent Aggressiveness* (vol. 3). Washington, D.C.: Government Printing Office, 1972: 316-371.

1313   Johnson, Rolland C. "Seldom Tested Variables in the Effects of Televised Violence on Aggressive Behavior: An Examination of Violence Placement, Non-Forced Response Choice, Fictional/Nonfictional Presentations, and Male/Female Response Differences." *Dissertation Abstracts International,* 1972, 32 (9-A): 5258.

1314   Johnson, W. O., Jr. *Super Spectator and the Electric Lilliputians.* Boston: Little, Brown and Company, 1971.

1315   Johnson, W. T., Kupperstein, L. R., and Peters, J. J. "Sex Offenders' Experience with Erotica." In *Technical Report of the Commission on Obscenity and Pornography: Erotica and Antisocial Behavior* (vol. 7) Washington, D.C.: Government Printing Office, 163-172.

1316   Johnstone, J.W.C. "Social Integration and Mass Media Use Among Adolescents: A Case Study." In J. G. Blumler and E. Katz (eds.), *The Uses of Mass Communications: Current Perspectives on Gratifications Research.* Beverly Hills: Sage, 1974: 35-47.

1317   Johnstone, J. and Katz, E. "Youth and Popular Music." *American Journal of Sociology,* 1957, 62, 6: 563-568.

1318   Johnstone, Ronald D. "Who Listens to Religious Radio Broadcasts Anymore?" *Journal of Broadcasting,* 1972, 16, 1: 91-102.

1319   Jones, G. W. "The Relationship of Screen-Mediated Violence to Anti-Social Behavior." Doctoral Dissertation, Syracuse University, 1971.

1320   Joint Commission on Mental Health of Children. *The Mental Health of Children: Services, Research and Manpower,* Reports of Task Forces IV and V and the Report of the Committee on Clinical Issues. New York: Harper and Row, 1973.

1321 _____ . *Mental Health: From Infancy Through Adolescence,* Reports from Task Forces I, II, and III and the Committees on Education and Religion. New York: Harper and Row, 1973.

K

1322 Kaid, Lynda Lee, Saunders, Keith R., and Hirsch, Robert. *Political Campaign Communication: A Bibliography and Guide to the Literature.* Metuchen, N.J.: Scarecrow Press, 1974. Contains roughly 1500 indexed citations of descriptive, analytical, evaluative, and experimental works. Fifty representative books are annotated.

1323 Kamen, Gary B. "A Second Look at the Effects of Stress-Producing Film on Adult Test Performance." *Journal of Clinical Psychology,* 1971, 27, 66: 465-467.

1324 Kane, T. R., Doerge, P., and Tedeschi, J. T. "When is Intentional Harm-Doing Perceived as Aggressive? A Naive Reappraisal of the Berkowitz Aggression Paradigm." *Proceedings of the 81st Annual Convention of the American Psychological Association.* Washington, D.C.: American Psychological Association, 1972: 113-114.

1325 Kaninga, Nancy, Scott, Thomas, and Gade, Eldon. "Working Women Portrayed on Evening Television Programs." *Vocational Guidance Quarterly.* 1974, 23, 2: 134-137.

1326 Kanter, D. L. "Research on the Effects of Over-the-Counter Drug Advertising." *Journal of Drug Issues,* 1974, 4, 3: 223-226.

1327 _____ . "Some Aspects of the Broadcast Anti-Drug Program." *Public Opinion Quarterly,* 1971, 35, 3: 459.

1328 Kaplan, D. M. "The Psychopathology of Television Watching." *Performance Magazine,* July/August, 1972: 21-29.

1329 Kaplan, M. *Leisure in America: A Social Inquiry.* New York: Wiley, 1960.

1330 _____ and Lazarsfeld, Paul. "The Mass Media and Man's Orientation to Nature." In *Trends in American Living and Outdoor Recreation; A Report to the Outdoor Recreation Resources Review Commission.* Study Report no. 22, Washington, D.C.: Government Printing Office, 1962.

1331 Kaplan, M., Gans, S. P., and Kahn, H. M. *Children and Urban Environment: A Learning Experience: Evaluation of the WGBH-TV Educational Project.* New York: Praeger, 1973.

1332 Kaplan, R. M. "On Television as a Cause of Aggression." *American Psychologist,* 1972, 27: 968-969.

1333 Karrby, G. *Child Rearing and the Development of Moral Structure.* Stockholm: Almqvis and Wiksell, 1971.

1334 Kassarjian, Harold H. "The Negro and American Advertising, 1946-1967." *Journal of Marketing Research,* 1969, 6: 29-39.

1335 Kasarjian, Waltraud M. "Blacks as Communicators and Interpreters of Mass Communication." *Journalism Quarterly,* 1973, 50, 2: 285-291, 305.

1336 Kato, Hidetoshe. *Japanese Research on Mass Communication: Selected Abstracts.* Honolulu: University of Hawaii Press, 1974. A collection of 97 abstracts emphasizing research on broadcast media.

1337 Katz, D. "The Functional Approach to the Study of Attitudes." *Public Opinion Quarterly,* 1960, 24: 163-204.

1338 Katz, Elihu. "Communication Research and the Image of Society: Convergence of Two Traditions." *American Journal of Sociology,* 1959, 65: 435-440.

1339 _____. "On Reopening the Question of Selectivity in Exposure to Mass Communications." In R. P. Abelson, et al. (eds.), *Theories of Cognitive Consistency: A Source Book.* Chicago: Rand McNally, 1968: 788-796.

1340 _____. "Platforms and Windows: Broadcasting's Role in Election Campaigns." *Journalism Quarterly,* 1971, 48: 304-314.

1341 _____. "Television as a Horseless Carriage." In G. Gerbner, L. Gross, and W. Melody (eds.), *Communications Technology and Social Policy: Understanding the New "Cultural Revolution."* New York: Wiley, 1973: 381-392.

1342 _____. "The Two-Step Flow of Communication: An Up-to-Date Report on an Hypothesis." *Public Opinion Quarterly,* 1957, 21, 1: 61-78.

1343 _____ and Feldman, J. "The Debates in Light of Research: A Survey of Surveys." In S. Kraus (ed.), *The Great Debates.* Bloomington: Indiana University Press, 1962: 173-223.

1344 Katz, Elihu and Foulkes, David. "On the Use of the Mass Media as 'Escape': Clarification of a Concept." *Public Opinion Quarterly,* 1962, 26, 3: 377-388. Points out the importance of peer group and family relationships to the use of media.

1345 Katz, Elihu and Lazarsfeld, Paul. *Personal Influence: The Part Played by People in the Flow of Mass Communication.* Glencoe, Ill.: The Free Press, 1955.

1346 Katz, Elihu, Blumler, Jay G., and Gurevitch, Micheal. "Uses and Gratifications Research." *Public Opinion Quarterly,* 1973, 37, 4: 509-523.

1347 _____. "Uses of Mass Communication by the Individual." In W. P. Davison and F. T. C. Yu (eds.) *Mass Communication Research: Major Issues and Future Directions.* New York: Praeger, 1974: 11-35.

1348 _____. "Utilization of Mass Communication by the Individual." In J. G. Blumler and E. Katz, *The Uses of Mass Communications.* Beverly Hills: Sage, 1974: 19-34.

1349 Katz, Elihu, Gurevitch, M., and Haas, H. "On the Use of Television for Important Things." *American Sociological Review,* 1973, 38: 164-181.

1350 Katz, Harvey A. "The Effects of Previous Exposure to Pornographic Film, Sexual Instrumentality, and Guilt on Male Verbal Aggression Against Women." *Dissertation Abstracts International,* 1971, 32 (1-B): 562.

1351 Katzman, Marshall. "Photograph Characteristics Influencing the Judgment of Obscenity." In *Technical Report of The Commission on Obscenity and Pornography: The Consumer and the Community* (vol. 9). Washington, D.C.: Government Printing Office, 1972: 9-26.

1352 Katzman, N. I. "Aggressive Violence: Definitions and Distinctions for Mass Media Studies." Michigan State University, Department of Communication, 1971.

1353 _____ . *One Week of Public Television: April 1972.* Washington, D.C.: Corporation for Public Broadcasting, 1973.

1354 _____ . *Public Television and Program Content: 1974.* Washington, D.C.: Corporation for Public Broadcasting, 1975.

1355 _____ . "Television Soap Operas: What's Been Going On Anyway?" *Public Opinion Quarterly,* 1972, 36, 2: 200-212.

1356 _____ . "Violence and Color Television: What Children of Different Ages Learn." In G. A. Comstock, E. A. Rubinstein, and J. P. Murray (eds.), *Television and Social Behavior: Television's Effects: Further Explorations* (vol. 5). Washington, D.C.: Government Printing Office, 1972: 253-308.

1357 _____ and Nyenhuis, James. "Color vs. Black-and White Effects on Learning, Opinion, and Attention." *Audio-Visual Communication Review,* 1972, 20, 1: 16-28.

1358 Kaufmann, H. *Aggression and Altruism.* New York: Holt, Rinehart and Winston, 1970.

1359 _____ . "Definitions and Methodology in the Study of Aggression." *Psychological Bulletin,* 1965, 64: 351-364.

1360 Kaufmann, H. and Feshbach, S. "Displaced Aggression and Its Modification Through Exposure to Anti-Aggressive Communications." *Journal of Abnormal and Social Psychology,* 1963, 67: 79-83.

1361 _____ . "The Influence of Anti-Aggressive Communications Upon the Response to Provocation." *Journal of Personality,* 1963, 31: 428-444.

1362 Kay, H. "Toward an Understanding of News-Reading Behavior." *Journalism Quarterly,* 1954, 31: 15-32.

1363 _____ . "Weaknesses in the Television-Causes Aggression Analysis by Eron, et al." *American Psychologist,* 1972, 27: 970-973.

1364 Kaye, E. *The Family Guide to Children's Television: What To Watch, What To Miss, What To Change.* New York: Pantheon Books, 1974.

1365 Keating, J. P. "Persuasive Impact, Attitudes, and Image: The Effect of Communication Media and Audience Size on Attitudes Toward a Source and Toward His Advocated Position." Doctoral Dissertation, Ohio State University, 1972.

1366 Keating, J. P. and Latane, B. "Distorted Television Reception, Distraction, and Attitude Change." *Proceedings of the 80th Annual Convention of the*

American Psychological Association. Washington, D.C.: American Psychological Association, 1972: 141-142.

1367 _____ . "Politicians on T.V.: The Image is the Message." University of Washington and Ohio State University, 1974.

1368 Keel, V. A. "Leisure and the Mass Media: A Study of the Communications Behavior of Participants in a Major Area." Doctoral Dissertation, University of Minnesota, 1973.

1369 Keilhacker, M., and Keilhacker, M. *Jugend und Spielfilm. Erlebnisweisen und Einflusse* [Youth and the Story Film. How Young People Experience Films and are Influenced by Them]. Stuttgart: Ernst Klett Verlag, 1953.

1370 Keilhacker, M., Brudny, W., and Lammers, P. *Kinder sehen Filme* [Children see films]. Munich: Ehrenwirth Verlag, 1957.

1371 Keller, S. "The Social World of the Urban Slum Child: Some Early Findings." *American Journal of Orthopsychiatry,* 1963, 33, 5: 823-831.

1372 Kelley, Stanley, Jr. "Campaign Debates: Some Facts and Issues." *Public Opinion Quarterly,* 1962, 26, 3: 351-366.

1373 Kempkes, Wolfgang, *International Bibliography of Comics Literature.* New York: R. R. Bowker, 1971.

1374 Kenny, C. T. and Elliott, L., Jr. "Selective Exposure and the Active Group Effect." *Journal of Psychology,* 1972, 82: 197-199.

1375 Kenny, David A. "Threats to the Internal Validity of Cross-Lagged Panel Inference, as Related to Television Violence and Child Aggression: A Follow-up Study." In G. A. Comstock and E. A. Rubinstein (eds.), *Television and Social Behavior: Television and Adolescent Aggressiveness* (vol. 3). Washington, D.C.: Government Printing Office, 1972: 136-140.

1376 Kerckhoff, Alan C. *Socialization and Social Class.* Englewood Cliffs, N.J.: Prentice-Hall, 1972.

1377 Kerpelman, Larry C. "Personality and Attitude Correlates of Political Candidate Preference." *Journal of Social Psychology,* 1968, 76: 2: 219-226.

1378 Kerrick, Jean S. "The Influence of Captions on Picture Interpretation." *Journalism Quarterly,* 1955, 32, 2: 177-182.

1379 Kessel, John H. "Cognitive Dimensions and Political Activity." *Public Opinion Quarterly,* 1965, 29, 3: 377-389.

1380 Kessen, W. "Research Design in the Study of Developmental Problems." In P. Musen (ed.), *Handbook of Research Methods in Child Development.* New York: Wiley, 1960.

1381 Key, V. O., Jr. *Public Opinion and American Democracy.* New York: Alfred A. Knopf, 1961.

1382 Key, Wilson B. *Subliminal Seduction: Ad Media's Manipulation of a Not-so-Innocent America.* Englewood Cliffs, N.J.: Prentice-Hall, 1973.

1383 Kilguss, Anne F. "Using Soap Operas as a Therapeutic Tool." *Social Casework,* 1974, 55, 9: 525-530.

1384 Kilpatrick, James J. *The Smut Peddlers.* Garden City, N.Y.: Doubleday, 1960.

1385 King, Charles W. and Summers, John O. "Attitudes and Media Exposure." *Journal of Advertising Research,* 1971, 11, 1: 26-32.

1386 Kinzer, Nora S. "Soapy Sin in the Afternoon." *Psychology Today,* 1973, 7, 3: 46-48.

1387 Kirkpatrick, Charles A. *Advertising: Mass Communication in Marketing.* Boston: Houghton Mifflin, 1959.

1388 Kirsch, A. D. and Banks, S. "Program Types Refined by Factor Analysis." *Journal of Advertising Research,* 1962, 2, 3: 29-32.

1389 Klapper, Joseph T. "The Comparative Effects of the Various Media." In W. Schramm (ed.), *The Process and Effects of Mass Communication.* Urbana: University of Illinois Press, 1954: 91:105.

1390 _____. *The Effects of Mass Communication.* Glencoe, Ill.: Free Press, 1960. A classic synthesis of the literature which concludes by emphasizing the multitude of mediating factors which intervene in the effects process.

1391 _____. "The Effects of Mass Communication." In B. Berelson and M. Janowitz (eds), *Reader in Public Opinion and Communication* (2nd ed.). New York: Free Press, 1966: 473-486.

1392 _____. "The Effects of Mass Communication; An Analysis of Research on the Effectiveness and Limitations of Mass Media In Influencing the Opinions, Values, and Behavior of their Audiences." Doctoral Dissertation, Columbia University, 1961.

1393 _____. "The Impact of Viewing 'Aggression': Studies and Problems of Extrapolation." In O. N. Larsen (ed.), *Violence and the Mass Media.* New York: Harper and Row, 1968: 131-139.

1394 _____. "Mass Communication, Attitude Stability and Change." In C. W. Sherif and M. Sherif (eds.), *Attitude, Ego-Involvement and Change.* New York: Wiley, 1967: 297-310.

1395 _____. "Mass Communications Research: An Old Road Resurveyed," *Public Opinion Quarterly,* 1963, 27, 4: 515-527. Reviews the effects literature from a functional point of view, emphasizing the need for a uses and gratifications orientation to effects research in the future.

1396 _____. "Studying Effects of Mass Communication: An Introduction to the Field as Viewed by the Behavioral Sciences." *Teachers College Record,* 1955, 57, 2: 95-103.

1397 _____. "What We Know About the Effects of Mass Communications: The Brink of Hope." *Public Opinion Quarterly,* 1957-1958, 4: 453-474.

1398 Klavan, G. *Turn That Damned Thing Off: An Irreverent Look At TV's Impact on the American Scene.* Indianapolis: Bobbs-Merrill, 1972.

1399 Kleemeier, R. W., ed. *Aging and Leisure.* New York: Oxford University Press, 1961.

1400 Kline, F. G. "Media Time Budgeting as a Function of Demographics and Life Style." *Journalism Quarterly,* 1971, 48, 2: 211-221.

1401 _____. "Theory in Mass Communication Research." In F. G. Kline and P. J. Tichenor (eds.), *Current Perspectives in Mass Communication Research.* Beverly Hills: Sage, 1972: 17-40.

1402 _____. "Urban-Suburban Family Structure and Media Use." Doctoral Dissertation, University of Minnesota, 1969.

1403 _____ and Clarke, P., eds. *Mass Communications and Youth: Some Current Perspectives.* Beverly Hills: Sage, 1971.

1404 Kline, F. G. and Tichenor, P. J., eds. *Current Perspectives in Mass Communication Research.* Beverly Hills: Sage, 1972. The first in the "Sage Annual Reviews of Communication Research." Presents articles on theory, socialization, politics, sex and violence, diffusion, and the effects of environment on communication.

1405 Kline, F. G., Miller, P. V., and Morrison, A. J. "Adolescents and Family Planning Information: An Exploration of Audience Needs and Media Effects." In J. G. Blumler and E. Katz (eds.), *The Uses of Mass Communications: Current Perspectives on Gratifications Research.* Beverly Hills: Sage, 1974: 113-136.

1406 _____ and Fredin, E. S. "The Basis for Adolescent Information Acquisition About Drugs and Alcohol: A Uses and Gratifications Approach." University of Michigan, 1974.

1407 Kline, J. A. "Evaluation of a Multimedia Drug Education program." *Journal of Drug Education,* 1972, 2, 3: 229-239.

1408 Kloskowska, Antonina. *Kuetura Masowa. Krytypa i obrana* [Mass Culture: Critique and Defense]. Warsaw, Poland: Panstwowe Wydawnicto Naukowe, 1964.

1409 _____. "The Effect of Rehearsal Delay on Long-Term Imitation of Filmed Aggression" *British Journal of Psychology,* 1973, 64: 259-265.

1410 _____. "Social Class and Imitation of Aggressive Adult and Peer Models." *Journal of Social Psychology,* 1973, 89: 311-312.

1411 _____. "The Very Young, and Television Violence." *Journal of Psychomatic Research,* 1974, 18, 4: 233-237.

1412 Kniveton, B. H. and Stephenson, G. M. "The Effect of Pre-Experience on Imitation of An Aggressive Film Model." *British Journal of Social and Clinical Psychology,* 1970, 9: 31-36.

1413 _____. "An Examination of Individual Susceptibility to the Influence of Aggressive Film Models." *British Journal of Psychiatry,* 1973, 122: 53-56.

1414 Knower, F. H. "Graduate Theses and Dissertations on Broadcasting: 1956-1958." *Journal of Broadcasting,* 1960, 4: 77-87.

1415 _____. "Graduate Theses and Dissertations on Broadcasting: 1959-1960." *Journal of Broadcasting,* 1961, 5: 355-370.

1416 _____. "Graduate Theses and Dissertations on Broadcasting: 1961-1962." *Journal of Broadcasting,* 1963, 7: 269-282.

1417 _____. "Graduate Theses and Dissertations on Broadcasting: 1963-1966." *Journal of Broadcasting,* 1967, 11: 153-181.

1418 Knutson, J. N. (ed.). *Handbook of Political Psychology.* San Francisco: Jossey-Bass, 1973.

1419 Koefoed, Peter, Linne, Olga, and Richardt, Aase. "Born og TV: Interesse, Indlaering og Seervaner. Et Eksperiment og en Feltundersogelse" [Children and TV: Interest Learning and Viewing Habits. An Experiment and a Field Study]. Kobenhavn: Danmarks Radio, no. 12B, 1974.

1420 Kolaja, Jiri. "American Magazine Cartoons and Social Control." *Journalism Quarterly,* 1953, 30, 1: 71-74.

1421 Komisar, Lucy. "The Image of Women in Advertising." In V. Gornick and B. K. Moran (eds.), *Woman in Sexist Society.* New York: Basic Books, 1971.

1422 Koppel, Mark A. "The Effects of Humor on Induced Anxiety." *Dissertation Abstracts International,* 1970, 30 (7-B): 3388.

1423 Koriat, A., Melkman, R., Averil, J. R., and Lazarus, R. S. "The Self-Control of Emotional Reactions to a Stressful Film." *Journal of Personality,* 1972, 40: 601-619.

1424 Kraus, S., ed. *The Great Debates.* Bloomington: Indiana University Press, 1962.

1425 _____. "Mass Communication and Political Socialization: A Reassessment of Two Decades of Research." *Quarterly Journal of Speech,* 1973, 59, 4: 390-400.

1426 _____. "The Political Use of Television." *Journal of Broadcasting,* 1964, 8, 3: 219-228.

1427 _____ and Chaffee, S. H., eds. "The Ervin Committee Hearings and Communication Research." *Communication Research,* 1974, 1, special issue.

1428 Kraus, S. and Smith, R. G. "Issues and Images." In S. Kraus (ed.), *The Great Debates.* Bloomington: Indiana University Press, 1962: 289-312.

1429 Kraus, S., Meyer, Timothy, and Shelby, Maurice. "Sixteen Months After Chappaquidick: Effects of the Kennedy Broadcast." *Journalism Quarterly,* 1974, 51, 3: 431-440.

1430 Krauss, R. M. and Gluksburg, S. "Socialization of Communication Skills." In R. A. Hoppe, G. A. Milton, and E. C. Simmel (eds.), *Early Experiences and the Process of Socialization,* New York: Academic Press, 1970.

1431 Krebs, D. "The Effects of Presentation of Violence in the Mass Media: Catharsis or Stimulation?" *Zeitschrift fur Sozialpsychologie,* 1973, 4: 318-332.

1432 Krieghbaum, Hillier. *Science and the Mass Media.* New York: New York University Press, 1967.

1433 Kronhausen, Eberhard and Kronhausen, Phyllis. *Pornography and the Law: The Psychology of Erotic Realism and Pornography* (2nd ed.). New York: Ballantine Books, 1964.

1434 Kroupa, E. A. "Use of Mass Media by U.S. Army Personnel." *Journal of Broadcasting,* 1973, 17, 3: 309-320.

1435 Krugman, Herbert E. "An Application of Learning Theory to TV Copy Testing." *Public Opinion Quarterly,* 1962, 26, 4: 626-634.

1436 _____. "Brain Wave Measure of Media Involvement." *Journal of Advertising Research,* 1971, 11, 1: 3-9. Shows greater effort and tension involved in processing print vs. television information.

1437 _____. "A Comparison of Physical and Verbal Responses to Television Commercials." *Public Opinion Quarterly,* 1965, 29, 2: 323-325.

1438 _____. "The Impact of Television Advertising: Learning Without Involvement." *Public Opinion Quarterly,* 1965, 29, 3: 349-356.

1439 _____. "The Measurement of Advertising Involvement." *Public Opinion Quarterly,* 1966, 30, 4: 583-596.

1440 _____. "Processes Underlying Exposure to Advertising." *American Psychologist,* 1968, 23, 4: 245-253.

1441 _____. " 'Temporary' Effects of Communication." *Journal of Advertising Research,* 1970, 10, 1: 15-18.

1442 _____ and Hartley, Eugene L. "Passive Learning from Television." *Public Opinion Quarterly,* 1970, 34, 2: 184-190.

1443 Ksobiech, Kenneth J. "An Exploratory Investigation of Cross-Modality Cueing and Stimulus-Response Associations in Selected ITV Programs." *Dissertation Abstracts International,* 1971, 32 (2-A): 995.

1444 Kuhn, D. Z. "Imitation Theory and Research From a Cognitive Perspective." *Human Development,* 1973, 16: 157-180.

1445 _____, Madsen, C. H., Jr., and Becker, W. C. "Effects of Exposure to An Aggressive Model and 'Frustration' on Children's Aggressive Behavior." *Child Development,* 1967, 38: 739-745.

1446 Kuhns, William. *Why We Watch Them: Interpreting TV Shows.* New York: Benzinger, 1970.

1447 Kulik, James A., Sarbin, Theodore R., and Stein, Kenneth B. "Language, Socialization, and Delinquency." *Developmental Psychology,* 1971, 4, 3: 434-439.

1448 Kupperstein, Lenore R. "The Role of Pornography in the Etiology of Juvenile Delinquency: A Review of the Research Literature." In W. C. Wilson (comp.), *Technical Report of the Commission on Obscenity and Pornography: Preliminary Studies* (vol. 1). Washington, D.C.: Government Printing Office, 1971: 103-114. Provides a review of the professional, theoretical, and research literature on the relationship between pornography and delinquency.

1449 _____ and Wilson, W. C. "Erotica and Antisocial Behavior: An Analysis of Selected Social Indicators Statistics." In *Technical Report of The Commission on Obscenity and Pornography: Erotica and Antisocial Behavior* (vol. 7). Washington, D.C.: Government Printing Office, 1971: 311-324.

1450 Kuroda, Yasumasa. "Newspaper Reading and Political Behavior in a Japanese Community." *Journal of Communication,* 1965, 15, 3: 171-181.

1451 Kurth, E. "Fernsehen Und Verhaltens Storungen" [TV and Behavior Disturbances]. *Zeitschrift fur Psychologie,* 1964, 170, 3-4: 261-269.

1452 Kurtz, N. R. "Gatekeepers: Agents in Acculturation." *Rural Sociology,* 1968, 33, 1: 63-70.

1453 Kutchinsky, Berl. "The Effect of Easy Availability of Pornography on the Incidence of Sex Crimes: The Danish Experience." *Journal of Social Issues,* 1973, 29, 3: 163-182.

L

1454 LaBlonde, Jeanne A. "A Study of the Relationship Between the Television Viewing Habits and Scholastic Achievement of Fifth Grade Children." Doctoral Dissertation, University of Minnesota, 1966.

1455 LaGuardia, Robert. *The Wonderful World of TV Soap Operas.* New York: Ballantine Books, 1974.

1456 Lahtinen, P. and Taipale, H. "The Effect of TV on Children's Drawings and Vocabulary." Jyvchaskyla, Finland: Institute for Educational Research, University of Jyvchaskyla, 1971.

1457 Land, H. W. "The Children's Television Workshop: How and Why it Works." Jericho, N.Y.: Nassau Board of Cooperative Educational Services, 1971.

1458 Land, Kenneth C. and Spilerman, S., eds. *Social Indicator Models.* New York: Russell Sage Foundation, 1975.

1459 Landau, Barbara. "This Column is About Women: Emotional Disturbances in Childhood." *Ontario Psychologist,* 1973, 5, 4: 46-49.

1460 Landy, David and Mettee, D. "Evaluation of an Aggressor as a Function of Exposure to Cartoon Humor." *Journal of Personality and Social Psychology,* 1969, 12, 11: 66-71.

1461 Lane, Jonathan P. "Functions of the Mass Media in Brazil's 1964 Crisis." *Journalism Quarterly,* 1967, 44: 297-306.

1462 Lane, R. E., *Political Life: Why People Get Involved in Politics.* Glencoe, Ill.: The Free Press, 1959.

1463 _____ and Sears, D. O. *Public Opinion.* Englewood Cliffs, N.J.: Prentice-Hall, 1964.

1464 Lang, Gladys E. and Lang, Kurt. "The Inferential Structure of Political Communications: A Study in Unwitting Bias." *Public Opinion Quarterly,* 1955, 19, 2: 168-183.

1465 _____. "Political Participation and the Television Perspective." *Social Problems,* 1956, 4, 2: 107-116.

1466 _____. "Some Pertinent Questions on Collective Violence and the News Media." *Journal of Social Issues,* 1972, 28, 1: 93-110.

1467 Lang, Kurt. "Areas of Radio Preference; A Preliminary Inquiry." *Journal of Applied Psychology,* 1957, 41, 1: 7-14.

1468 _____. "Images of Society: Media Research in Germany." *Public Opinion Quarterly,* 1974, 38, 3: 335-351.

1469 _____. "Mass Appeal and Minority Tastes." In B. Rosenberg and D. M. White (eds.), *Mass Culture.* Glencoe, Ill.: Free Press, 1957: 379-384.

1470   Lang, Kurt and Lang, G. E. "The Mass Media and Voting." In E. Burdick and A. J. Brodbeck (eds.), *American Voting Behavior.* Glencoe, Ill.: Free Press, 1959: 217-235.

1471   _____ . "Ordeal by Debate: Viewer Reactions." *Public Opinion Quarterly,* 1961, 25, 2: 277-288.

1472   _____ . *Politics and Television.* Chicago: Quadrangle Books, 1968. Explores television's role in the creation of "reality" and the possible distortion of same in the political arena. Summarizes the Lang's findings in their research on TV's political impact.

1473   _____ . "Reactions of Viewers." In S. Kraus (ed.), *The Great Debates.* Bloomington: Indiana University Press, 1962: 313-330.

1474   _____ . "The Television Personality in Politics: Some Considerations." *Public Opinion Quarterly,* 1956, 20, 1: 103-112.

1475   _____ . "The Unique Perspective of Television and Its Effects: A Pilot Study." *American Sociological Review,* 1953, 18: 3-12.

1476   _____ . *Voting and Nonvoting: Implications of Broadcasting Returns Before Polls are Closed.* Waltham, Mass.: Blaisdell Publishing Co., 1968.

1477   Langton, K. P. *Political Socialization.* New York: Oxford, 1969.

1478   Lanzetta, J. T. and Driscoll, J. M. "Uncertainty and Importance as Factors in Information Search." *Journal of Personality and Social Psychology,* 1968, 10: 479-486.

1479   LaPlante, W. A. "An Investigation of the Sight Vocabulary of Pre-School Children as Measured By Their Ability to Recognize Words Shown Frequently on Commercial Television." Doctoral Dissertation, Temple University, 1968.

1480   Larder, D. L. "Effect of Aggressive Story Content on Nonverbal Play Behavior." *Psychological Reports,* 1962, 11: 14.

1481   Larkin, Ernest F. "A Q-Analysis of Values and Attitudes Toward Advertising." *Journalism Quarterly,* 1971, 48, 1: 68-72.

1482   Larrabbe, E. and Meyersohn, R. *Mass Leisure.* Glencoe, Ill.: Free Press, 1958.

1483   Larsen, Otto. "Controversies About the Mass Communication of Violence." In M. E. Wolfgang (ed.), *Patterns of Violence: Annals of the American Academy of Political and Social Science,* 1966, 364: 37-49.

1484   _____ . "Innovators and Early Adopters of Television." *Sociological Inquiry,* 1962, 32, 1: 16-33.

1485   _____ . "Posing the Problem of Effects." In R. K. Baker and S. J. Ball (eds.), *Violence and the Media.* A Staff Report to the National Commission on the Causes and Prevention of Violence. 1969: 237-246.

1486   _____ . "Social Effects of Mass Communication." In R.E.L. Faris (ed.), *Handbook of Modern Sociology.* Chicago: Rand McNally, 1964: 348-381. Examines the media from a sociological, process orientation, emphasizing television's potential in the socialization process.

1487   _____ , ed. *Violence and the Mass Media.* New York. Harper & Row, 1968.

1488 Larsen, Otto and DeFleur, Melvin L. "The Comparative Role of Children and Adults in Propaganda Diffusion." *American Sociological Review,* 1954, 19: 593-602.

1489 Larsen, Otto and Hill, R. "Mass Media and Interpersonal Communication in the Diffusion of a News Event." *American Sociological Review,* 1954, 19: 426-433.

1490 Larsen, Otto, Gray, Louis, and Fortis, J. Gerald. "Goals and Goal-Achievement Methods in Television Content: Models for Anomie?" *Sociological Inquiry,* 1963, 33, 2: 180-196. Documents the heavy use of socially disapproved means to achieve socially approved ends.

1491 Larson, C. U. "A Content Analysis of Media Reporting of the Watergate Hearings." *Communication Research,* 1974, 1, 4: 440-448.

1492 Lasswell, Harold D. "Communications Research and Public Policy." *Public Opinion Quarterly,* 1972, 36, 3: 301-310.

1493 _____. "The Structure and Function of Communication in Society." In W. Schramm (ed.), *Mass Communications.* Urbana: University of Illinois Press, 1960.

1494 _____, Ward, L. S., and Tancill, K. "Alienation and Use of Mass Media." *Public Opinion Quarterly,* 1965-1966, 29: 583-594.

1495 Lauter, Paul, ed. *Theories of Comedy.* Garden City, N.Y.: Doubleday, 1964.

1496 Lavidge, R. and Steiner, G. A. "A Model for Predicting Measurements of Advertising Effectiveness." *Journal of Marketing,* 1961, 24: 59-62.

1497 Lawrence, G. C. "Media Effects in Congressional Election Campaigns." Doctoral Dissertation, Stanford University, 1972.

1498 Lazarsfeld, Paul F. "Afterword: Some Reflections on Past and Future Research on Broadcasting." In G. Steiner, *The People Look at Television.* New York: Knopf, 1963: 409-422.

1499 _____. "Research Argumentation and Action in the Media Field." *Journalism Quarterly,* 1950, 27, 3: 263-267.

1500 _____. "A Researcher Looks at Television." *Public Opinion Quarterly,* 1960, 24, 1: 24-31.

1501 _____. "Trends in Broadcasting Research." In *Studies of Broadcasting* (no. 1). Tokyo: Radio and Television Culture Research Institute, Nippon Hoso Kyokai, 1963: 49-64.

1502 _____. "Why Is So Little Known About the Effects of Television on Children and What Can Be Done?" *Public Opinion Quarterly,* 1955, 19, 3: 243-251.

1503 _____ and Merton, R. K. "Mass Communication, Popular Taste, and Organized Social Action." In W. Schramm and D. F. Roberts (eds.), *The Process and Effects of Mass Communication* (2nd ed.). Urbana: University of Illinois Press, 1971: 554-578.

1504 Lazarus, H. R. and Bienlein, D. K. "Soap Opera Therapy." *International Journal of Group Psychotherapy,* 1967, 17, 252-256.

1505 Lazarus, R. S., Speisman, J. C., Mordkoff, A. M., and Davison, L. A. "A Laboratory Study of Psychological Stress Produced by a Motion Picture Film." *Psychological Monographs,* 1962, 76, 34.

1506 Leab, Daniel J. *From Sambo to Superspade. The Black Experience in Motion Pictures.* Boston: Houghton Mifflin, 1975.

1507 Leavitt, Clark. "A Multidimensional Set of Rating Scales for Television Commercials." *Journal of Applied Psychology,* 1970, 54, 5: 427-429.

1508 Lee, A. McClung. *La Sociologia delle Communicazoni [The Sociology of Communication].* Torino, Italy: Taylor, 1960.

1509 Lee, Richard W., ed. *Politics and the Press.* Washington, D.C.: Acropolis Books, 1970. Stems from the University of Maryland Distinguished Journalism lecture series. Includes lectures on press and presidential politics, press credibility, reporting standards, television distortion, politics, blacks and the press.

1510 Lefcourt, H. M., Barnes, K., Parke, R. D., and Schwartz, F. "Anticipated Social Censure and Aggression-Conflict as Mediators of Response to Aggression Induction." *Journal of Social Psychology,* 1966, 70: 251-263.

1511 Lefever, E. W. *TV and National Defense: An Analysis of CBS News, 1972-1973,* Boston, Va.: Institute for American Strategy Press, 1974.

1512 Lefkowitz, M., Eron, L. D., Walder, L. O., and Huesmann, L. R. "Television Violence and Child Aggression: A Follow-up Study." In G. A. Comstock and E. A. Rubinstein (eds.), *Television and Social Behavior: Television and Adolescent Aggressiveness* (vol. 3). Washington, D.C.: Government Printing Office, 1972: 35-135.

1513 _____ . "Environmental Variables as Predictors of Aggressive Behavior." *International Journal of Group Tensions,* 1973, 3 (3-4): 30-47.

1514 _____ . "Preference for Televised Contact Sports as Related to Sex Differences in Aggression." *Developmental Psychology,* 1973, 9, 3: 417-420.

1515 Lehmann, D. R. "Television Show Preference: Application of a Choice Model." *Journal of Marketing Research,* 1971, 8: 47-55.

1516 Leifer, A. D. "Research on the Socialization Influence of Television in the United States." In *Television and Socialization Processes in the Family,* Proceedings of the Prix Jeunesse Seminar, 1975: 26-53.

1517 _____ . "The Use of Television to Encourage Socially Valued Behaviors in Preschoolers." Cambridge, Mass.: Harvard University, 1974.

1518 _____ and Roberts, D. F. "Children's Responses to Television Violence." In J. P. Murray, E. A. Rubinstein, and G. A. Comstock (eds.), *Television and Social Behavior: Television and Social Learning* (vol. 2). Washington, D.C.: Government Printing Office, 1972: 43-180.

1519 Leifer, A. D., Gordon, N. J., and Graves, S. B. "Children and Television: Recommended Future Efforts." Boston: Harvard University, Center for Research in Children's Television, 1973. Recommends more research on diversity of portrayals, prosocial effects, modification of the impact of current programming, formation of a Television Information Center, TV viewing as an activity, and the meaning of new video technologies for child development.

1520 _____ . "Children's Television: More Than Mere Entertainment." *Harvard Educational Review,* 1974, 44, 2: 213-245.

1521 Leifer, A. D., Collins, W. A., Gross, B. M., Taylor, P. H., Andrews, L., and Blackmer, E. R. "Developmental Aspects of Variables Relevant to Observational Learning." *Child Development,* 1971, 42: 1509-1516.

1522 Lejins, P. "Crime, Violence, and Horror Movies and TV Shows and Juvenile Delinquency." New York: National Council on Crime and Delinquency, 1960.

1523 Leith, James A. *Media and Revolution: Molding a New Citizenry in France During the Terror.* Toronto: Canadian Broadcasting Corp., 1968.

1524 Lemert, James B. "Components of Source 'Image': Hong Kong, Brazil, North America." *Journalism Quarterly,* 1969, 46: 306-313, 418.

1525 _____ . "Two Studies of Status Conferral." *Journalism Quarterly,* 1966, 43, 1: 25-33.

1526 LeMoal, P. and Faugere, M. M. "Le Cinema et L'Enfant" [The Cinema and the Child]. *La Sauvegarde de L'Enfance,* 1947, 2: 66-77.

1527 Leopold, W. F. *Bibliography of Child Language.* Bloomington: Indiana University Press, 1972.

1528 Lerner, Daniel. "Mass Communication and the Nation State." In W. P. Davison and F.T.C. Yu (eds.), *Mass Communication Research: Major Issues and Future Directions.* New York: Praeger, 1974: 83-92. A summary article synthesizing contextual variables, communication variables, mass communication and development, and ending with suggestions for research.

1529 _____ . *The Passing of Traditional Society.* New York: Free Press, 1958.

1530 _____ . *Propaganda in War and Crisis.* New York: George Stewart, 1951.

1531 _____ and Schramm, W., eds. *Communication and Change in the Developing Countries.* Honolulu: East-West Center Press, 1967.

1532 Lerner, L. and Weiss, R. L. "Role of Value of Reward and Model Affective Response in Vicarious Reinforcement." *Journal of Personality and Social Psychology,* 1972, 21: 93-100.

1533 LeRoy, David J. and Sterling, Christopher H., eds. *Mass News: Practices, Controversies, and Alternatives.* Englewood Cliffs, N.J.: Prentice-Hall, 1973.

1534 LeRoy, David J., Uram, Eugene, and Williams, Wenmouth. "Use of Operant Methodology in Measuring Mass Media Effects." *Journalism Quarterly,* 1971, 51, 1: 102-106.

1535 LeRoy, David J., Wotring, C. Edward, and Lyle, Jack. "The Public Television Viewer and the Watergate Hearings." *Communication Research,* 1974, 1, 4: 406-425.

1536 _____ . "Today in the Legislature: The Florida Story." *Journal of Communication,* 1974, 24, 3: 92-98.

1537 LeRoy, David J., Wotring, C. E., and Williams, W. "Mediated Violence and Victim Consequences: A Behavioral Measure of Attention and Interest." Tallahassee: Florida State University, Communication Research Center, 1974.

1538 Lesser, G. S. *Children and Television: Lessons from Sesame Street.* New York: Random House, 1974. Reviews the evidence which shows that such educational shows can be entertaining, popular, and effective.

1539 _____ . "Learning, Teaching, and Television Production For Children: The Experience of Sesame Street." *Harvard Educational Review,* 1972, 42: 232-272.

1540 Leventhal, Howard and Mace, William. "The Effect of Laughter on Evaluation of a Slapstick Movie." *Journal of Personality,* 1970, 38, 1: 16-30.

1541 Levonian, Edward. "Need for Control Data in Studies of Self-Esteem and Persuasibility." *Psychological Reports,* 1970, 27, 2: 527-544.

1542 _____ . "Personality and Communication-Mediated Opinion Change: The Influence of Control." *Journal of Communication,* 1969, 19, 3: 217-226.

1543 Levy, Sheldon G. "Communications During the Detroit Riot." *Journalism Quarterly,* 1971, 48, 2: 339-342.

1544 _____ . "How Population Subgroups Differed in Knowledge of Six Assassinations." *Journalism Quarterly,* 1969, 46, 4: 685-698.

1545 Lewels, F. J. *The Uses of the Media by the Chicano Movement: A Study in Minority Access.* New York: Praeger, 1974.

1546 Lewis, John D. "Feedback in Mass Communication: Its Nature and Use in Decision Making." *Dissertation Abstracts,* 1966, 27 (6-A): 1929.

1547 Leyens, J. P. and Camino, Leoncio. "Violence on the Screen and Among the Spectators: Some Processes or Mediation at the Individual and Group Level." *Revue de Psychologie et des Sciences de L'Education,* 1974, 9, 3: 279-300.

1548 Leyens, J. P., Parke, R. D., Camino, L., and Berkowitz, L. "Effects of Movie Violence on Aggression in a Field Setting as a Function of Group Dominance and Cohesion." *Journal of Personality and Social Psychology,* 1975, 32, 2: 346-360.

1549 Leymore, V. L. *Hidden Myth: Structure and Symbolism in Advertising.* New York: Basic Books, 1975. Contends that advertising in modern society functions as myth did in ancient times—to reinforce accepted modes of behavior. Applies structuralism via Levi-Strauss to advertising.

1550 Lichty, L. W. "'The Real McCoys' and its Audience: A Functional Analysis." *Journal of Broadcasting,* 1965, 9: 157-166.

1551 _____ , comp. *World and International Broadcasting: A Bibliography.* Washington: Broadcast Education Association, 1971.

1552 _____ and LeRoy, D. J. "Missing the Newscaster: Reactions to the 1967 AFTRA Strike." *Journal of Broadcasting,* 1972, 16: 175-184.

1553 Lichty, L. W., Ripley, J. M., and Summers, H. B. "Political Programs on National Television Networks: 1960 and 1964." *Journal of Broadcasting,* 1965, 9: 217-229.

1554 Lickona, T., ed. *Man and Morality: Theory, Research, and Social Issues.* New York: Holt, Rinehart and Winston, 1974.

1555 Lieberman, S. "Children's Reactions To Violent Material on Television." Second year report prepared by Leiberman Research, Inc. New York: American Broadcasting Co., Inc., 1973.

1556 _____ . "Children's Reactions To Violent Material on Television." Third year report prepared by Lieberman Research, Inc. New York: American Broadcasting Co., Inc., 1974.

1557 Liebert, Robert M. "Modeling and the Media." *School Psychology Digest,* 1975, 4, 1: 22-29.

1558 _____ . "Observational Learning: Some Social Applications." In P. J. Elich (ed.), *Social Learning: Fourth Western Symposium on Learning.* Bellingham, Wash.: Western Washington State College, 1972: 59-73.

1559 _____ . "Television and Children's Aggressive Behavior: Another Look." *American Journal of Psychoanalysis,* 1975, 45, 3: 99-107.

1560 _____ . "Television and Social Learning: Some Relationships Between Viewing Violence and Behaving Aggressively (Overview)." In J. P. Murray, E. A. Rubinstein, and G. A. Comstock (eds.), *Television and Social Behavior: Television and Social Learning* (vol. 2). Washington, D.C.: Government Printing Office, 1972: 1-42.

1561 Liebert, Robert M. and Baron, Robert A. "Short-Term Effects of Televised Aggression on Children's Aggressive Behavior." In J. P. Murray, E. A. Rubinstein, and G. A. Comstock (eds.), *Television and Social Behavior: Television and Social Learning* (vol. 2), Washington, D.C.: Government Printing Office, 1972, 181-201.

1562 _____ . "Some Immediate Effects of Televised Violence on Children's Behavior." *Developmental Psychology,* 1972, 6, 3: 469-475. The effects evident included greater preference for aggressive toys and greater interpersonal aggression.

1563 Liebert, Robert M. and Fernandez, L. E. "Imitation as a Function of Vicarious and Direct Reward." *Developmental Psychology,* 1970, 2: 230-232.

1564 Liebert, R. M. and Poulos, R. W. "Television as a Moral Teacher." In T. Lickona (ed.), *Man and Morality: Theory, Research, and Social Issues.* New York: Holt, Rinehart and Winston, 1974. Reviews the literature to make a case for the potential prosocial effects of television.

1565 _____ . "TV For Kiddies: Truth, Goodness, Beauty—and a Little Bit of Brainwash." *Psychology Today,* 1972, 6, 6: 123-128.

1566 Liebert, R. M., Davidson, E. S., and Neale, J. M. "Aggression in Childhood: The Impact of Television." In V. B. Cline (ed.), *Where Do You Draw the Line?: An Exploration into Media Violence, Pornography, and Censorship.* Provo, Utah: Brigham Young University, 1974: 113-128.

1567 Liebert, R. M., Davidson, E. S., and Sobol, M. P. "Catharsis of Aggression Among Institutionalized Boys: Further Discussion." In G. A. Comstock, E. A. Rubinstein, and J. P. Murray (eds.), *Television and Social Behavior. Television's Effects: Further Explorations* (vol. 5). Washington, D.C.: Government Printing Office, 1972: 366-373.

1568 Liebert, Robert M., Neale, John M., and Davidson, Emily S., *The Early Window: The Effects of Television on Children and Youth.* New York: Pergamon, 1973. Presents theory and research bearing on TV and children's attitudes, development, and behavior. Three of the nine chapters deal with the violence question. Also explores the political and social questions surrounding these issues.

1569 Liebert, Robert M., Poulos, Rita W., and Rubinstein, Eli A. "Positive Social Learning: The Effects of Television on Children and Adolescents." *Journal of Communication,* 1975, 25, 4: 90-97.

1570 Liebert, R. M., Sobol, M. P., and Copemann, C. D. "Effects of Vicarious Consequences and Race of Model Upon Imitative Performance by Black Children." *Developmental Psychology,* 1972, 6, 3: 453:456.

1571 Liebert, R. M., Sobol, M. P., and Davidson, E. S. "Catharsis of Aggression Among Institutionalized Boys: Fact or Artifact." In G. A. Comstock, E. A. Rubinstein, and J. P. Murray (eds.), *Television and Social Behavior: Television's Effects; Further Explorations* (vol. 5). Washington, D.C.: Government Printing Office, 1972: 351-359.

1572 Liebert, R. M., Sprafkin, H. N., and Poulos, R. W. "Selling Cooperation to Children." State University of New York, 1975.

1573 Light, Marvin L. "An Experimental Study of the Effects of Repeated Persuasive Communications Upon Awareness and Attitudes." *Dissertation Abstracts,* 1968, 28 (12-B): 5226.

1574 Lindley, William R. "Communications Theories and Racial Tensions." *Journalism Quarterly,* 1969, 46, 11: 147-149.

1575 Lindsley, Ogden Richardson. "A Behavioral Measure of Television Viewing." *Journal of Advertising Research,* 1962, 2, 3: 2-12.

1576 Linne, O. *Reactions of Children to Scenes of Violence on T.V.* Stockholm: Sveriges Radio Audience and Programme Research Department, 1971.

1577 Linsky, Arnold S. "The Changing Public Views of Alcoholism." *Quarterly Journal of Studies on Alcohol,* 1970, 31 (3-A): 692-704.

1578 _____ . "Theories of Behavior and the Image of the Alcoholic in Popular Magazines, 1900-1966." *Public Opinion Quarterly,* 1970, 34, 4: 573-581.

1579 Lismonde, Henry. "Comportements et Attitudes de L'Homme Televisionnaire" [Behavior and Attitudes of the TV Man]. *Etudes de Radio-Television,* 1965, 11/12: 65-76.

1580 Littner, N. "A Psychiatrist Looks at Television and Violence." *Television Quarterly,* 1969, 8: 7-23.

1581 Liu, Alan P. *Communications and National Integration in Communist China.* Berkeley: University of California Press, 1971.

1582 _____. "Mass Communication and Media in China's Cultural Revolution." *Journalism Quarterly,* 1969, 46, 2: 314-319.

1583 _____. "Movies and Modernization in Communist China," *Journalism Quarterly,* 1966, 43, 2: 319-324.

1584 Livolsi, Marino. "Mass Communication and Interpersonal Communication: An Apparent Antimony." *Ikon,* 1966, 19: 167-200.

1585 Loevinger, L. "The Ambiguous Mirror: The Reflective-Projective Theory of Broadcasting and Mass Communications." *Journal of Broadcasting,* 1968, 12: 97-116.

1586 _____. *The Politics of Advertising: An Address Before the International Radio and Television Society.* New York: Television Information Office, 1973.

1587 Long, B. H. and Henderson, E. H. "Children's Use of Time: Some Personal and Social Correlates." *Elementary School Journal,* 1973, 73, 4: 193-199.

1588 Long, Michele L. and Simon, Rita J. "The Roles and Statuses of Women on Children and Family TV Programs." *Journalism Quarterly,* 1974, 51, 1: 107-110. A content analysis supporting the contention that the image of women is considerably less positive than that of the male.

1589 "Looking at Violence." *British Medical Journal,* 1973, 5866, 2: 565-566.

1590 Lopiccolo, John. "An Examination of Heart Rate and Conscious Responses to Selected Televised Dramatic Segments." *Dissertation Abstracts International,* 1972, 32 (12-A): 7022.

1591 Lorimor, E. S. and Dunn, S. W. "Use of the Mass Media in France and Egypt." *Public Opinion Quarterly,* 1968, 32, 4: 680-684.

1592 LoSciuto, Leonard A. "A National Inventory of Television Viewing Behavior." In E. A. Rubinstein, G. A. Comstock and J. P. Murray (eds.), *Television and Social Behavior: Television in Day-to-Day Life: Patterns of Use* (vol. 4). Washington, D.C.: Government Printing Office, 1972: 33-86.

1593 Louis, R. and Rovan, J. *Television and Tele-Clubs in Rural Communities: An Experiment in France.* Paris: UNESCO, 1955.

1594 Lovaas, I. "Effect of Exposure to Symbolic Aggression on Aggressive Behavior." *Child Development,* 1961, 32: 37-44.

1595 Lovibond, S. H. "The Effect of Media Stressing Crime and Violence Upon Children's Attitudes." *Social Problems,* 1967, 15, 1: 91-100. A before-and-after study of the effects of the introduction of television into a community. Revealed attitude shifts consistent with the media content and a subsequent decrease in book and comic reading and movie-going.

1596 Lowin, A. "Approach and Avoidance: Alternative Models of Selective Exposure to Information." *Journal of Personality and Social Psychology,* 1967, 6: 1-9.

1597 Lowry, Dennis T. "Agnew and the Network TV News: A Before/After Content Analysis." *Journalism Quarterly,* 1971, 48, 2: 205-210.

1598 _____. "Gresham's Law and Network TV News Selection." *Journal of Broadcasting,* 1971, 15: 397-408.

1599 _____. "Measures of Network News Bias in the 1972 Presidential Campaign." *Journal of Broadcasting,* 1974, 18, 4: 387-402.

1600 Lucas, Darrell Blaine and Britt, Stewart Henderson. *Advertising Psychology and Research.* New York: McGraw-Hill, 1950.

1601 _____. *Measuring Advertising Effectiveness.* New York: McGraw-Hill, 1963.

1602 Lull, James T. "Counter-Advertising: Persuasibility of the Anti-Bayer TV Spot." *Journal of Broadcasting,* 1974, 18, 3: 353-360.

1603 Lumsdaine, A. A. "Gauging the Effects of Films on Reading Interests." In M. A. May and A. A. Lumsdaine (eds.), *Learning From Films.* New Haven, Conn.: Yale University Press, 1958: 185-194.

1604 Lyle, Jack. "Attitude Measurement in Communication Research." *Journalism Quarterly,* 1965, 42, 4: 606-614.

1605 _____. "Contemporary Functions of the Mass Media." In R. K. Baker and S. J. Ball (eds.), *Violence and the Media.* A Staff Report to the National Commission on the Causes and Prevention of Violence. Washington, D.C.: Government Printing Office, 1969, 187-216.

1606 _____. "Immediate vs. Delayed Reward Use of Newspapers by Adolescents." *Journalism Quarterly,* 1962, 39, 1: 83-85.

1607 _____. "The Negro and the News Media." In J. Lyle, *The News in Megalopolis.* San Francisco: Chandler, 1967: 163-182.

1608 _____. *The News in Megalopolis.* San Francisco: Chandler, 1967.

1609 _____. "Television in Daily Life: Patterns of Use (Overview)." In E. A. Rubinstein, G. A. Comstock, and J. P. Murray (eds.), *Television and Social Behavior: Television in Day-to-Day Use: Patterns of Use* (vol. 4). Washington, D.C.: Government Printing Office, 1972, 1-32.

1610 _____. "Why Adults Do or Do Not Watch Educational Television." *Journal of Broadcasting,* 1961, 1, 54: 325-334.

1611 Lyle, Jack and Hoffman, H. R. "Children's Use of Television and Other Media." In E. A. Rubinstein, G. A. Comstock, and J. P. Murray (eds.), *Television and Social Behavior: Television in Day-to-Day Life: Patterns of Use* (vol. 4). Washington, D.C.: Government Printing Office, 1972: 129-256.

1612 _____. "Explorations in Patterns of Television Viewing by Preschool Age Children." In E. A. Rubinstein, G. A. Comstock, and J. P. Murray (eds.), *Television and Social Behavior: Television in Day-to-Day Life: Patterns of Use* (vol. 4). Washington, D.C.: Government Printing Office, 1972: 257-273.

1613 _____. "Television in the Lives of Our Children: The 1970s." *Educational and Industrial Television,* 1972, 5, 5: 10.

1614 Lynch, J. E. "Seven Days With 'All in the Family': Case Study of the Taped TV Drama." *Journal of Broadcasting,* 1973, 17: 259-274.

1615   Lyness, P. I. "Patterns in the Mass Communications Tastes of the Young Audience." *Journal of Educational Psychology,* 1951, 42: 449-467.

1616 _____. "The Place of the Mass Media in the Lives of Boys and Girls." *Journalism Quarterly,* 1952, 29, 1: 43-55.

1617   Lynn, Jerry R. "Effects of Persuasive Appeals in Public Service Advertising." *Journalism Quarterly,* 1974, 51: 622-630.

1618 _____. "Perception of Public Service Advertising: Source, Message and Receiver Effects." *Journalism Quarterly,* 1973, 50: 673-679, 689.

Mc

1619   McAllister, William H. "The Effects of Bylines on News Story Credibility." *Journalism Quarterly,* 1966, 43, 2: 331-333.

1620   McArthur, Leslie Z. and Resko, Beth G. "The Portrayal of Men and Women in American Television Commercials." *Journal of Social Psychology,* 1975, 97, 2: 209-220.

1621   McCain, Thomas A. "A Functional Analysis of Network Television News Viewing." Doctoral Dissertation, University of Wisconsin, 1972.

1622   McCall, G. and Simmons, J. L. *Identities and Interactions.* New York: Free Press, 1966.

1623   McCasland, B. W. "The Relation of Aggressive Fantasy to Aggressive Behavior in Children." Doctoral Dissertation, Syracuse University, 1961.

1624   McClure, Robert D. and Patterson, Thomas E. "Television News and Political Advertising: The Impact of Exposure on Voter Beliefs." *Communication Research,* 1974, 1: 3-31.

1625   MacConkey, D. "Teens and the Mass Media: A Study of Black and White Adolescents and Their Use of Mass Media." Doctoral Dissertation, University of Maryland, 1974.

1626   McCombs, Maxwell E. "Editorial Endorsements: A Study of Influence." *Journalism Quarterly,* 1967, 44, 3: 545-548.

1627 _____. "Mass Communication In Political Campaigns: Information, Gratification, and Persuasion." In F. G. Kline and P. J. Tichenor (eds.), *Current Perspectives in Mass Communication Research.* Beverly Hills: Sage, 1972: 169-194.

1628 _____. "Negro Use of Television and Newspapers for Political Information, 1952-1964." *Journal of Broadcasting,* 1968, 12, 3: 261-266. Documents a marked increase in blacks' use of media for political information between 1952 and 1964, with television being the favored medium.

1629 _____. "Role of Television in the Acquisition of Language." Doctoral Dissertation, Stanford University, 1966.

1630 _____ and Mullins, L. E. "Consequences of Education: Media Exposure, Political Interest and Information-Seeking Orientations." *Mass Comm Review,* 1973, 1, 1: 27-31.

1631 McCombs, Maxwell E. and Shaw, Donald L. "The Agenda-Setting Function of Mass Media." *Public Opinion Quarterly,* 1972, 36, 2: 176-187. Shows exceptionaly strong correlation between media content in a community and voters' judgments of news item salience.

1632 McCombs, Maxwell E. and Wilcox, W. "Media Use in Presidential Election Campaigns." In C. Bush (ed.), *News Research for Better Newspapers,* 1968, 3: 36-39.

1633 McConville, Maureen N. and Leavitt, Clark. "Predicting Product Related Recall from Verbal Response." *Proceedings of the 76th Annual Convention of the American Psychological Association,* 1968, 3: 677-678.

1634 McCormack, Thelma. "Social Theory and the Mass Media." *Canadian Journal of Economics and Political Science,* 1961, 27, 4: 479-489.

1635 McCroskey, J. C. and Prichard, S.V.O. "Selective-Exposure and Lyndon B. Johnson's 1966 'State of the Union' Address." *Journal of Broadcasting,* 1967, 11: 331-337.

1636 McDaniel, D. "Film's Presumed Advantage in Presenting Television News." *Journalism Quarterly,* 1973, 50: 146-148.

1637 MacDonald, N. W. "Television Drama Preference Choice." Doctoral Dissertation, University of Minnesota, 1966.

1638 McDonaugh, Edward, et al. "Television and the Family." *Sociology and Social Research,* 1950, 35, 2: 113-122.

1639 McEwen, W. J. and Greenberg, Bradley S. "The Effects of Message Intensity on Receiver Evaluations of Source, Message and Topic." *Journal of Communication,* 1970, 20, 4: 340-350.

1640 McEwen, W. J. and Hanneman, G. J. "The Depiction of Drug Use in Television Programming." *Journal of Drug Education,* 1974, 4, 3: 281-293.

1641 _____. "An Experimental Analysis of Reaction to Filmed Drug Abuse Information." Drug Abuse Information Research Project Report no. 8. Storrs: University of Connecticut, Communication Research Program, 1972.

1642 McGinnis, J. *The Selling of the President, 1968.* New York: Trident Press, 1969. A behind-the-scene description on the molding of Richard Nixon's image in the 1968 Presidential campaign.

1643 McGonnies, Elliot. "Communication Viewed as Social Control." In A. Silverstein (ed.), *Human Communication: Theoretical Explorations.* New York: Wiley, 1974: 185-202.

1644 McGrath, K. "An Agenda-Setting Approach to Covering the 1974 Elections." Medill School of Journalism, Northwestern University, 1974.

1645 McGuire, Delbert. "The Effectiveness of the Presidential Press Conference as a Medium of Communication Between the President and the Nation Through the Mass Media." Doctoral Dissertation, University of Iowa, 1966.

1646 McGuire, W. J. "An Information-Processing Approach to Advertising Effectiveness." In H. Davis and A. J. Silk(eds.),*The Behavioral and Management Sciences in Marketing.* New York: Ronald Press, 1974.

1647 _____ . "Psychological Motives and Communication Gratification." In J. G. Blumler and E. Katz (eds.), *The Uses of Mass Communications: Current Perspectives on Gratifications Research.* Beverly Hills: Sage, 1974: 167-196.

1648 _____ . "Selective Exposure: A Summing Up." In R. P. Abelson, et al. (eds.), *Theories of Cognitive Consistency: A Source Book,* Chicago: Rand McNally, 1968.

1649 McIntyre, Anne. "Sex Differences in Children's Aggression." *Proceedings of the Annual Convention of the American Psychological Association,* 1972, 7: 93-94.

1650 McIntyre, J. J. and Teevan, J. J., Jr. "Television Violence and Deviant Behavior." In G. A. Comstock and E. A. Rubinstein (eds.), *Television and Social Behavior: Television and Adolescent Aggressiveness.* (vol. 3). Washington, D.C.: Government Printing Office, 1972: 383-435.

1651 McKerns, J. P., McNall, C. L., and Johnson, E. M. "Mass Media Criticism: An Annotated Bibliography." *Mass Comm Review,* 1975/76, 3, 1: 9-18.

1652 McLaughlin, James. "The Doctor Shows." *Journal of Communication,* 1975, 25, 3: 181-184.

1653 MacLean, Malcolm S. "Mass Media Audiences: City, Small City, Village and Farm." *Journalism Quarterly,* 1952, 29, 3: 271-282.

1654 Maclean, R. *Television in Education.* London: Methuen, 1968.

1655 McLeod, J. M. and Becker, L. B. "Testing the Validity of Television Gratification and Avoidances Through Political Effects Analysis." In J. G. Blumler and E. Katz (eds.), *The Uses of Mass Communications.* Beverly Hills: Sage, 1974: 137-166.

1656 _____ and Chaffee, S. H. "The Construction of Social Reality." In J. Tedeschi (ed.), *The Social Influence Processes.* Chicago: Aldine, 1971.

1657 McLeod, J. M. and O'Keefe, G. J. "The Socialization Perspective and Communication Behavior." In F. G. Kline and P. J. Tichenor (eds.), *Current Perspectives in Mass Communication Research.* Beverly Hills: Sage, 1972: 121-168.

1658 _____ . "The Use of Aggregate Data in Analyzing Primary Elections." *Journalism Quarterly,* 1969, 46, 2: 287-293.

1659 McLeod, J. M., Atkin, C. K., and Chaffee, S. H. "Adolescents, Parents, and Television Use: Adolescent Self-Support Measures From Maryland and Wisconsin Samples." In G. A. Comstock and E. A. Rubinstein (eds.), *Television and Social Behavior: Television and Adolescent Aggressiveness* (vol. 3). Washington, D.C.: Government Printing Office, 1972: 173-238.

1660 McLeod, J. M., Becker, L. B., and Byrnes, J. E. "Another Look at the Agenda-Setting Function of the Press." *Communication Research,* 1974, 1, 1: 131-166.

1661 McLeod, Jack, Rush, Ramona R., and Friederich, Karl H. "The Mass Media and Poltical Information in Quito, Ecuador." *Public Opinion Quarterly,* 1968, 32, 4: 575-587.

1662 McLeod, Jack, Ward, Scott, and Tancill, Karen. "Alienation and Uses of Mass Media." *Public Opinion Quarterly,* 1965, 29, 4: 583-594.

1663 McLuhan, Marshall. *Counter Blast.* New York: Harcourt, Brace and World, 1969.

1664 _____ . *Culture is Our Business.* New York: McGraw-Hill, 1970.

1665 _____ . "Effects of the Improvements of Communication Media," *Journal of Economic History,* 1960, 20, 4: 566-575.

1666 _____ . *From Cliche to Archetype.* New York: Viking Press, 1970.

1667 _____ . *The Gutenberg Galaxy: The Making of Typographic Man.* Toronto: University of Toronto Press, 1962.

1668 _____ . *The Mechanical Bride: Folklore of Industrial Man.* New York: Vanguard Press, 1951.

1669 _____ . "Radio: The Tribal Drum." *Audio-Visual Communication Review,* 1964, 12, 2: 133-145.

1670 _____ . *Understanding Media: The Extensions of Man.* Toronto: McGraw-Hill, 1965. The key book presenting his philosophy. Includes examples of how the medium is the message.

1671 _____ and Carpenter, E. S. *Explorations in Communication.* Boston: Beacon Press, 1960.

1672 McLuhan, Marshall and Fiore, Q. *The Medium is the Message.* Toronto: Bantam Books, 1967.

1673 McMartin, P. A. "A Cross-Lag Test of Lerner's Model of Modernization." *Journalism Quarterly,* 1974, 51: 120-121.

1674 McNeil, Jean C. "Feminism, Femininity and the Television Series: A Content Analysis." *Journal of Broadcasting,* 1975, 19, 3: 259-271.

1675 McNeil, Elton Burbank. *Human Socialization.* Belmont, Calif., Brooks/ Cole Publishing Co., 1969.

1676 MacNeil, Robert E. *The People Machine: The Influence of Television on American Politics.* New York: Harper and Row, 1968. A former newsman's discussion of the "exploitation" of television by those in power and political hopefuls.

1677 McNelly, J. T., Rush, R. R., and Bishop, M. E. "Cosmopolitan Media Usage in the Diffusion of International Affairs News." *Journalism Quarterly,* 1968, 45: 329-332.

1678 McPhee, W. N. *Formal Theories of Mass Behavior.* New York: Free Press, 1963.

1679 McQuail, D. *Sociology of Mass Communications: Selected Readings.* Baltimore: Penguin Books, 1972. Most of these 20 readings are from non-U.S. sources (French, German, Italian, Polish, and Russian included). Content areas involve general perspectives, mass media and mass society, audiences, institutions, structural analyses, and issues of policy or social concern.

1680 _____ . "Television and Education." In J. Halloran (ed.), *The Effects of Television.* London: Panther, 1970: 181-219.

1681 _____ . *Toward a Sociology of Mass Communications.* New York: Collier-MacMillan, 1969. Besides a thorough review of the literature and conceptualization of media within social systems, presents specific suggestions for studying media in context rather than isolation.

1682 _____ . "Uncertainty About the Audience and the Organization of Mass Communications." *Sociological Review Monograph,* 1969, 13: 75-84.

1683 _____ and Gurevitch, M. "Explaining Audience Behavior: Three Approaches Considered." In J. G. Blumler and E. Katz (eds.), *The Uses of Mass Communications: Current Perspectives on Gratifications Research.* Beverly Hills: Sage, 1974: 287-301.

1684 McQuail, D., Blumler, J. G., and Brown, J. R. "The Television Audience: A Revised Perspective." In D. McQuail (ed.), *Sociology of Mass Communications.* London: Penguin, 1972: 135-165.

1685 McVey, G. F. "Television: Some Viewer-Display Considerations." *Audio-Visual Communication Review,* 1970, 18, 3: 277-290.

M

1686 Maccoby, E. E. "Effects of the Mass Media." In M. Hoffman and L. W. Hoffman (eds.), *Review of Child Development Research* (vol. 1). New York: Russell Sage Foundation, 1964: 323-348.

1687 _____ . "The Effects of Television on Children." In W. Schramm (ed.), *The Science of Human Communication.* New York: Basic Books, 1963: 116-127.

1688 _____ . "Pitfalls in the Analysis of Panel Data: A Research Note on Some Technical Aspects of Voting." *American Journal of Sociology,* 1956, 59: 359-362.

1689 _____ . "Television: Its Impact on School Children." *Public Opinion Quarterly,* 1951, 15, 3: 421-444.

1690 _____ . "Why Do Children Watch Television?" *Public Opinion Quarterly,* 1954, 18, 3: 239-244.

1691 _____ and Wilson, W. C. "Identification and Observational Learning from Films." *Journal of Abnormal and Social Psychology,* 1957, 55: 76-87. Children tended to identify with like-sex characters, especially if in a social class to which the child aspires. Given identification, recall of words and actions increased.

1692 Maccoby, E. E., Levin, H., and Selya, B. M. "Effects of Emotional Arousal on Retention of Aggressive and Nonaggressive Movie Content." *American Psychologist,* 1955, 20: 359.

1693 _____ . "The Effects of Emotional Arousal on the Retention of Film Content: A Failure to Replicate." *Journal of Abnormal and Social Psychology,* 1966, 53: 373-374.

1694   Macoby, E. E., Wilson, W. C., and Burton, R. V. "Differential Movie-Viewing Behavior of Male and Female Viewers." *Journal of Personality,* 1958, 26, 2: 259-267.

1695   Maccoby, N. and Markle, D. G. "Communication and Learning." In I. de Sola Pool and W. Schramm (eds.), *Handbook of Communication.* Chicago: Rand McNally, 1973: 153-173.

1696   Madden, Lowell E. "Impact of Information About Negroes on Attitude Change." *Dissertation Abstracts International,* 1971, 31 (10-A): 5039-5040.

1697   Maddison, John. "Radio and Television in Literacy: A Survey of the Use of the Broadcasting Media in Combating Illiteracy Among Adults." Paris: UNESCO, 1971.

1698   Madsen, Roy. *The Impact of Film: How Ideas are Communicated Through Cinema and Television.* New York: Macmillan, 1973.

1699   Magil, Adriano. "Suggestione Ipnotica ed Esperienza Spettacolore nel Pubblico della Televisione" [Hypnotic Suggestion and Viewing Experience of the Television Audience]. *Rassegna Italiana di Sociologia,* 1966, 7, 2: 271-278.

1700   Magnin, W. "Les Emissions pour la Jeunesse" [Programs for Young People] *Cahiers d'Etudes de Radiotelevision,* 1968, 23: 307-310.

1701   Maisel, R. "The Decline of Mass Media." *Public Opinion Quarterly,* 1973, 37: 159-170.

1702   Maletzke, Gerhard. *Fernsehen im Leben der Jugen* [Television in the Life of Youth]. Hamburg, Germany: Hans Bredow Institut, 1959.

1703   Maloney, J. C. "Advertising Research and an Emerging Science of Mass Persuasion." *Journalism Quarterly,* 1964, 41, 4: 517-528.

1704   _____. "Is Advertising Believability Really Important?" *Journal of Marketing,* 1963, 27: 1-8.

1705   Maloney, M. "Black is the Color of Our New TV." *TV Guide,* November 16, 1968.

1706   Mandell, L. M. and Shaw, D. L. "Judging People in the News—Unconsciously: Effect of Camera Angle and Bodily Activity." *Journal of Broadcasting,* 1973, 17: 353-362.

1707   Mander, Jerry. "The Media and Environmental Awareness." In G. Bell (ed.), *The Environmental Handbook,* New York: Ballantine, 1970.

1708   Manes, Audrey L. and Melnyk, Paula. "Televised Models of Female Achievement." *Journal of Applied Social Psychology,* 1974, 4, 4: 365-374.

1709   Mann, J., Sidman, J., and Starr, S. "Effects of Erotic Films on the Sexual Behavior of Married Couples." In *Technical Report of The Commission on Obscenity and Pornography: Erotica and Social Behavior* (vol. 8). Washington, D.C.: Government Printing Office, 1971: 170-254.

1710   _____. "Evaluating Social Consequences of Erotic Films: An Experimental Approach." *Journal of Social Issues,* 1973, 29: 113-132.

1711   Mann, J., Berkowitz, L., Sidman, J., Starr, S., and West S. "Satiation of the Transient Stimulating Effects of Erotic Films." *Journal of Personality and*

Social Psychology, 1974, 30: 729-735. Decreasing effects of erotic films on the sexual activities of married couples over time.

1712   Manning, S. A. and Taylor, D. A. "The Effects of Viewed Violence and Aggression: Stimulation and Catharsis." *Journal of Personality and Social Psychology,* 1975, 31: 180-188.

1713   Mapp, Edward. *Blacks in American Films: Today and Yesterday.* Metuchen, N.J.: Scarecrow Press, 1972.

1714   Marceau, F. Jane. "Communication and Development: A Reconsideration." *Public Opinion Quarterly,* 1972, 36, 2: 235-245.

1715   Markel, Lester. *What You Don't Know Can Hurt You: A Study of Public Opinion and Public Emotion.* Washington, D.C.: Public Affairs Press, 1972.

1716   Markham, David. "The Dimensions of Source Credibility of Television Newscasters." *Journal of Communication,* 1968, 18, 1: 57-64.

1717   Martin, Cora A. and Benson, Leonard. "Parental Perceptions of the Role of Television in Parent-Child Interaction." *Journal of Marriage and the Family,* 1970, 32, 3: 410-414.

1718   Martin, E. M. "The Mass Media and the Human Condition: World, Play and Ego." *Communication,* 1974, 1, 2: 223-232.

1719   Marting, Leeda P. "An Empirical Study of the Images of Males and Females During Prime-Time Television Drama." Doctoral Dissertation, Ohio State University, 1973.

1720   Maslog, Crispin. "Images and the Mass Media." *Journalism Quarterly,* 1971, 48: 519-525.

1721   Mason, Robert. "The Use of Information Sources by Influentials in the Adoption Process." *Public Opinion Quarterly,* 1963, 27: 455-466.

1722   Masson, Peter. "The Effects of Television on Other Media." In J. Halloran (ed.), *The Effects of Television.* London: Panther, 1970: 138-180.

1723   Mast, Benjamin. "The Impact of Television on the Control of Broadcasting in Canada." *Journal of Broadcasting,* 1959, 3, 3: 263-288.

1724   Matranga, J. T. "Reaction to Film Violence in Delinquent Boys as a Function of Aggressive Predisposition Level of Fantasy Aggression and Perceived Reality of the Film Material." Doctoral Dissertation, Catholic University of America, 1973.

1725   Matraux, G. S., ed. *Music and Society.* Paris: UNESCO, 1973. The first in UNESCO's Cultures Series. Explores the relationship between sound and the environment as an interactive communication process.

1726   Mattelart, A. "Mass Media and the Socialist Revolution: The Experience of Chile." In G. Gerbner, L. Gross, and W. Melody (eds.), *Communications Technology and Social Policy: Understanding the New "Cultural Revolution."* New York: Wiley, 1973: 425-440.

1727   Matteoni, Louise. "TV Cartoons In Initial Reading Experiences with Culturally Deprived Children." Doctoral Dissertation, New York University, 1967.

1728 Mattese, Anthony M. "A Descriptive Study of Children's Programming on Major American Television Networks from 1950 through 1964." Doctoral Dissertation, Ohio University, 1967.

1729 May, M. A. and Lumsdaine, A. A. *Learning from Films.* New Haven: Yale University Press, 1958.

1730 Mayer, Philip. *Socialization: The Approach from Social Anthropology.* New York: Tavistock, 1970.

1731 Maynard, Richard A., ed. *The Black Man on Film: Racial Stereotyping.* Rochelle Park, N.J.: Hayden Book Co., 1974.

1732 Mayo, C. G. "The Mass Media and Campaign Strategy in a Mayoralty Election." *Journalism Quarterly,* 1964, 41: 353-359.

1733 Mazo, E., Moos, M., Hoffman, H., and Wheeler, H. *The Great Debates.* Santa Barbara, Calif.: Center for the Study of Democratic Institutions, 1962.

1734 Medalia, Nahum Z. and Larsen, Otto N. "Diffusion and Belief in a Collective Delusion: The Seattle Windshield Pitting Epidemic." *American Sociological Review,* 1958, 23, 2 (April): 180-186.

1735 Meerloo, J. A. M. "Television Addiction and Reactive Apathy." *Journal of Nervous and Mental Disease,* 1954, 120: 290-291.

1736 Mehling, Reuben. "Television's Value to the American Family Member," *Journal of Broadcasting,* 1960, 4, 4: 307-313. Documents that the majority of school children, if permitted to keep only one medium, would prefer television over all others.

1737 _____ , Kraus, S., and Yoakam, R. D. "Pre-Debate Campaign Interest and Media Use." In S. Kraus (ed.), *The Great Debates.* Bloomington: Indiana University Press, 1962: 224-231.

1738 Meier, Richard. "Communications and Social Change." *Behavioral Science,* 1956, 11: 43-58.

1739 Melnick, Daniel. "Intensive Politicization Episodes: Movies, Melas, and Political Attitudes in a North Indian District." *American Behavioral Scientist,* 1974, 17, 3: 439-476.

1740 Melody, William. *Children's Television: The Economics of Exploitation.* New Haven, Conn.: Yale University Press, 1973. Reviews the institutions, markets, history, policy, and unique characteristics of children's television.

1741 _____ . *Children's Television: Economics and Public Policy.* Newtonville, Mass.: Action for Children's Television, no date.

1742 Mendelson, Gilbert and Young, Morissa. "Network Children's Programming: A Content Analysis of Black and Minority Treatment on Children's Television." Washington, D.C.: Black Efforts for Soul in Television, 1972.

1743 Mendelsohn, Harold. "Behaviorism, Functionalism, and Mass Communications Policy." *Public Opinion Quarterly,* 1974, 38, 3: 379-389.

1744 _____ . "Broadcast vs. Personal Sources of Information in Emergent Public Crises: The Presidential Assassination." *Journal of Broadcasting,* 1964, 8: 147-156.

1745 _____ . "Election-Day Broadcasts and Terminal Voting Decisions," *Public Opinion Quarterly,* 1966, 30, 2: 212-225.

1746 _____ . *Mass Entertainment.* New Haven, Conn.: College University Press, 1966. Defends the concept and function of mass entertainment through a review of positive and negative media effects.

1747 _____ . "Measuring the Process of Communications Effect." *Public Opinion Quarterly,* 1962, 26, 3: 411-416.

1748 _____ . "Operation Stop-Gap: A Study of the Application of Communication Techniques in Reaching the Unreachable Poor." University of Denver, February, 1968.

1749 _____ . "Plan 13. The Process of the Effect of Television in Inducing Action." In L. Arons and M. A. May (eds.), *Television and Human Behavior: Tomorrow's Research in Mass Communication.* New York: Appleton-Century-Crofts, 1963: 220-228.

1750 _____ . "Sociological Perspective on the Study of Mass Communications." In L. A. Dexter and D. M. White (eds.), *People, Society, and Mass Communications.* New York: Free Press, 1964: 29-36.

1751 _____ . "Socio-Psychological Perspectives on the Mass Media and Public Anxiety," *Journalism Quarterly,* 1963, 40, 4: 511-516.

1752 _____ . "Some Policy Implications of the Uses and Gratifications Paradigm." In J. G. Blumler and E. Katz (eds.), *The Uses of Mass Communications: Current Perspectives on Gratifications Research.* Beverly Hills: Sage, 1974: 303-318.

1753 _____ . "Some Reasons Why Information Campaigns Can Succeed," *Public Opinion Quarterly,* 1973, 37, 1: 50-61.

1754 _____ : "TV and Youth: New Style for Politics." *Nation,* June 6, 1966, 202: 669-673.

1755 _____ and Crespi, I. *Polls, Television, and the New Politics.* San Francisco: Chandler Publishing Co., 1970. Discusses television's influence on politics in the areas of nominating conventions, campaigning, party operations, and the challenging of traditional procedures.

1756 Mendelsohn, Harold and O'Keefe, G. J. *The People Choose a President: Influences on Voter Decision Making.* New York: Praeger, 1975. Presents research on the 1972 presidential election. Chapters profile the electorate, the voting process, issues, images and voting decisions, as well as campaigns and media influences.

1757 Mendelson, G. and Young, M. *Network Children's Programming: A Content Analysis of Black and Minority Treatment on Children's Television.* Newtonville, Mass.: Action for Children's Television, 1972.

1758 Mendieta y Nuñez, L. "Aspectos Sociológicos de la Televisión" [Sociological Aspects of Television]. *Revista Interamericana de Sociología,* 1967, 1, 4: 13-40.

1759 Menzel, H. and Katz, E. "Social Relations and Innovation in the Medical Profession: The Epidemiology of a New Drug." *Public Opinion Quarterly,* 1955, 19, 4: 337-352.

1760   Menzies, E. S. "The Effects of Repeated Exposure to Televised Violence Upon Attitudes Towards Violence Among Youthful Offenders." Doctoral Dissertation, Florida State University, 1973.

1761   Merelman, R. M. "Mass Culture and Political Ideology: The Television Western." Doctoral Dissertation, Yale University, 1965.

1762   Merki, Donald J., et al. "The Effects of Two Educational Methods and Message Themes on Rural Youth Smoking Behavior." *Journal of School Health,* 1968, 38, 7: 448-454.

1763   Merrill, Irving R. "Attitude Films and Attitude Change." *Audio-Visual Communication Review,* 1962, 10, 1: 3-13.

1764   _____. "Broadcast Viewing and Listening by Children." *Public Opinion Quarterly,* 1961, 25, 2: 263-276.

1765   Merrill, J. C. and Lowenstein, R. L. *Media, Messages and Men: New Perspectives in Communication.* New York: McKay, 1971.

1766   Merritt, R. L., ed. *Communication in International Politics.* Urbana: University of Illinois Press, 1972. Compiles 18 articles on a variety of topics, including the transmission of values and meaning across national boundaries through people to people campaigns, government to government, and coverage of events abroad.

1767   Meyer, Timothy P. "Children's Perceptions of Favorite Television Characters as Behavioral Models." *Educational Broadcasting Review,* 1973, 7, 1: 25-33.

1768   _____. "Children's Perceptions of Justified/Unjustified and Fictional/ Real Film Violence." *Journal of Broadcasting,* 1973, 17, 3: 321-332.

1769   _____. "The Effects of Sexually Arousing and Violent Films on Aggressive Behavior." *Journal of Sex Research,* 1972, 8: 324-331.

1770   _____. "The Effects of Verbally Violent Film Content on Aggressive Behavior." *Audio-Visual Communication Review,* 1972, 20, 2: 160-169.

1771   _____. "Effects of Viewing Justified and Unjustified Real Film Violence on Aggressive Behavior." *Journal of Personality and Social Psychology,* 1972, 23, 1: 21-29.

1772   _____. "News Reporter Bias: A Case Study in Selective Perception." *Journal of Broadcasting,* 1972, 16: 195-203.

1773   _____. "Some Effects of Real Newsfilm Violence on the Behavior of Viewers." *Journal of Broadcasting,* 1971, 15: 275-285. News film violence presented as justified was rated as justified by the student viewers and produced more aggressive reactions than when presented as unjustified.

1774   Meyer, Timothy P. and Anderson, James A. "Media Violence Research: Interpreting the Findings." *Journal of Broadcasting,* 1973, 17, 4: 447-458.

1775   _____. "A Response to Pryluck." *Journal of Broadcasting,* 1975, 19, 4: 421-424. See #64 for original article, and #2016 and #2017.

1776   Meyer, Timothy P. and Miller, William C. "Emphasis and Non-Emphasis Radio Newscast Delivery." *Journalism Quarterly,* 1970, 47, 1: 144-147.

1777 Meyerson, Leonard J. "The Effects of Filmed Aggression on the Aggressive Responses of High and Low Aggressive Subjects." *Dissertation Abstracts,* 1967, 27 (9-B): 3291.

1778 Meyersohn, Rolf. "A Critical Examination of Commercial Entertainment." In Robert W. Kleemeier (ed.), *Aging and Leisure.* New York: Oxford University Press, 1961.

1779 _____ . "Leisure and Television: A Study In Compatibility." Doctoral Dissertation, Columbia University, 1965.

1780 _____ . "Social Research in Television." In B. Rosenberg and D. M. White (eds.), *Mass Culture.* Glencoe, Ill.: Free Press, 1957: 345-357.

1781 _____ . "Television and the Rest of Leisure." *Public Opinion Quarterly,* 1968, 32, 1: 102-112.

1782 _____ . *Television Research: An Annotated Bibliography.* New York: Columbia University, Bureau of Applied Social Research, 1954.

1783 _____ . "What We Know About Audiences." *Journal of Broadcasting,* 1957, 1, 3: 220-231.

1784 Miami University, Department of Marketing. *The Influence of Television on the Election of 1952.* Oxford, Ohio: Oxford Research Associates, Inc., 1954.

1785 Michael, D. N. and Maccoby, N. "Factors Influencing Verbal Learning From Films Under Varying Conditions of Audience Participation." *Journal of Experimental Psychology,* 1953, 46: 411-418.

1786 Mickelson, Sig. *The Electric Mirror: Politics in an Age of Television.* New York: Dodd, Mead, 1972. A descriptive look, by a former network news president, at the role of TV in political campaigns since 1952.

1787 Middleton, Russell. "Fertility Values In American Magazine Fiction 1916-1956." *Public Opinion Quarterly,* 1960, 24, 1: 139-143.

1788 _____ . "National TV Debates and Presidential Voting Decisions." *Public Opinion Quarterly,* 1962, 26, 3: 429-434.

1789 _____ . "Negro and White Reactions to Racial Humor." *Sociometry,* 1959, 22: 175-183.

1790 Mielke, Keith W. "Education Level as a Correlate of Attitudes Toward Television." *Journal of Broadcasting,* 1965, 9, 4: 313-321.

1791 _____ . "Evaluation of Television as a Function of Self-Beliefs." *Dissertation Abstracts,* 1966, 26, 7: 4105.

1792 Milavsky, J. R. and Pekowsky, B. "Exposure to TV 'Violence' and Aggressive Behavior in Boys, Examined as Process: A Status Report of a Longitudinal Study." New York: Department of Social Research, National Broadcasting Company, 1973.

1793 _____ and Stipp, H. "TV Drug Advertising and Proprietary and Illicit Drug Use Among Teenage Boys." *Public Opinion Quarterly,* 1975, 39: 457-481. Exposure to TV advertising was positively related to drug use, but negatively related to use of illicit drugs.

1794 Milbrath, Lester W. *Political Participation: How and Why Do People Get Involved in Politics?* Chicago: Rand McNally and Co., 1971.

1795 Milgram, S. and Shotland, R. L. *Television and Antisocial Behavior: Field Experiments.* New York: Academic Press, 1973. A report on eight field experiments designed to test the short-term effects of television through actual manipulation of network programming ("Medical Center"). Represents a major field test effort. See #571 for reaction.

1796 Miller, Gerald R. and Roberts, Kenn. "Communicator Race, Open and Closed Mindedness, and Response to Informative Communications." *Audio-Visual Communication Review,* 1965, 13: 259-269.

1797 Miller, Gerald R., Bender, D., Florence, T., and Nicholson, H. "Real versus Reel: What's the Verdict?" *Journal of Communication,* 1974, 24, 3: 99-111.

1798 Miller, J. *Marshall McLuhan.* New York: Viking Press, 1971. Traces his life and theories, with bibliography of works.

1799 Miller, Kenneth M. and Nicol, Margaret A. *Occupational Status, Sex and Age as Factors in Radio Programme Choice.* Hobart, Tasmania: University of Tasmania, 1958.

1800 Miller, Susan H. "The Content of News Photos: Women's and Men's Roles." *Journalism Quarterly,* 1975, 52: 70-75.

1801 Miller, W. E. "Analysis of the Effect of Election Night Predictions on Voting Behavior." University of Michigan, Survey Research Center (Political Behavior Program), 1965.

1802 Mills, Donald B. "An Exploration of the Relationship Between Television Habits, Preferences, and Aggression in Sixth-Grade Boys." *Dissertation Abstracts International,* 1972, 32 (9-A): 4842.

1803 Mills, K. "Fighting Sexism on the Airwaves." *Journal of Communication,* 1974, 24, 2: 150-156.

1804 Millum, Trevor. *Images of Woman: Advertising in Women's Magazines.* Totawa, N.J.: Rowman & Littlefield, 1975.

1805 Mindak, W. H. and Hursh, G. D. "Television Functions on the Assassination Weekend." In B. S. Greenberg and E. B. Parker (eds.), *The Kennedy Assassination and the American Public: Social Communication in Crisis.* Stanford: Stanford University Press, 1965: 130-141.

1806 Minghi, Julian. "Television Preference and Nationality in a Boundary Region." *Sociological Inquiry,* 1963, 33, 2: 165-179.

1807 Minkinnen, Sirkka. Experiments on Comprehension and Impact of Movies Among Children and Youth People. Helsinki: Oy. Yleisradio Ab, LSP, 1969.

1808 _____ . "Why Mass Media Education is Needed in Schools?" In Yrjo Littunen, Sirkka Minkkinen, and Kaarle Nordenstreng (eds.), *Approaching Mass Media Education through Communication Research.* Tampere, Finland: Institute of Journalism and Mass Communication, Research Institute for Social Sciences, University of Tampere, 1974: 14-32.

1809 Minow, Newton N., et al. *Presidential Television.* New York: Basic Books, 1973.

1810 Minton, J. H. "The Impact of Sesame Street on Reading Readiness of Kindergarten Children." Doctoral Dissertation, Fordham University, 1972.

1811 Mirams, G. "Drop That Gun." In *Quarterly of Film, Radio, and Television,* 1951, 6, 1.

1812 Mishra, Vishwa M. *Communication and Modernization in Urban Slums.* New York: Asia Publishing House, 1972. The first three chapters deal with the processes of urbanization and the media in general. The remaining three present the results of a media-related survey of urban villagers in India's Greater Delhi area.

1813 _____. "Mass Media Use and Modernization in Greater Delhi Basties." *Journalism Quarterly,* 1970, 47, 2: 331-339.

1814 _____. "Mass Media Variables Related to Urbanization and Modernization in Developing Areas." *Journalism Quarterly,* 1971, 48, 3: 513-518.

1815 Mitchell, John D. "Socialization and the Mass Media in China and Japan." *Journalism Quarterly,* 1969, 46, 3: 576-582.

1816 Monaghan, Robert. "Television Preference and Viewing Behavior." Doctoral Dissertation, Michigan State University, 1964.

1817 _____, Hsueh, S., Layne, C. E., and Seguin, J. A. *"Mister Rogers' Neighborhood* and the Handicapped Child Interface: Exploring and Assessing Integration of Educational Media and Professional Services to the Handicapped Child." Final Report, Ohio State University, September, 1974.

1818 Monaghan, Robert R., Plummer, Joseph T., Rarick, David L., and Williams, Dwight A. "Predicting Viewer Preference for New TV Program Concepts." *Journal of Broadcasting,* 1974, 18, 2: 131-142.

1819 Mooney, Hughson F. "Popular Music Since the 1920s: The Significance of Shifting Taste." *American Quarterly,* 1968, 20, 1: 67-85.

1820 _____. "Songs, Singers and Society." *American Quarterly,* 1954, 6, 3: 221-232.

1821 Moore, F. J., Chernell, E., and West, M. J. "Television as a Therapeutic Tool." *Archives of General Psychiatry,* 1965, 12: 217-220.

1822 Moore, J. L., Tuchin, M.S., and Birren, J. E. "A Bibliography of Doctoral Dissertations on Aging from American Institutions of Higher Learning." *Journal of Gerontology,* 1971, 26: 391-422.

1823 More, D. M. and Roberts, A. F. "Societal Variations in Humor Responses to Cartoons." *Journal of Social Psychology,* 1957, 45: 233-243.

1824 Morgan, James N. "Some Pilot Strides of Communication and Concensus in the Family." *Public Opinion Quarterly,* 1968, 32, 1: 113-121.

1825 Morris, L. W., Spiegler, N, D., and Liebert, R. M. "Effects of a Therapeutic Modeling Film on Cognitive and Emotional Components of Anxiety." *Journal of Clinical Psychology,* 1974, 30: 219-223.

1826 Morris, Monica B. "Newspapers and the New Feminists: Black-Out as Social Control?" *Journalism Quarterly,* 1973, 50, 1: 37-42.

1827 Morris, N. S. *Television's Child.* Boston, Mass.: Little, Brown & Co., 1971.

1828 Morris, W. N., Marshall, H. M., and Miller, R. S. "The Effect of Vicarious Punishment on Prosocial Behavior in Children." *Journal of Experimental Child Psychology,* 1973, 15: 222-236.

1829 Mortensen, C. David. "A Comparative Analysis of Political Persuasion on Four Telecast Program Formats in the 1960 and 1964 Presidential Campaigns." Doctoral Dissertation, University of Minnesota, 1967.

1830 _____. "The Influence of Television on Policy Discussion." *Quarterly Journal of Speech,* 1968, 54, 3: 277-281.

1831 Mortensen, C. David and Sereno, K. K., eds. *Advances in Communication Research.* New York: Harper and Row, 1973.

1832 _____. "Influence of Ego-Involvement and Discrepancy on Perceptions of Communication." *Speech Monographs,* 1970, 37, 2: 127-134.

1833 Mosher, D. L. "Pornographic Films, Male Verbal Aggression Against Women, and Guilt." In *Technical Report of the Commission on Obscenity and Pornography: Erotica and Social Behavior* (vol. 8). Washington, D.C.: Government Printing Office, 1971: 357-379.

1834 _____. "Psychological Reactions to Pornographic Films." In *Technical Report of the Commission on Obscenity and Pornography: Erotica and Social Behavior* (vol. 8). Washington, D.C.: Government Printing Office, 1971, 255-312.

1835 _____. "Sex Differences, Sex Experience, Sex Guilt, and Explicitly Sexual Films." *Journal of Social Issues,* 1973, 29: 95-112. After viewing pornographic films, females, high sex-guilt subjects, and lesser experienced subjects reacted more negatively and were less aroused.

1836 Mosse, Hilde L. "The Influence of Mass Media on the Sex Problems of Teenagers." *Journal of Sex Research,* 1966, 2, 1: 27-35.

1837 Motto, Jerome A. "Newspaper Influence on Suicide: A Controlled Study." *Archives of General Psychiatry,* 1970, 23, 2: 143-148.

1838 _____. "Suicide and Suggestibility: The Role of the Press." *American Journal of Psychiatry,* 1967, 124, 2: 252-256.

1839 Mowlana, H. *International Communication: A Selected Bibliography.* Dubuque, Iowa: Kendall/Hunt, 1971. A collection of nearly 1500 unannotated items.

1840 Mueller, Claus. *The Politics of Communication: A Study in the Political Sociology of Language, Socialization, and Legitimation.* New York: Oxford University Press, 1973. Analyzes the role of political processes in advanced industrial societies.

1841 Mullen, James J. "The Congruity Principle and Television Commercials." *Journal of Broadcasting,* 1962-63, 7, 1: 35-42.

1842 Munn, Mark. "The Effect on Parental Buying Habits of Children Exposed to Children's Television Programs," *Journal of Broadcasting,* 1958, 2, 3: 253-258.

1843 Murdock, G. and Phelps, G. "Responding to Popular Music: Criteria of Classification and Choice Among English Teenagers." *Popular Music and Society,* 1972, 1, 3: 144-151.

1844 Murray, James P. *To Find an Image: Black Films from Uncle Tom to Superfly.* Indianapolis: Bobbs-Merrill, 1973.

1845 Murray, John P. "Television in Inner-City Homes: Viewing Behavior of Young Boys." In E. A. Rubinstein, G. A. Comstock and J. P. Murray (eds.), *Television and Social Behavior: Television in Day-to-Day Life: Patterns of Use* (vol. 4). Washington, D.C.: Government Printing Office, 1972: 345-394.

1846 _____. "Television and Violence: Implications of the Surgeon General's Research Program." *American Psychologist,* 1973, 28, 6: 472-478.

1847 _____, Nayman, Oguz B., and Atkin, Charles K. "Television and the Child: A Comprehensive Research Bibliography." *Journal of Broadcasting,* 1972, 16, 1: 3-20.

1848 Murray, John P., Rubinstein, E. A., and Comstock, G. A., eds. *Television and Social Behavior: Television and Social Learning* (vol. 2). Washington, D.C.: Government Printing Office, 1972.

1849 Murray, Randall L., Cole, Richard R., and Fedler, Fred. "Teenagers and TV Violence: How They Rate and View It." *Journalism Quarterly,* 1970, 47, 2: 247-255.

1850 Muse, William V. "Product Related Response to Use of Black Models in Advertising." *Journal of Marketing Research,* 1971, 8: 107-109.

1851 Musgrave,P. W. "How Children Use Television." *New Society,* 1969, 13, 334: 277-278.

1852 Muson, Howard. *Media Violence.* New York: Harper and Row, 1972.

1853 Mussen, P. H. and Sutherford, E. "Effects of Aggressive Cartoons on Children's Aggressive Play." *Journal of Abnormal and Social Psychology,* 1961, 62: 461-464.

1854 Myers, Lawrence, Jr. "An Examination of Television Audience Measurement Methods and an Application of Sequential Analysis to the Telephone Interview Method." *Dissertation Abstracts,* 1956, 16: 1955-1956.

N

1855 Nafziger, Ralph O., Engstrom, Warren C., and MacLean, Malcolm S. "The Mass Media and an Informed Public." *Public Opinion Quarterly,* 1951, 15, 1: 105-114.

1856 Nakamura, Masara. "On The Relation Between the Viewers' Attitude to Television Programs and Their Opinions on Crimes: The Case of Junior and Senior High School Students." *Japanese Journal of Experimental Social Psychology,* 1973, 13, 2: 148-167.

1857 Napolitan, J. *The Election Game and How to Win It.* Garden City, N.Y.: Doubleday and Co., 1969.

1858   Narut, Thomas E. "The Use of a Symbolic Model and Verbal Intervention in Inducing and Reducing Stress." *Dissertation Abstracts International,* 1972, 32 (9-B): 5453-5454.

1859   Nathan, Peter E. and Wallace, Wallace H. "An Operant Behavioral Measure of TV Commercial Effectiveness." *Journal of Advertising Research,* 1965, 5, 4: 13-20.

1860   National Association for Better Broadcasting. *Crime on Television: A Survey Report.* Los Angeles: National Association for Better Broadcasting, 1964.

1861   National Commission on the Causes and Prevention of Violence. *Statement on Violence in Television Entertainment Programming.* Washington, D.C.: Government Printing Office, 1969. Concludes that television violence can stimulate aggressive behavior.

1862   National Institute of Mental Health. *Report of Special Consultation on the Development of Measures of TV Violence.* Bethesda, Md.: National Institute of Mental Health, June 1972.

1863   National Organization for Women. "A Study of the Treatment of Females and Males in WRC-TV Programming Aired During a Composite Week." In *Women in the Wasteland Fight Back: A Report on the Image of Women Portrayed in TV Programming.* Washington, D.C.: National Organization for Women, National Capitol Area Chapter, 1972.

1864   ———— . "Survey of WRC-TV Public Affairs and News Programming Since February, 1972." In *Women in the Wasteland Fight Back: A Report on the Image of Women Portrayed in TV Programming.* Washington, D.C.: National Organization for Women, National Capitol Area Chapter, 1972.

1865   Nawy, Harold. "In the Pursuit of Happiness?: Consumers of Erotica in San Francisco." *Journal of Social Issues,* 1973, 29, 3: 147-162.

1866   Nayman, Oguz B., Atkin, Charle K., and Gillette, Bill. "The Four-Day Workweek and Media Use: A Glimpse of the Future." *Journal of Broadcasting,* 1973, 17, 3: 301-308.

1867   Neale, John M. "Comment on 'Television Violence and Child Aggression: A Follow-up Study'." In G. A. Comstock and E. A. Rubinstein (eds.), *Television and Social Behavior: Television and Adolescent Aggressiveness* (vol. 3). Washington, D.C.: Government Printing Office, 1972: 141-148.

1868   Neely, J. J., Heckel, R. V., and Leichtman, H. M. "The Effect of Race of Model and Response Consequences to the Model on Imitation in Children." *Journal of Social Psychology,* 1973, 89: 225-231.

1869   Neill, S. D. "McLuhan's Media Charts Related to the Process of Communication." *Audio-Visual Communication Review,* 1973, 21, 3: 277-297.

1870   Nelson, Bardin H. "Seven Principles in Image Formation." *Journal of Marketing,* 1962, 26, 1: 67-71.

1871 Nelson, R. J. "Relationships of Reported Television Viewing to Selected Characteristics Reported by Superior High School Students." Doctoral Dissertation, University of Wisconsin, 1963.

1872 New Jersey, Division of Aging. *Uses of Free Time for Senior Citizens.* Trenton, N.J.: Division of Aging, 1962.

1873 Newcomb, Horace. *TV: The Most Popular Art.* New York: Doubleday Anchor, 1974.

1874 Nicholas, Karen B., McCarter, Robert E., and Heckel, Robert V. "The Effects of Race and Sex on the Imitation of Television Models." *Journal of Social Psychology,* 1971, 85, 2: 315-316.

1875 _____ . "Imitation of Adult and Peer Television Model by White and Negro Children." *Journal of Social Psychology,* 1971, 85, 2: 317-318.

1876 Nicosia, F. M. *Consumer Decision Processes: Marketing and Advertising Implications.* Englewood Cliffs, N.J.: Prentice-Hall, 1966.

1877 Nielsen, Richard P. "A Generalized Attitude Model for Television Programs." *Journal of Broadcasting,* 1974, 18, 2: 153-160.

1878 Niemi, R. G. "Political Socialization." In J. N. Knutson (ed.), *Handbook of Political Psychology.* San Francisco: Jossey-Bass, 1973: 117-138.

1879 Nimmo, Dan. *The Political Persuaders: The Techniques of Modern Election Campaigns.* Englewood Cliffs, N.J.: Prentice-Hall, 1970. Discusses campaign management, campaign research, and its effects on the electoral process.

1880 Nimmo, Dan and Bonjean, Charles M., eds. *Political Attitudes and Public Opinion.* New York: McKay, 1972. A reader containing 36 articles covering basic concepts and methods of attitude formation, political socialization, consistency theories of attitude change, and consideration of sub-group differences.

1881 Niven, Harold. "Who in the Family Selects the TV Program?" *Journalism Quarterly,* 1960, 37, 1: 110-111.

1882 Noble, Grant. *Children in Front of the Small Screen.* Beverly Hills: Sage, 1975. Discusses the author's research on children in Britain, Ireland, and Canada. Covers television's popularity, identification processes, media as escape, role modeling, violence and deviant behavior, and the gatekeeper role of the producer.

1883 _____ . "Concepts of Order and Balance in a Children's TV Program." *Journalism Quarterly,* 1970, 47, 1: 101-108.

1884 _____ . "Discrimination Between Different Forms of Televised Aggression by Delinquent and Non-Delinquent Boys." *British Journal of Criminology,* 1970, 11, 3: 230-244.

1885 _____ . "Effects of Different Forms of Filmed Aggression on Children's Constructive and Destructive Play." *Journal of Personality and Social Psychology,* 1973, 26: 56-59.

1886 _____ . "Film-Mediated Aggressive and Creative Play." *British Journal of Social and Clinical Psychology,* 1970, 9, 1: 1-7.

1887 _____ . "Some Comments on the Nature of Delinquents' Identification with Television Heroes, Fathers and Best Friends." *British Journal of Social and Clinical Psychology,* 1971, 10: 172-180.

1888 _____ . "Younger Children's Comprehension of a Televised Film." In W. Dunn (ed.), *Aspects of Education Technology,* London: Methuen, 1969.

1889 Noelle-Neumann, Elisabeth. "Mass Communication Media and Public Opinion." *Journalism Quarterly,* 1959, 36, 4: 401-409.

1890 _____ . "The Spirit of Silence: A Theory of Public Opinion." *Journal of Communication,* 1974, 24, 2: 43:51.

1891 Nogee, Philip and Levin, Murray B. "Some Determinants of Political Attitudes Among College Voters." *Public Opinion Quarterly,* 1958-59, 22, 4: 449-463.

1892 Nolan, M. J. "Effects of Justified Aggression Upon Children of Different Ages." Stanford, Calif.: Institute for Communication Research, Stanford University, 1971.

1893 Nordenstreng, K. "Comments on 'Gratifications Research' in Broadcasting." *Public Opinion Quarterly,* 1970, 34: 130-132.

1894 _____ . "Consumption of Mass Media in Finland." *Gazette,* 1969, 15: 249-259.

1895 Nordenstreng, K. and Varis, T. "The Nonhomogeneity of the National State and the International Flow of Communication." In G. Gerbner, L. Gross, and W. Melody (eds.), *Communications Technology and Social Policy: Understanding the New "Cultural Revolution."* New York: Wiley, 1973: 393-412.

1896 _____ . "Television Traffic: A One-Way Street?" *Reports and Papers on Mass Communication, no. 70.* Paris: UNESCO (New York: UNIPUB), 1974.

1897 NORDICOM. *Bibliography of Works on Mass Communications.* Tampere, Finland, Nordic Documentation Center for Mass Communication Research, University of Tampere, 1975.

1898 Nordlie, David A. "The Socialization of Achievement Values." *Dissertation Abstracts International,* 1971, 32 (5-A): 2811.

1899 North, Robert C. "Communication as an Approach to Politics." *American Behavioral Scientist,* 1967, 10, 8, 12: 21-23.

1900 Northcott, Herbert C., Seggar, John F., and Hinton, James L. "Trends in TV Portrayal of Blacks and Women." *Journalism Quarterly,* 1975, 52: 741-744.

1901 Novak, Michael. "Television Shapes the Soul." In D. Cater (ed.), *Television as a Social Force: New Approaches to TV Criticism.* New York: Praeger, 1975: 9-22.

1902 Novic, Kenneth and Sandman, Peter M. "How Use of Mass Media Affects Views on Solutions to Environmental Problems." *Journalism Quarterly,* 1974, 51, 3: 448-452.

1903 Nunnally, J. "The Communication of Mental Health Information: A Comparison of the Opinions of Experts and the Public with Mass Media Presentations." *Behavioral Science,* 1957, 2, 3: 222-230.

1904 _____. "Mental Illness: What the Media Present." In S. Cohen and J. Young (eds.), *The Manufacture of News: A Reader.* Beverly Hills: Sage, 1973: 136-145.

O

1905 Oboler, E. M. *The Fear of the Word: Censorship and Sex.* Metuchen, N.J.: Scarecrow Press, 1974. The anthropological, linguistic, sociological, psychological, philosophical, and theological origins of censorship are examined.

1906 O'Brien, T. "Stages of Consumer Decision Making." *Journal of Marketing Research,* 1971, 8: 283-289.

1907 O'Bryan, K. G. and Silverman, H. "Report on Children's Television Viewing Strategies." Ontario, Canada: Ontario Institute for Studies in Education, October 1972.

1908 O'Connor, R. D. "Modification of Social Withdrawal Through Symbolic Modeling." *Journal of Applied Behavior Analysis,* 1969, 2: 15-22.

1909 Ogden, D. M., Jr. and Peterson, A. L. *Electing the President* (rev. ed.). San Francisco: Chandler, 1968.

1910 Oglesbee, Frank W. "The Basis for Marshall McLuhan's Concepts of the Effects of Television Viewing." *Dissertation Abstracts,* 1970, 30 (8-A): 3571.

1911 Ohara, Haruko. "Comparative Preferences of Radio and Television Programs." *Sociology and Social Research,* 1953, 37, 5: 305-311.

1912 Ohliger, John and Gueulette, David. "Media and Adult Learning: A Bibliography with Abstracts, Annotations, and Quotations." New York: Garland Publishing, 1975. Collects roughly 1700 citations.

1913 Okabe, K. "Broadcasting Research in Post-War Japan." In *Studies of Broadcasting* (no. 1). Tokyo: Radio and Television Culture Research Institute, Nippon Hoso Kyokai, 1963: 7-47.

1914 O'Keefe, Garrett J. and Mendelsohn, Harold. "Voter Selectivity, Partisanship, and the Challenge of Watergate." *Communication Research,* 1974, 1, 4: 345-367.

1915 _____ and Spetnagel, H. T. "Patterns of College Undergraduates' Use of Selected News Media." *Journalism Quarterly,* 1973, 50, 3: 543-548.

1916 O'Keefe, M. Timothy. "The Anti-Smoking Commercials: A Study of Television's Impact on Behavior." *Public Opinion Quarterly,* 1971, 35, 2: 242-248.

1917 _____. "Some Allies: The Mass Media and Drug Abuse Education." In M. S. Goodstadt (ed.), *Research on Methods and Programs of Drug Education.* Toronto, Canada: Alcoholism and Drug Addiction Research Foundation of Ontario, 1974.

1918 _____ and Kissel, Bernard C. "Visual Impact: An Added Dimension in the Study of News Diffusion." *Journalism Quarterly,* 1971, 48, 2: 298-303.

1919 O'Keefe, M. Timothy and Sheinkopf, Kenneth G. "The Voter Decides: Candidate Image or Campaign Issue?" *Journal of Broadcasting,* 1974, 18, 4: 403-412.

1920 O'Kelly, Charlotte G. "Sexism in Children's Television." *Journalism Quarterly,* 1974, 51, 4: 722-724.

1921 Olesen, V. L. and Whittaker, E. W., *The Silent Dialogue: A Study in the Social Psychology of Professional Socialization.* San Francisco: Jossey Bass, 1968.

1922 Olkinuora, Erkki. "The Effect of Television on Personal Norms." University of Jyvaskyla, Institute for Educational Research, no. 105, 1971.

1923 Olley, A. K. *Post-Television Social Survey: The Effects of Television Upon the Interests and Activities of Families and Persons in Sydney, Australia.* University of New South Wales, 1962.

1924 Olsen, Marvin. "Motion Picture Attendance and Social Isolation." *Sociological Quarterly,* 1960, 1, 2: 107-116.

1925 _____ . "Social and Political Participation of Blacks." *American Sociological Review,* 1970, 35, 4: 682-697.

1926 Olson, David R. ed. *Media and Symbols: The Forms of Expression, Communication and Education.* Chicago: University of Chicago Press, 1974. As the 73rd Yearbook of the National Society for the Study of Education, this volume presents 18 significant articles by major scholars in the field.

1927 _____ and Bruner, Jerome S. "Learning Through Experience and Learning Through Media." In D. Olson (ed.), *Media and Symbols: The Forms of Expression, Communication, and Education.* Chicago: University of Chicago Press, 1974: 125-150.

1928 Onder, J. J. *The Manual of Psychiatric Television: Theory, Practice, Imagination.* Ann Arbor: Maynard House, 1970.

1929 Opotowsky, S. *TV the Big Picture: A Close Hard Look at the World of Television.* New York: Collier, 1961.

1930 Orme, F., ed. *Violence is a Saleable Commodity.* Los Angeles: National Association for Better Broadcasting, 1973.

1931 Ormiston, L. H. and Williams, S. *Saturday Children's Programming in San Francisco, California: An Analysis of the Presentation of Racial and Cultural Groups on Three Network Affiliated San Francisco Television Stations.* San Francisco: Committee on Children's Television, 1973.

1932 Osborn, D. K. and Endsley, R. C. "Emotional Reactions of Young Children to TV Violence." *Child Development,* 1971, 42, 1: 321-331. Preschool children showed greater reaction to and remembered more from violent films and cartoons.

1933 _____ and Hale, W. "Television Violence." *Childhood Education,* 1969, 45: 505-507.

1934   Otto, Herbert A. "The Pornograhic Fringeland on the American News-stand." *Journal of Human Relations,* 1964, 12, 3: 375-390.

1935 _____ . "Sex and Violence on the American Newsstand." *Journalism Quarterly,* 1963, 40, 1: 19-26.

1936 _____ . "Sex and Violence in Contemporary Media—Three Studies." *Journal of Human Relations,* 1968, 16, 4: 571-590.

1937   Owen, Bruce M. "Measuring Violence on Television: The Gerbner Index." Staff Research Paper, Office of Telecommunications Policy. Springfield, Va.: National Technical Information Service, 1972.

P

1938   Packard, Vance. *The Hidden Persuaders.* New York: McKay, 1965.

1939   Paisley, M. B. "Social Policy Research and the Realities of the System: Violence Done to TV Research." Stanford, Calif.: Institute of Communication Research, Stanford University, 1972.

1940   Palda, K. S. *The Measurement of Cumulative Advertising Effects.* Englewood Cliffs, N.J.: Prentice-Hall, 1964.

1941   Paletz, D. L. "Delegates' Views of TV Coverage of the 1968 Democratic Convention." *Journal of Broadcasting,* 1972, 16: 441-451.

1942 _____ and Dunn, R. "Press Coverage of Civil Disorders: A Case Study of Winston-Salem, 1967." *Public Opinion Quarterly,* 1969, 33, 3: 328-345.

1943   Paletz, D. L., Reichert, P., and McIntyre, B. "How the Media Support Local Governmental Authority." *Public Opinion Quarterly,* 1971, 35: 80-92.

1944   Paletz, D. L., Koon, J., Whitehead, E., and Hagens, R. B. "Selective Exposure: The Potential Boomerang Effect." *Journal of Communication,* 1972, 22: 48-53.

1945   Palmer, Edward L. "Formative Research in the Production of Television for Children." In D. Olson (ed.), *Media and Symbols: The Forms of Expression, Communication, and Education.* Chicago: University of Chicago Press, 1974: 303-329.

1946   Panzarella, Marion A. "A Study to Develop a Cognitive Preference Test Based on Motion Picture Stimuli." *Dissertation Abstracts International,* 1971, 32 (1-A): 101.

1947   Pariat, M. "De l'Efficacite du Message Publicitaire" [The Effectiveness of Advertising]. *Revue Francaise du Marketing,* 1964, 10, 1: 45-47.

1948   Parke, R. D. "The Role of Punishment in the Socialization Process." In R. A. Hoppe, G. A. Milton, and E. C. Simmel (eds.), *Early Experiences and the Processes of Socialization.* New York: Academic Press, 1970.

1949 _____ , Berkowitz, L., Leyens, J. P., West, S., and Sebastian, R. J. "The Effects of Repeated Exposure to Movie Violence on Aggressive Behavior in Juvenile Delinquent Boys: Field Experimental Studies." In L. Berkowitz (ed.), *Advances in Experimental Social Psychology* (vol. 8). New York: Academic Press, 1975.

1950   Parker, Edwin B. "Changes in the Function of Radio with the Adoption of Television." *Journal of Broadcasting,* 1961, 5, 1: 39-48.

1951   _____ . "The Effects of Television on Magazine and Newspaper Reading: A Problem in Methodology." *Public Opinion Quarterly,* 1963, 27, 2: 315-320.

1952   _____ . "The Effects of Television on Public Library Circulation." *Public Opinion Quarterly,* 1963, 27, 4: 578-589.

1953   _____ . "The Functions of Television for Children." *Dissertation Abstracts,* 1961, 21: 2813-2814.

1954   _____ . "The Impact of a Radio Book Review Program on Public Library Circulation." *Journal of Broadcasting,* 1964, 8, 4: 363-361.

1955   _____ . "Implications of New Information Technology." *Public Opinion Quarterly,* 1973, 37, 4: 590-600.

1956   _____ . "Implications of New Information Technology." In W. P. Davison and F.T.C. Yu (eds.), *Mass Communication Research: Major Issues and Future Directions.* New York: Praeger, 1974: 171-183.

1957   _____ . "Information and Society." In C. A. Cuadra (ed.), *Annual Review of Information Science and Technology.* Washington, D.C.: American Society for Information Science,`1973.

1958   _____ . "Subliminal Stimulation and Voting Behavior." *Journalism Quarterly,* 1960, 37, 4: 588-590.

1959   _____ . "Television and the Process of Cultural Change." *Journalism Quarterly,* 1961, 38, 4: 537-540.

1960   Parris, Helen E. "Facilitating India's Family Planning Program Through Television; A Study of Source Effectiveness." Doctoral Dissertation, Michigan State University, 1971.

1961   Parsons, Talcott and Bales, R. F. *Family Socialization and Interaction Process.* New York: Free Press, 1955.

1962   Parsons, Talcott and White, Winston. "Commentary I: The Mass Media and the Structure of American Society." *Journal of Social Issues,* 1960, 16, 3: 67-77.

1963   Patterson, Thomas and McClure, R. "Political Advertising on Television: Spot Commercials in the 1972 Presidential Election." *Maxwell Review,* 1973, 9: 57-69.

1964   _____ . *Political Advertising: Voter Reaction to Televised Political Commercials.* Princeton, N.J.: Citizens' Research Foundation, 1974.

1965   Paulsen, K. "Was bleibt? Kinder besinnen sich auf einem Film" [What Remains? Children Recall a Film]. *Film-Bild-Ton* (Munich), 1957, 7: 8-13.

1966   Paulson, F. Leon. "Live versus Televised Observations of Social Behavior." *Proceedings of the Annual Convention of the American Psychological Association,* 1972, 7: 135-136.

1967   _____ . "Teaching Cooperation on Television: An Evaluation of Sesame Street Social Goals Programs." *Audio-Visual Communication Review,* 1974, 22, 3: 229-246.

1968 _____ , McDonald, D. L., and Whittemore, S. L. "An Evaluation of Sesame Street Programming Designed to Teach Cooperative Behavior." Monmouth, Oregon: Teaching Research, 1972.

1969 Paulu, Burton. "Audiences for Broadcasting in Britain and America." *Journalism Quarterly,* 1955, 32, 2: 329-334.

1970 Pearce, A. "Economics of Children's Television: An Assessment of the Impact of a Reduction in the Amount of Advertising." Washington, D.C.: Federal Communications Commission, 1974.

1971 _____ . "The Economics of Network Children's Television Programming." Washington, D.C.: Federal Communications Commission, 1972.

1972 Pearce, M., Cunningham, Scott, and Miller, Avon. *Appraising the Economic and Social Effects of Advertising.* Cambridge, Mass.: Marketing Science Institute Staff Report, 1971.

1973 Pearlin, Leonard I. "Social and Personal Stress and Escape Television Viewing." *Public Opinion Quarterly,* 1959, 23, 2: 255-259. Supports the escapist function for higher stress subjects.

1974 _____ . "The Social and Psychological Setting of Communications Behavior: An Analysis of Television Viewing." *Dissertation Abstracts,* 1957, 17: 1142-1143.

1975 Peatman, John and Hallonquist, T. "Geographical Sampling in Testing the Appeal of Radio Broadcasts." *Journal of Applied Psychology,* 1950, 34, 4: 270-279.

1976 Peled, T. and Katz, E. "Media Functions in Wartime: The Israel Home Front in October 1973." In J. G. Blumler and E. Katz (eds.), *The Uses of Mass Communications: Current Perspectives on Gratifications Research.* Beverly Hills: Sage, 1974: 49-69.

1977 Penn, Roger. "Effects of Motion and Cutting-Rate In Motion Pictures." *Audio-Visual Communication Review,* 1971, 19, 1: 29-50.

1978 Pepper, R. "Election Night 1972: TV Network Coverage." *Journal of Broadcasting,* 1973, 18: 27-38.

1979 Perrow, M. V. "A Description of Similarity of Personality Between Selected Groups of Television Viewers and Certain Television Roles Regularly Viewed by Them." Doctoral Dissertation, University of Southern California, 1968.

1980 Peterson, Marilyn. "The Visibility and Image of Old People on Television." *Journalism Quarterly,* 1973, 50, 3: 569-573.

1981 Petrov, John V. "Readership Study of the Influence of Printed Commercial Messages on Negro Readers in Atlanta, Georgia." *Phylon,* 1967, 28, 4: 399-407.

1982 Petzel, T. P. and Michaels, E. J. "Perception of Violence as a Function of Levels of Hostility." *Journal of Consulting and Clinical Psychology,* 1973, 41: 35-36.

1983 Pfautz, H. W. "Image of Alcohol in Popular Fiction: 1900-1904 and 1946-1950." *Quarterly Journal of Studies on Alcohol,* 1962, 23, 1: 131-146.

1984 Pfuhl, E. H. "The Relationship of Mass Media to Reported Delinquent Behavior." Doctoral Dissertation, Washington State University, 1960.

1985 Phillips, Kevin P. *Mediacracy: American Parties and Politics in the Communication Age.* Garden City, N.Y.: Doubleday, 1975.

1986 Pickles, W. "Political Attitudes in the Television Age." *Political Quarterly,* 1959, 30, 1: 54-66.

1987 Piepe, Anthony, Emerson, M., and Lannon, J. *Television and the Working Class.* Lexington, Mass.: Lexington Books, 1975.

1988 Pillard, Richard C., Atkinson, Kim W., and Fisher, Seymour. "The Effect of Different Preparations on Film-Induced Anxiety." *Psychological Record,* 1967, 17, 1: 35-41.

1989 Pillard, Richard C., Carpenter, James, Atkinson, Kim W., and Fisher, Seymour. "Palmar Sweat Prints and Self-Ratings as Measures of Film-Induced Anxiety." *Perceptual and Motor Skills,* 1966, 23, 3: 771-777.

1990 Pinderhughes, C. A. "Televised Violence and Social Behavior." *Psychiatric Opinion,* 1972, 9, 2: 28-36.

1991 Pittman, D. J. "Mass Media and Juvenile Delinquency." In J. S. Roucek (ed.), *Juvenile Delinquency.* New York: Philosophical Library, 1958: 230-247.

1992 Plummer, Joseph T. "Life-Style Patterns: A New Constraint for Mass Communications Research." *Journal of Broadcasting,* 1972, 16, 1: 79-89.

1993 Polak, Fred L. "Television and Leisure." *Journal of Communication,* 1952, 22: 15-25.

1994 Polsby, Nelson W. and Wildavsky, Aaron B., *Presidential Elections.* New York: Charles Scribner Sons, 1968.

1995 Polsky, R. M. "The Children's Television Workshop, 1966-1968." Doctoral Dissertation, Teacher's College, 1973.

1996 ———. *Getting to Sesame Street: Origins of the Children's Television Workshop.* New York: Praeger, 1974.

1997 Pool, Ithiel. "The Mass Media and Their Interpersonal Social Functions in the Process of Modernization." In L. Pye (ed.), *Communications and Political Development.* Princeton: Princeton University Press, 1963.

1998 ———. "The Mass Media and Politics in the Modernization Process." In L. W. Pye (ed.), *Communications and Political Development.* Princeton: Princeton University Press, 1963: 234-253.

1999 ———. "TV: A New Dimension in Politics." In E. Burdick and A. J. Brodbeck (eds.), *American Voting Behavior.* Glencoe, Ill.: Free Press, 1959: 197-208.

2000 ———. "The Rise of Communications Policy Research." *Journal of Communication,* 1974, 24, 2: 31-42.

2001 ——— and Alexander, H. E. *Politics in a Wired Nation.* New York: Alfred P. Sloan Foundation, 1971.

2002 Pool, Ithiel, et al. *The Prestige Press: A Comparative Study of Political Symbols.* Cambridge, Mass.: Massachusetts Institute of Technology Press, 1970.

2003   Porter, Richard. "A Quantification of the Program Preferences of a Television Audience." *Journal of Broadcasting,* 1959, 3, 1: 56-63.

2004   Poussaint, Alvin F. "Blaxploitation Movies: Cheap Thrills that Degrade Blacks." *Psychology Today,* 1974, 7, 9: 22-32, 98.

2005   Powell, Len S. *Communication and Learning.* New York: American Elsevier, 1969.

2006   Powers, Anne, ed., *Blacks in American Movies: A Selected Bibliography.* Metuchen, N.J.: Scarecrow Press, 1974.

2007   Prawat, Dorothy M. and Prawat, Richard S. "Preschoolers' Learning Behavior While Watching Two Types of Television Fare." *Perceptual and Motor Skills,* 1975, 40, 2: 575-582.

2008   Preston, Ivan L. *The Great American Blow-Up: Puffery in Advertising and Selling.* Madison: University of Wisconsin Press, 1975.

2009   _____ . "Theories of Behavior and the Concept of Rationality in Advertising." *Journal of Communication,* 1967, 17, 3: 211-222.

2010   _____ and Bowen, Lawrence. "Perceiving Advertisements as Emotional, Rational and Irrational." *Journalism Quarterly,* 1971, 48: 73-84.

2011   Price, Frank T. "Some Effects of Film-Mediated Professional Models on the Self-Perceptions of Black School Children." *Dissertation Abstracts International,* 1971, 31 (7-B): 4318.

2012   Price, T., ed. "Drug Advertising Hearings." *Journal of Drug Issues,* 1974, 4, 3: 203-205.

2013   Price, Warren C. and Rickett, C. M. *An Annotated Journalism Bibliography: 1958-1968. Minneapolis: University of Minnesota Press, 1970.*

2014   Pride, Richard A. and Clarke, Daniel H. "Race Relations in Television News: A Content Analysis of the Networks." *Journalism Quarterly,* 1973, 50, 2: 319-328.

2015   Prosser, Michael H., ed. *Intercommunication Among Nations and Peoples.* New York: Harper and Row, 1973.

2016   Pryluck, Calvin. "Functions of Functional Analysis: Comments on Anderson-Meyer." *Journal of Broadcasting,* 1975, 19, 3: 413-421.

2017   _____ . "Rejoinder to Anderson-Meyer." *Journal of Broadcasting,* 1975, 19, 4: 424-425.

2018   Pye, L. W., ed. *Communications and Political Development.* Princeton: Princeton University Press, 1963.

2019   Pyke, S. W. and Stewart, J. C. "This Column is About Women: Women and Television." *Ontario Psychologist,* 1974, 6, 5: 66-69.

Q

2020   Quera, Leon. *Advertising Campaigns: Formulation and Tactics.* Columbus, Ohio: Grid, Inc., 1973.

R

2021 Rabinovitch, Martin S. "Violence Perception as a Function of Entertainment Value and TV Violence." *Psychonomic Science,* 1972, 29: 360-362. Presenting violent slides in the context of positive entertainment reduced the degree of perceived violence.

2022 _____ , MacLean, Malcom S., Markham, James W., and Talbot, Albert D. "Children's Violence Perception as a Function of Television Violence." In G. A. Comstock, E. A. Rubinstein, and J. P. Murray (eds.), *Television and Social Behavior: Television Effects: Further Explorations* (vol. 5). Washington, D.C.: Government Printing Office, 1972: 231-252.

2023 Radio and Television Culture Research Institute. "Children's Viewing Patterns and Factors Influencing Their Program Choices." *Annual Bulletin of the Radio and Television Culture Research Institute,* no. 6, 1961.

2024 _____ . "An Effect Study of TV on Children's Behavior with Cultural Environment as an Intervening Variable." *Annual Bulletin of the Radio and Television Culture Research Institute,* no. 7, 1962.

2025 _____ . "An Effect Study of TV on Children's Behavior with the Difference of Intelligence as an Intervening Variable." *Annual Bulletin of the Radio and Television Culture Research Institute,* no. 6, 1961.

2026 Rafi-Zadeh, Hassau. *International Mass Communications: Computerized Annotated Bibliography.* Carbondale, Illinois: Honorary Relation-Zone, 1972.

2027 Ramsdell, M. L. "The Trauma of TV's Troubled Soap Families." *Family Coordinator,* 1973, 22, 2: 299-304.

2028 Randall, R. S. *Censorship of the Movies: The Social and Political Control of a Mass Medium.* Madison: University of Wisconsin Press, 1968.

2029 Rarick, David L. "Expressed Preferences and Desirability Judgments of Parents and Their Children for Eighteen Types of Television Violence." Doctoral Dissertation, Ohio State University, 1970.

2030 _____ , Townsend, James E., and Boyd, Douglas A. "Adolescent Perceptions of Police: Actual and as Depicted in TV Drama." *Journalism Quarterly,* 1973, 50, 3: 438-446. Evidences marked discrepancies between the real world and the television world.

2031 Rarick, Galen. "Political Persuasion: The Newspaper and the Sexes." *Journalism Quarterly,* 1970, 47, 2: 360-364.

2032 Ray, M. L. "Marketing Communication and the Hierarchy-of-Effects." In P. Clarke (ed.), *New Models for Mass Communication Research.* Beverly Hills: Sage, 1973: 147-176.

2033 _____ and Ward, Scott. eds. *Communicating with Consumers: The Information Processing Approach.* Beverly Hills: Sage, 1975.

2034 Ray, M. L. and Wilkie, W. L. "Fear: The Potential of an Appeal Neglected by Marketing." *Journal of Marketing,* 1970, 34: 54-62.

2035 Ray, M. L., Sawyer, A. G., and Strong, E. C. "Frequency Effects Revisited." *Journal of Advertising Research,* 1971, 11: 14-20.

2036 Ray, M. L., Ward, S., and Lesser, G. "Experimentation to Improve Pretesting of Anti-Drug Abuse Education and Information Campaigns." Cambridge: Marketing Science Institute, 1974.

2037 Reagor, Pamela A. "Delinquency, Socialization, and Type of Social Reinforcement." *Dissertation Abstracts International,* 1971, 31 (12-B): 7608.

2038 Redd, Lawrence N. *Rock as Rhythm and Blues: The Impact of Mass Media.* East Lansing: Michigan State University Press, 1974. An assessment of the impact of mass media on the musical culture of Black America.

2039 Reed, J. B. "Planned Social Advertising: Testing for Effects of Appeals, Distraction, Involvement, and Competition." Doctoral Dissertation, Graduate School of Business, Stanford University, 1974.

2040 Rees, M. B., and Paisley, W. J. *Social and Psychological Predictors of Information Seeking and Media Use. A Multivariate Reanalysis.* Stanford, Calif.: Institute for Communication Research, Stanford University, 1967.

2041 Reeves, B. F. *The First Year of Sesame Street: The Formative Research.* New York: Children's Television Workshop, 1970.

2042 _____ . *The Responses of Children in Six Small Viewing Groups to Sesame Street Shows nos. 261-274.* New York: Children's Television Workshop, 1971.

2043 Reeves, Rosser. *Reality in Advertising.* New York: Knopf, 1961.

2044 Reich, Carol and Meisner, Alan. "A Comparison of Colour and Black and White TV." Ontario: Toronto University, 1972.

2045 Religious Television Associates. "Research From a Shopping Bag: A Summary of 400+ Informal Interviews About Children and Television in Canada." Toronto, Ontario: Religious Television Associates, 1973.

2046 Rembar, Charles. *The End of Obscenity: The Trials of Lady Chatterley, Tropic of Cancer, and Fanny Hill.* New York: Random House, 1968.

2047 Remond, R. and Neuschwander, C. "Television et Comportment Politique" [Television and Political Behavior]. *Revue Francaise de Science Politique.* 1963, 13, 2: 325-347.

2048 Repath, A. V. *Mass Media and You.* London: Longmans, Green & Company, 1966.

2049 Reynolds, James C. "The Effect of Viewer Distance on Film-Induced Anxiety." *Dissertation Abstracts,* 1969, 29 (10-A): 3341.

2050 Rhine, Ramon J. "The 1964 Presidential Election and Curves of Information Seeking and Avoidance." *Journal of Personality and Social Psychology,* 1967, 5, 4: 416-423.

2051 Ricciuti, E. A. "Children and Radio." *Genetic Psychology Monographs,* 1951, 64: 69-140.

2052 Rice, Susan and Mukerji, Rose. *Children are Centers for Understanding Media.* Washington, D.C.: Association for Childhood Education International, 1973. An examination of the ways to develop a more selective and intelligent audience of young viewers by involving the media in traditional educational schemes.

2053 Richards, Ivor Armstrong. *Design for Escape: World Education Through Modern Media.* New York: Harcourt, Brace and World, 1968.

2054 Richards, M., ed. *The Integration of a Child into a Social World.* New York: Cambridge University Press, 1974.

2055 Richards, Michael P. *The Making of the American Citizenry: An Introduction to Political Socialization.* New York: Chandler, 1973.

2056 Rider, John R. "The Charleston Study: The Television Audience of the Nixon-Kennedy Debates." Doctoral Dissertation, Michigan State University, 1963.

2057 Riedel, James A. and Dunne, James R. "When the Voter Decides." *Public Opinion Quarterly,* 1969, 33, 4: 619-621.

2058 Riggs, F. L. "The Changing Role of Radio." *Journal of Broadcasting,* 1964, 8, 4: 331-339.

2059 Riley, Matilda and Flowerman, Samuel. "Group Relations as a Variable in Communications Research." *American Sociological Review,* 1951, 16, 2: 174-180.

2060 Riley, Matilda and Riley, John W. "A Sociological Approach to Communications Research." *Public Opinion Quarterly,* 1951, 15, 3: 445-460. Emphasizes studying the formation of attitudes and opinions within the socio-cultural context of which they are a part.

2061 Rinder, Irwin D. "A Sociological Look into the Negro Pictorial." *Phylon,* 1959, 20, 2: 169-177.

2062 Rissover, F. and Birch, D. C., comps. *Mass Media and The Popular Arts.* New York: McGraw Hill, 1971.

2063 Rist, Ray C., comp. *The Pornography Controversy: Changing Moral Standards in American Life.* New Brunswick, N.J.: Transaction Books, 1975.

2064 Rivers, William L., Peterson, Theodore, and Jensen, Jay W. *The Mass Media and Modern Society* (2nd ed.). Corte Madera, Calif.: Rinehart Press, 1970.

2065 Roberts, Churchill. "The Portrayal of Blacks on Network Television." *Journal of Broadcasting,* 1971, 15, 1: 45-53.

2066 _____. "The Presentation of Blacks in Television Network Newscasts." *Journalism Quarterly,* 1975, 52: 50-55.

2067 Roberts, D. F. "Communication and Children: A Developmental Approach." In I. Pool, et al. (eds)., *Handbook of Communication.* Chicago: Rand McNally, 1973: 174-215. Places the development of the child and the nature of the information being processed in a developmental vs. a behavioral paradigm.

2068 _____ . "A Developmental Study of Opinion Change: Source Orientation vs. Content Orientation at Three Age Levels." Doctoral Dissertation, Stanford University, 1968.

2069 _____ . "The Nature of Human Communication Effects." In W. Schramm and D. F. Roberts (eds.), *The Process and Effects of Mass Communication* (2nd ed.). Urbana: University of Illinois Press, 1971: 347-387.

2070 _____ and Schramm, W. "Children's Learning from the Mass Media." In W. Schramm and D. F. Roberts (eds.), *The Process and Effects of Mass Communication* (2nd ed.). Urbana: University of Illinois Press, 1971: 596-611.

2071 Roberts, D. F., Hawkins, Robert P., and Pingree, Suzanne. "Do the Mass Media Play a Role in Political Socialization?" *Australian and New Zealand Journal of Sociology,* 1975, 11, 2: 37-43.

2072 Roberts, D. F., Herold, C., Hornby, M., King, S., Sterne, D., Whitely, S., and Silverman, L. T. "Earth's a Big Blue Marble: A Report of the Impact of a Children's Television Series on Children's Opinions." Stanford, Calif.: Institute for Communication Research, Stanford University, 1974.

2073 Roberts, Edwin A., Jr. *The Smut Rakers: A Report in Depth on Obscenity and the Censors.* Silver Springs, Md.: National Observer, 1966.

2074 Robertson, Thomas S. "The Impact of Television Advertising on Children." *Wharton Quarterly,* Fall, 1972: 38-41.

2075 _____ . *Innovative Behavior and Communication.* New York: Holt, Rinehart, Winston, 1971.

2076 _____ and Rossiter, John R. "Children and Commercial Persuasion: An Attribution Theory Analysis." *Journal of Consumer Research,* 1974, 1, 1: 13-20.

2077 Robertus, Patricia and Simon, Rita James. "The Movie Code: A View from Parents and Teenagers." *Journalism Quarterly,* 1970, 47, 3: 568-569, 629.

2078 Robinson, Campbell D. "Television/Film Attitudes of Upper-Middle Class Professionals." *Journal of Broadcasting,* 1975, 19, 2: 195-209.

2079 Robinson, Edward J. "Analyzing the Impact of Science Reporting." *Journalism Quarterly,* 1963, 60, 3: 306-314.

2080 Robinson, Gertrude Joch. "Mass Media and Ethnic Strife in Multi-National Yugoslavia." *Journalism Quarterly,* 1974, 51, 3: 490-497.

2081 Robinson, John P. "The Audience for National TV News Programs." *Public Opinion Quarterly,* 1971, 35, 3: 403-405.

2082 _____ . "Mass Communication and Information Diffusion." In F. G. Kline and P. J. Tichenor (eds.), *Current Perspectives in Mass Communication Research.* Beverly Hills: Sage, 1972: 71-94.

2083 _____ . "Perceived Media Bias and the 1968 Vote: Can the Media Affect Behavior After All?" *Journalism Quarterly,* 1972, 49, 2: 239-246.

2084 _____ . "The Press as King-Maker: What Surveys from Last Five Campaigns Show." *Journalism Quarterly,* 1974, 51, 4: 587-594, 606.

2085 _____ . "Public Opinion During the Watergate Crisis." *Communication Research,* 1974, 1, 4: 391-405.

2086 _____ . "Television and Leisure Time: Yesterday, Today, and (Maybe) Tomorrow." *Public Opinion Quarterly,* 1969, 33, 3: 210-222. Documents how television has usurped both American's and European's leisure time.

2087 _____ . "Television's Impact on Everyday Life: Some Cross-National Evidence." In E. A. Rubinstein, G. A. Comstock, and J. P. Murray (eds.), *Television and Social Behavior: Television in Day-to-Day Life: Patterns of Use* (vol. 4). Washington, D.C.: Government Printing Office, 1972: 410-431.

2088 _____ . "Toward Defining the Functions of Television." In E. A. Rubinstein, G. A. Comstock, and J. P. Murray (eds.), *Television and Social Behavior: Television in Day-to-Day Life: Patterns of Use* (vol. 4). Washington, D.C.: Government Printing Office, 1972: 568-601. Entertainment wins out over information as a major function.

2089 _____ . "World Affairs Information and Mass Media Exposure." *Journalism Quarterly,* 1967, 44, 1: 23-31.

2090 _____ and Bachman, J. G. "Television Viewing Habits and Aggression." In G. A. Comstock and E. A. Rubinstein (eds.), *Television and Social Behavior: Television and Adolescent Aggressiveness* (vol. 3). Washington, D.C.: Government Printing Office, 1972: 372-382.

2091 Robinson, John P. and Converse, P. E. "The Impact of Television on Mass Media Usages: A Cross-National Comparison." In A. Szalai (ed.), *The Use of Time: Daily Activities of Urban and Suburban Populations in Twelve Countries.* The Hague: Mouton and Co., 1972: 197-212.

2092 Robinson, John P. and Hirsch, Paul M. "Teenage Response to Rock and Roll Protest Songs." Ann Arbor: University of Michigan Survey Research Center, 1970.

2093 Robinson, M. J. "The Impact of the Televised Watergate Hearings." *Journal of Communication,* 1974, 24, 2: 17-30.

2094 _____ and Burgess, P. M. "The Edward M. Kennedy Speech: The Impact of a Prime Time Television Appeal." *Television Quarterly,* 1970, 9, 1: 29-39.

2095 Roetter, Charles. *The Art of Psychological Warfare: 1914-1945.* New York: Stein and Day, 1974.

2096 Rogers, E. M. *Bibliography on the Diffusion of Innovations.* East Lansing: Department of Communication, Michigan State University, 1967.

2097 _____ . *Communication Strategies for Family Planning.* New York: Free Press, 1973. Places the family planning problem within the context of both communication and diffusion, with specific strategy suggestions.

2098 _____ . "Mass Media and Interpersonal Communication." In I. de Sola Pool and W. Schramm (eds.), *Handbook of Communication.* Chicago: Rand McNally, 1973: 290-310.

2099 _____ . "Mass Media Exposure and Modernization Among Colombian Peasants." *Public Opinion Quarterly,* 1965, 29, 4: 614-625.

2100 _____ . *Modernization Among Peasants: The Impact of Communication.* New York: Holt, Rinehart and Winston, 1969.

2101 _____ . *Supplement to the Bibliography on the Diffusion of Innovations.* East Lansing, Mich.: Department of Communication, Michigan State University, 1968.

2102 _____ and Shoemaker, Floyd F., *Communication of Innovations: A Cross-Cultural Approach* (2nd ed.). New York: Free Press, 1971. Synthesizes more than 1500 studies of the diffusion process, with the full bibliography appended.

2103 _____ and Smith, Leticia. "Bibliography on the Diffusion of Innovations." East Lansing: Michigan State Univ. Department of Communication, 1965.

2104 Rogers, Rosemarie. "The Soviet Audience Expects and Gets More from Its Media." *Journalism Quarterly,* 1969, 46, 4: 767-776, 783.

2105 Rogers, R. W. "An Analysis of Fear Appeals and Attitude Change." Final report. University of South Carolina, August, 1973.

2106 Rokeach, M. *Beliefs, Attitudes, and Values.* San Francisco: Jossey-Bass, 1968.

2107 The Roper Organization, Inc. *Trends in Public Attitudes Toward Television and Other Mass Media, 1959-1974.* New York: Television Information Office, 1975. Television comes through as the most preferred source of news, and most content is approved.

2108 Rose, Arnold M. "Mental Health Attitudes of Youth as Influenced by a Comic Strip." *Journalism Quarterly,* 1958, 35, 3: 333-342.

2109 _____ . "The Study of the Influence of the Mass Media on Public Opinion." *Kyklos,* 1962, 15, 2: 465-484.

2110 Rose, R. *Influencing Voters: A Study of Campaign Rationality.* New York: St. Martin's Press, 1967.

2111 Rosekrans, M. A. "Imitation in Children as a Function of Perceived Similarities to a Social Model of Vicarious Reinforcement." *Journal of Personality and Social Psychology,* 1967, 7: 307-315. Increased similarity produced increased aggressive responses.

2112 _____ and Hartup, W. W. "Imitative Influences of Consistent and Inconsistent Response Consequences to a Model on Aggressive Behavior in Children." *Journal of Personality and Social Psychology,* 1967, 7, 4: 429-434.

2113 Rosen, I. C. "The Effects of the Motion Picture 'Gentlemen's Agreement' on Attitudes Toward Jews." *Journal of Psychology,* 1948, 26: 525-536.

2114 Rosenbaum, W. B., Rosenbaum, L. L., and McGinnies, E. "Sex Differences in Selective Exposure." *Journal of Social Psychology,* 1974, 92: 85-89.

2115 Rosene, J. M. "The Effects of Violent and Sexually Arousing Film Content: An Experimental Study." Doctoral Dissertation, Ohio University, 1971.

2116 Rosengren, K. E. "News Diffusion: An Overview." *Journalism Quarterly,* 1973, 50: 83-91.

2117 _____ . "Uses and Gratifications: A Paradigm Outlined." In J. G. Blumler and E. Katz (eds.), *The Uses of Mass Communications: Current Perspectives on Gratifications Research.* Beverly Hills: Sage, 1974: 269-286.

2118 _____ and Windahl, S. "Mass Media Consumption as a Functional Alternative." In D. McQuail (ed.), *Sociology of Mass Communications: Selected Readings.* Baltimore: Penguin Books, 1972.

2119 Rosenhan, D. L. "Prosocial Behavior of Children." In W. W. Hartup and N. L. Smothergill (eds.), *The Young Child* (vol. 2). Washington, D.C.: National Association for the Education of Young Children, 1972: 340-359.

2120 _____ and White, G. M. "Observation and Rehearsal as Determinants of Prosocial Behavior." *Journal of Personality and Social Psychology,* 1967, 5: 424-431.

2121 Rosenkoetter, L. I. "Resistance to Temptation: Inhibitory and Disinhibitory Effects of Models." *Developmental Psychology,* 1973, 8: 80-84.

2122 Rosenthal, Paul I. "Ethos in the Presidential Campaign of 1960: A Study of the Persuasive Process of the Kennedy-Nixon Television Debates." Doctoral Dissertation. University of California, L.A., 1963.

2123 Roses, James M. "The Effects of Violent and Sexually Arousing Film Content: An Experimental Study." *Dissertation Abstracts International,* 1972, 32 (11-A): 6469-6470.

2124 Roshier, R. "Crime and the Press." Doctoral Dissertation, University of New Castle, 1969.

2125 Rosow, I. *Socialization to Old Age.* Berkeley: University of California Press, 1974.

2126 Ross, John E. and Bostian, Lloyd R. "Communications Activities of Wisconsin Farm Families in Wintertime." *Journal of Broadcasting,* 1958, 2, 4: 319-328.

2127 Ross, L. B. "The Effect of Aggressive Cartoons on the Group Play of Children." Doctoral Dissertation, Miami University, 1972.

2128 Rossi, Peter H., ed. *The New Media and Education: Their Impact on Society.* Chicago: Aldine, 1966.

2129 Rossiter, John R. "Children's Susceptibility to Television Advertising: A Behavioral Test of Cognition and Attitude." Doctoral Dissertation, Annenberg School of Communications, University of Pennsylvania, 1974.

2130 _____ and Robertson, Thomas S. "Children's TV Commercials: Testing the Defenses." *Journal of Communication,* 1974, 24, 4: 137-144. Suggests that concentrated advertising such as that at Christmas time may wear down the defenses of children who show strong cognitive and attitudinal defenses before the heavy campaigns.

2131 _____ . "Children's Television Viewing: An Examination of Parent-Child Consensus." *Sociometry,* 1975, 33, 3: 308-326.

2132 Rossman, Jules. "The TV Critic Column: Is it Influential?" *Journal of Broadcasting,* 1975, 19, 4: 401-411.

2133 Rothman, L. J. and Rauta, I. "Towards a Typology of the Television Audience." *Journal of the Market Research Society,* 1969, 11: 45-69.

2134 Rothschild, M. L. "The Effects of Political Advertising upon the Voting Behavior of a Low Involvement Electorate." Doctoral Dissertation, Graduate School of Business, Stanford University, 1974.

2135 Rothschild, M. L. and Ray, M. L. "Involvement and Political Advertising Effects." *Communication Research,* 1974, 1, 3: 264-285.

2136 Roucek, Joseph S. "The Influence of Television on American Politics." *Politico,* 1963, 28, 1: 124-134.

2137 Rowley, Susan L. "Film Cartoon Violence and Children's Aggressive Behavior." *Dissertation Abstracts International,* 1971, 32 (4-B): 2384-2385.

2138 Rubin, B. *Political Television.* Belmont, Calif.: Wadsworth Publishing Company, 1967.

2139 Rubin, D. M. and Sachs, D. P. *Mass Media and the Environment: Water Resources, Land Use and Atomic Energy in California.* New York: Praeger, 1973.

2140 Rubinstein, Eli A. "Television and the Young Viewer." New York: State University at Stony Brook, Department of Psychiatry, 1973.

2141 _____ . "The TV Violence Report: What's Next?" *Journal of Communication,* 1974, 24, 1: 80-88.

2142 _____ , Comstock, G. A., and Murray, J. P., eds. *Television and Social Behavior: Television in Day-to-Day Life: Patterns of Use* (vol. 4). Washington, D.C.: Government Printing Office, 1972.

2143 Rubinstein, Eli A., Liebert, R. M., Neale, J. M., and Poulos, R. W. "Assessing Television's Influence on Children's Prosocial Behavior." Stony Brook, N.Y.: Brookdale International Institute, 1974.

2144 Rue, Vincent M. "Retooling Information Systems for Aging." *International Journal of Aging and Human Development.* 1973, 4, 4: 361-374.

2145 _____ . "Television and the Family: The Question of Control." *Family Coordinator,* 1974, 23, 1: 73-81.

2146 Ruffner, Marguerite Anne. "Women's Attitudes Toward Progressive Rock Radio." *Journal of Broadcasting,* 1973, 17, 1: 85-94.

2147 Rummer, Joseph T. "A Theoretical View of Advertising Communication." *The Journal of Communication,* 1971, 21, 4: 315-325.

2148 Runciman, Alexander. "A Stratification Study of Television Programs." *Sociology and Social Research,* 1960, 44, 4: 257-261.

2149 _____ . "Selected Social Psychological Factors Related to Viewers of Television Programs." Doctoral Dissertation, University of Southern California, 1969.

2150 Rush, Ramona R. "Interpersonal Communication and Cognitive Modernity: A Study of Socialization in Lima, Peru." *Journalism Quarterly,* 1972, 49: 327-339.

2151 Rush, Wilmer S. "Some Factors Influencing Children's Use of the Mass Media of Communication" *Journal of Experimental Education,* 1965, 33, 3: 301-304.

2152 Rushton, J. Philippe and Owen, Diane. "Immediate and Delayed Effects of Television Modelling and Preaching on Children's Generosity." *British Journal of Social and Clinical Psychology,* 1975, 14: 309-310.

2153 Russett, B., Alker, H., Jr., Deutsch, K., and Lasswell, H. *World Handbook of Political and Social Indicators.* New Haven, Conn.: Yale University Press, 1965.

2154 Russo, F. D. "A Study of Bias in TV Coverage of the Vietnam War: 1969 and 1970." *Public Opinion Quarterly,* 1971, 35: 539-543.

2155 Rutko, Victor. "Radio in Family Planning Education in Africa." *Educational Broadcasting International,* 1971, 5: 243-245.

2156 Rutstein, Nat. *"Go Watch TV!": What and How Much Should Children Really Watch?* New York: Sheed and Ward, 1974.

2157 Ryan, M. "News Content, Geographical Origin and Perceived Media Credibility." *Journalism Quarterly,* 1973, 50: 312-318.

2158 Ryan, Paul M. "An Empirical Study of the Relationship of Personal Values, News Content and Media Credibility Perception." Doctoral Dissertation, Southern Illinois University, 1971.

S

2159 Sachsman, David B. "Mass Media and the Urban Environment." *Mass Comm Review,* 1974, 1, 3: 3-12.

2160 Saenger, Gerhart. "Male and Female Relations in the American Comic Strip." *Public Opinion Quarterly,* 1955, 19, 2: 195-205.

2161 Salant, Richard S. "The Television Debates: A Revolution that Deserves a Future." *Public Opinion Quarterly,* 1962, 26, 3: 335-350.

2162 Salber, Wilhelm. *Film and Sexualitat: Untersuchungen zur Filmpsychologie* [Films and Sexuality: Investigations Concerning Film Psychology]. Bonn, W. Germany: H. Bouvier, 1970.

2163 Salcedo, Rodolfo N., Read, Hadley, Evans, James F., and Kong, Ana E. "A Successful Information Campaign on Pesticides." *Journalism Quarterly,* 1974, 51: 91-95, 110.

2164 Salomon, G. "Can We Affect Cognitive Skills Through Visual Media? An Hypothesis and Initial Findings." *AV Communication Review,* 1972, 20: 401-422.

2165 _____ . "Cross-Cultural Distribution of Television: A Study of Its Effects on Mental Skills." Jerusalem: The Hebrew University of Jerusalem, 1974.

2166 _____ . "What is Learned and How it is Taught: The Interaction Between Media, Messages, Task, and Learner." In D. Olson (ed.), *Media and Symbols: The Forms of Expression, Communication, and Education.* Chicago: University of Chicago Press, 1974: 383-406.

2167 _____ , Eglstein, S., Finkelstein, R., Finkelstein, I., Mintzberg, E., Malve, D., and Velner, L. "Educational Effects of Sesame Street on Israeli

Children." New York: Children's Television Workshop and Israel Institute of Applied Social Research, 1972.

2168 Sampson, John J. "Commercial Traffic in Sexually Oriented Materials in the United States." In *Technical Report of the Commission on Obscenity and Pornography; The Marketplace; The Industry* (vol. 3). Washington, D.C.: Government Printing Office, 1971: 3-203.

2169 Samuels, B. "The First Year of Sesame Street: A Summary of Audience Surveys." New York: Children's Television Workshop, 1970.

2170 Samuelson, M., Carter, R., and Ruggels, L. "Education, Available Time, and Use of Mass Media." *Journalism Quarterly,* 1963, 40: 491-496.

2171 Sanabria, Francisco. "La Responsabilidad Social de los Medios de Comunicación de Masas" [The Social Responsibility of Mass Communications Media]. *Revista Española de la Opinión Pública,* 1966, 4, April-June: 149-171.

2172 Sandage, C. H. "The Role of Advertising in Modern Society." *Journalism Quarterly,* 1951, 28, 1: 31-38.

2173 Sanders, J. T. "A Developmental Study of Preferences for Television Cartoons." Doctoral Dissertation, Ohio State University, 1969.

2174 Sandford, D. A. "Patterns of Sexual Arousal in Heterosexual Males." *Journal of Sex Research,* 1974, 10, 2: 150-155.

2175 Sargent, Leslie W. "Communicator Image and News Reception." *Journalism Quarterly,* 1965, 42, 1: 35-42.

2176 _____ and Stempel, Guido H. "Poverty, Alienation and Mass Media Use." *Journalism Quarterly,* 1968, 45, 2: 324-326.

2177 Sarson, Evelyn. "Growing Grass Roots in Viewerland." *Television Quarterly,* 1970, 9, 3: 50-57.

2178 Satterfield, J. R. "Televiewing Practices as a Function of Certain Personality Variables and Reading Achievement Levels of Middle Socio-Economic Status Fourth Grade Children." Doctoral Dissertation, University of Oklahoma, 1972.

2179 Savitsky, J. C., Rogers, R. W., Izard, C. E., and Liebert, R. M. "Role of Frustration and Anger in the Imitation of Filmed Aggression Against a Human Victim." *Psychological Reports,* 1971, 29: 807-810.

2180 Sawin, D. B. "Aggressive Behavior Among Children in Small Playgroup Settings with Violent Television." Doctoral Dissertation, University of Minnesota, 1974.

2181 Sawyer, A. G. "The Effects of Repetition of Refutational and Supportive Advertising Appeals." *Journal of Marketing Research,* 1972, 10: 23-33.

2182 Saxer, Ulrich. "Contributions of Research in the German-language Areas to the Subject: Television and Socialization Processes in the Family." In *Television and Socialization Processes in the Family.* Proceedings of the Prix Jeunesse Seminar, 1975: 85-99.

2183 Scanlon, T. J. "Color Television: New Language?" *Journalism Quarterly,* 1967, 44, 2: 225-230.

2184 _____ . "Viewer Perceptions on Color, Black and White TV: An Experiment." *Journalism Quarterly,* 1970, 47: 366-368.

2185 Schalinske, Theo F. "Role of Television in the Life of the Aged Person." Doctoral Dissertation, Ohio State University, 1968.

2186 Schary, Dore. "The Mass Media and Prejudice." In C. Glock and E. Siegelman (eds.), *Prejudice USA.* New York: Praeger, 1969.

2187 Schatzman, L. and Strauss, A. "Social Class and Modes of Communication." *American Journal of Sociology,* 1955, 60, 4: 329-338.

2188 Scherer, Klaus R. "Stereotype Change Following Exposure to Counter-Stereotypical Media Heroes." *Journal of Broadcasting,* 1971, 15, 1: 91-100.

2189 Schickel, R. "Violence in the Movies." *Review of Existential Psychology and Psychiatry,* 1968, 8, 3: 169-178.

2190 Schiff, William. "Perceived and Remembered Duration of Films." *Perceptual and Motor Skills,* 1970, 30, 3: 903-906.

2191 Schiller, H. I. "Authentic National Development versus the Free Flow of Information and the New Communications." In G. Gerbner, L. Gross, and W. Melody (eds.), *Communications Technology and Social Policy; Understanding the New "Cultural Revolution."* New York: Wiley, 1973: 467-480.

2192 _____ . "Mind Management: Mass Media in the Advanced Industrial State." *Quarterly Review of Economics and Business,* 1971, 11, 1: 39-52.

2193 _____ . *The Mind Managers.* Boston: Beacon Press, 1973. Takes a critical look at the manipulative use of media through chapters on the manipulative process, the knowledge industry (government and military-industrial), the reinforcement function of entertainment, public opinion, and mind management overseas.

2194 Schiller, Patricia. "Effects of Mass Media on the Sexual Behavior of Adolescent Females." In W. C. Wilson (comp.), *Technical Report of the Commission on Obscenity and Pornography: Preliminary Studies* (vol. 1) Washington, D.C.: Government Printing Office, 1971: 191-195. Supports the hypothesis that love and sex are closely associated for most adolescent females.

2195 Schlater, Robert. "Effect of Irrelevant Visual Cues on Recall of Television Messages." *Journal of Broadcasting,* 1970, 14, 1: 63-69.

2196 _____ . "Effects of Speed of Presentation on Recall of Television Messages." *Journal of Broadcasting,* 1970, 14, 2: 207-214.

2197 Schlinger, Mary Jane. "Responses to Advertising: Varieties of Liking and Disliking." *Journalism Quarterly,* 1970, 47, 1: 46-56.

2198 _____ and Plummer, Joseph T. "Advertising in Black and White." *Journal of Marketing Research,* 1972, 9: 149-153.

2199 Schlottmann, R. S., Shore, S. L., and Palazzo, R. F. "The Effects of Factual vs. Emotional Wording in Printed Accounts of Violence on Aggression." *Journal of Social Psychology,* 1975, 96, 2: 221-228.

2200 Schmelck, R. "Violence on French Television." *Annales Medicine Legale et de Criminologie, Police Scientifique et Toxicologie,* 1967, 47: 677-679.

2201   Schmidt, Gunter and Sigusch, Volkmar. "Sex Differences in Responses to Psychosexual Stimulation by Films and Slides." *Journal of Sex Research,* 1970, 6, 4: 268-283.

2202   Schneider, Lawrence. "Television in the Lives of Teenagers and Their Parents." Doctoral Dissertation, University of Iowa, 1967.

2203   Schneier, Edward V. "Intellectuals and the New Politics." *Bulletin of the Atomic Scientist,* 1968, 24, 8: 15-18.

2204   Schonbach, Peter. "James Bond: Anreiz Zur Aggression?" [James Bond: Incentive to Aggression?] In F. Merz (ed.), *Bericht Uber Den 25 Kongress Der Deutschen Gesellschaft Fur Psychologie Munster, 1966:* 570-575.

2205   Schramm, W. "Aging and Mass Communication." In M. Riley, et al. (eds.), *Aging and Society: Aging and the Professions* (vol. 1). New York: Russell Sage Foundation, 1969: 352-375.

2206   _____. "Channels and Audiences." In I. Pool, et al. (eds.), *Handbook of Communication.* Chicago: Rand McNally, 1973: 116-140.

2207   _____. "Communication in Crisis." In B. S. Greenberg and E. B. Parker (eds.), *The Kennedy Assassination and the American Public.* Stanford, Calif.: Stanford University Press, 1965: 1-25.

2208   _____. "The Effects of Television on Children and Adolescents." *Reports and Papers on Mass Communication, no. 43.* Paris: UNESCO (New York: UNIPUB), 1964.

2209   _____. "Leisure Roles." In M. W. Riley and A. Foner (eds.), *Aging and Society* (vol. 1). *An Inventory of Research Findings.* New York: Russell Sage Foundation, 1968: 511-535.

2210   _____. *Mass Media and National Development: The Role of Information in the Developing Countries.* Stanford, Calif.: Stanford University Press, 1964.

2211   _____. *Men, Messages, and Media: A Look at Human Communication.* New York: Harper and Row, 1974.

2212   _____. "Motion Pictures and Real-Life Violence: What The Research Says." A Working Paper for the Motion Picture Association of America. Stanford, Calif.: Institute for Communication Research, Stanford University, 1968.

2213   _____, ed. *Quality in Instructional Television.* Honolulu: University of Hawaii Press, 1972.

2214   _____, ed. *The Science of Human Communication: New Directions and New Findings in Communication Research.* New York: Basic Books, 1963.

2215   _____ and Carter, R. F. "The Effectiveness of a Political Telethon." *Public Opinion Quarterly,* 1959, 23, 1: 121-127.

2216   _____ and Roberts, D. F., eds. *The Process and Effects of Mass Communication* (2nd ed.). University of Illinois Press, 1971.

2217   Schramm, W., Lyle, J., and Parker, E. B. "Children's Learning from Television." *Studies in Public Communication,* 1961, 3: 86-98.

2218 _____ . "Patterns in Children's Reading of Newspapers." *Journalism Quarterly,* 1960, 37, 1: 35-40.

2219 _____ . *Television in the Lives of Our Children.* Stanford, Calif.: Stanford University Press, 1967. See volume four of the *Television and Social Behavior* series (E. Rubinstein, G. Comstock, and J. Murray, eds.) for the update.

2220 Schramm, W., Lyle, J., and Pool, I. *The People Look At Educational Television.* Stanford, Calif.: Stanford University Press, 1963.

2221 Schuck, Solomon A., et al. "Sex Differences in Aggressive Behavior Subsequent to Listening to a Radio Broadcast of Violence." *Psychological Reports,* 1971, 28, 3: 931-936.

2222 Schuller, G., Devai, M., and Kadar, J. "A Televizio Hatasa a Gyermekekre" [The Effect of Television on Children]. *Pszichologiai Tanulmanyok,* 1968, 11: 257-268.

2223 Schuman, Howard and Harding, John. "Sympathetic Identification with the Underdog." *Public Opinion Quarterly,* 1963, 27, 2: 230-241.

2224 Schuneman, R. Smith. "Visual Aspects of Television News: Communicator, Message, Equipment." *Journalism Quarterly,* 1966, 43, 2: 281-286.

2225 Schwartz, Alvin. *What do You Think? An Introduction to Public Opinion: How it Forms, Functions, and Affects Our Lives.* New York: E. P. Dutton, 1966.

2226 Schwartz, E. S., Feinglass, S. J., and Drucker, C. "Popular Music and Drug Lyrics: Analysis of a Scapegoat." In National Commission on Marihuana and Drug Abuse, *Drug Use in America: Problem in Perspective: Social Responses to Drug Use* (vol. 2). Washington, D.C.: Government Printing Office, 1973: 718-746.

2227 Schwartz, H. J., Eckert, J., and Bastine, R. "Die Wirkung Eines Aggressiven Films Auf Jugendliche Unter Varlierten Ausseren Bedingungen" [Effects of an Aggressive Film on Adolescents Under Varying External Conditions]. *Zeitschrift fur Entwicklungspsychologie und Padagogische Psychologie,* 1971, 3: 304-315.

2228 Schwartz, R. D. and Skolnick, J. H. "Plan 9. Televised Communication and Income Tax Compliance." In L. Arons and M. A. May (eds.), *Television and Human Behavior: Tomorrow's Research in Mass Communication.* New York: Appleton-Century-Crofts, 1963: 155-165.

2229 Schwartz, Tony. *The Responsive Chord.* Garden City, N.Y.: Anchor Press, 1973.

2230 Schweitzer, H. C., Jr. "Comparison of Color and Black and White Films in the Modification of Attitudes." Doctoral Dissertation, Fordham University, 1963.

2231 Scollon, R. W. "A Study of Some Communicator Variables Related to Attitude Restructuring through Motion Picture Films." Doctoral Dissertation, Pennsylvania State University, 1956.

2232 Scotch, Norman A. "The Vanishing Villains of Television." *Phylon,* 1960, 21, 1: 58-62.

2233 Scott, G. R. *"Into Whose Hands": An Examination of Obscene Libel in its Legal, Sociological and Literary Aspects.* New York: Waron Press, 1961.

2234 Scott, J. P. *The Process of Primary Socialization in Canine and Human Infants.* Lafayette, Indiana: Child Development Publications, 1963.

2235 Scott, L.F. "Relationships Between Selected Characteristics of Children and their Television Viewing." Doctoral Dissertation, University of California, 1955.

2236 _____ . "Social Attitudes of Children Revealed by Responses to Television Programs." *California Journal of Elementary Education,* 1954, 22: 176-179.

2237 _____ . "Television and School Achievement." *Phi Delta Kappa,* 1956, 38: 25-28.

2238 Scott, Joseph E. and Franklin, Jack L. "The Changing Nature of Sex References in Mass Circulation Magazines." *Public Opinion Quarterly,* 1972, 36, 1: 80-86.

2239 _____ . "Sex References in the Mass Media." *Journal of Sex Research,* 1973, 9, 3: 196-209.

2240 Scupham, John. *The Revolution in Communications.* New York: Holt, Rinehart and Winston, 1970.

2241 Seagoe, M. V. "Children's Television Habits and Preferences." *Quarterly of Film, Radio and Television,* 1951, 6: 143-152.

2242 _____ . "Some Current Research in Television for Children." *California Journal of Educational Research,* 1952, 3: 151-153.

2243 Searcy, Ellen and Chapman, Judith. *The Status of Research in Children's Television.* Washington, D.C.: George Washington University, 1972.

2244 Sears, David O. "The Paradox of De Facto Selective Exposure Without Preference for Supportive Information." In R. P. Abelson, et al. (eds.), *Theories of Cognitive Consistency: A Source Book.* Chicago: Rand McNally, 1968: 777-787.

2245 _____ . "Selective Exposure to Information: A Critical Review." *Public Opinion Quarterly,* 1967, 31, 2: 194-213.

2246 Sears, David O. and Whitney, Richard W. "Political Persuasion." In I. Pool, et al. (eds.), *Handbook of Communication.* Chicago, Ill.: Rand McNally, 1973: 253-289.

2247 Sears, R. R. "Relation of Early Socialization Experiences to Aggression in Middle Childhood." *Journal of Abnormal Social Psychology,* 1961, 63, 3: 466-492.

2248 _____ , Maccoby, E. E., and Levin, H. *Patterns of Child Rearing.* New York: Harper and Row, 1957.

2249 Seasonwein, Roger and Sussman, L. R. "Can Extremists Using TV Move An Audience?" *Journalism Quarterly,* 1972, 49, 1: 61-64, 78.

2250 Sebald, Hans. "Limitations of Communication: Mechanisms of Image Maintenance in the Form of Selective Perception, Selective Memory, and Selective Distortion." *Journal of Communication,* 1962, 12, 3: 142-149.

2251   See, Carolyn. *Blue Money: Pornography and the Pornographers—An Intimate Look at the Two-Billion Dollar Fantasy Industry.* New York: McKay, 1974.

2252   Seggar, John F. "Imagery as Reflected Through TV's Cracked Mirror." *Journal of Broadcasting,* 1975, 19, 3: 297-299.

2253   _____ . "Imagery of Women in Television Drama: 1974." *Journal of Broadcasting,* 1975, 19, 3: 283-288.

2254   _____ . "Women's Imagery on TV: Feminist, Fair Maiden, or Maid?" *Journal of Broadcasting,* 1975, 19, 3: 289-294.

2255   _____ and Wheeler, Penny. "World of Work on TV: Ethnic and Sex Representation in TV Drama." *Journal of Broadcasting,* 1973, 17, 2: 201-214. Compares occupational representation on TV with real world statistics.

2256   Sekerak, Robert M. "Mass Communication Media, Reading, Comprehension, and Intelligence." *Audio-Visual Communication Review,* 1957, 5, 2: 468-475.

2257   Servan-Schreiber, Jean L. *The Power to Inform: Media, The Information Business.* New York: McGraw-Hill, 1974. Translated from the French, this volume examines American media from the outside looking in. Functions, effects, successes and failures are compared to other media abroad.

2258   Sethi, S. Prakash. "An Investigation into the Mediating Effects of Socio-Psychological Variables Between Advertising Stimulus and Brand Loyalty." *Dissertation Abstracts,* 1968, 29 (6-B): 2227-2228.

2259   Seymour-Ure, Colin. *The Political Impact of Mass Media.* Beverly Hills: Sage, 1974. Examines media impact on political and media institutions as opposed to the effects on the individual.

2260   Shaffer, Helen B. "Censorship of Movies and TV." *Editorial Research Reports,* 1961, 1: 265-282.

2261   Sharon, Amiel T. "Racial Differences in Newspaper Readership." *Public Opinion Quarterly,* 1973, 37, 4: 611-617.

2262   Shaw, Colin. "Television and Popular Morality: The Predicament of the Broadcasters." *Sociological Review: Monograph No. 13,* 1969: 117-128.

2263   Shaw, Eugene F. "Media Credibility: Taking the Measure of a Measure." *Journalism Quarterly,* 1973, 50, 2: 306-311.

2264   Shayon, R. L. *Television and Our Children.* New York: Longmans, Green, 1951.

2265   Sheikh, Anees A., Prasad, V. K., and Rao, T. R. "Children's TV Commercials: A Review of Research." *Journal of Communication,* 1974, 24, 4: 126-136.

2266   Sheinkopf, K. G. "Family Communication Patterns and Anticipatory Socialization." *Journalism Quarterly,* 1973, 50, 1: 24-30, 133.

2267   Sheinkopf, K. G., Atkin, C. K., and Bowen, L. "The Functions of Political Advertising for Campaign Organizations." *Journal of Marketing Research,* 1972, 9: 401-405.

2268 _____ . "How Political Party Workers Respond to Political Advertising." *Journalism Quarterly,* 1973, 50, 2: 334-339.

2269 Shelby, M. "Children's Programming Trends on Network Television." *Journal of Broadcasting,* 1964, 8, 3: 247-256.

2270 _____ . "The Possible Influence of Criticism on Network Radio Programming for Children." *Journal of Broadcasting,* 1970, 14: 215-227.

2271 Shepherd, John R. and Scheidel, T. M. "Differences in Demand and Use of TV Programming Variety." *Journal of Broadcasting,* 1962, 6, 2: 143-147.

2272 Sherburne, E. G. "Science on Television: A Challenge to Creativity." *Journalism Quarterly,* 1963, 60, 3: 300-305.

2273 Sherrington, Richard. *Television and Language Skills.* London: Oxford University Press, 1973. Covers technological considerations, theories and methods of language teaching, language skills, and TV and listening, speaking, reading, and writing skills.

2274 Sherrod, Drury R. "Selective Perception of Political Candidates." *Public Opinion Quarterly,* 1971, 35, 4: 554-562.

2275 Shinar, Dov. "Structure & Content of Television Broadcasting in Israel." In G. A. Comstock and E. A. Rubinstein (eds.), *Television and Social Behavior: Media Content and Control* (vol. 1). Washington, D.C.: Government Printing Office, 1972: 493-532.

2276 Shipley, Linda J. "Communication Behavior of Persons Living in a Megalopolis: A Study of Mass Media Use and Interpersonal Communications of Commuters and Local Workers." Doctoral Dissertation, University of Pennsylvania, 1974.

2277 Shirley, K. W. "The Prosocial Effects of Publicly Broadcast Children's Television." Boys Town Center, Stanford, Calif.: Stanford University, 1974.

2278 _____ . "Television and Children: A Modeling Analysis Review Essay." Doctoral Dissertation, University of Kansas, 1973.

2279 Shosteck, Herschel. "Factors Influencing Appeal of TV News Personalities." *Journal of Broadcasting,* 1974, 18, 1: 63-72.

2280 _____ . "Some Influences of Television on Civil Unrest." *Journal of Broadcasting,* 1969, 13, 4: 371-385.

2281 Shuey, Audrey. "Stereotyping of Negroes and Whites: An Analysis of Magazine Pictures." *Public Opinion Quarterly,* 1953, 17, 2: 281-287.

2282 Sicher, F. "An Evaluation of Lindsley's New Measure of TV Viewing Behavior." *Journal of Advertising Research,* 1963, 3, 1: 44-47.

2283 Siebert, J. C., et al. *The Influence of Television on the Election of 1952.* Oxford: Oxford Research Associates, 1954.

2284 Siegel, A. E. "Alternatives to Direct Censorship." In V. B. Cline (ed.), *Where Do You Draw the Line?* Provo, Utah: Brigham Young University Press, 1974: 289-291.

2285 _____ . "Communicating With the Next Generation: Effects of Television on Children and Adolescents." *Journal of Communication,* 1975, 25, 4: 14-24.

2286 _____ . "The Effect of Film-Mediated Fantasy Aggression on Strength of Aggressive Drive in Young Children." Doctoral Dissertation, Stanford University, 1955.

2287 _____ . "The Effects of Media Violence on Social Learning." In R. K. Baker and S. J. Ball (eds.), *Violence and the Media.* A Staff Report to the National Commission on the Causes and Prevention of Violence. Washington, D.C.: Government Printing Office, 1969: 261-283.

2288 _____ . "Film-Mediated Fantasy Aggression and Strength of Aggressive Drive." *Child Development,* 1956, 27, 3: 365-378.

2289 _____ . "The Great Brain Robbery." *Johns Hopkins Magazine,* 1974, 25: 19-23.

2290 _____ . "The Influence of Violence in the Mass Media Upon Children's Role Expectations." *Child Development,* 1958, 29, 1: 35-56.

2291 _____ . "Violence in the Mass Media." In D. N. Daniels, M. F. Gilula, and F. M. Ochberg (eds.), *Violence and the Struggle for Existence.* Boston: Little, Brown, 1970: 193-239.

2292 Siepmann, Charles. "Moral Aspects of Television." *Public Opinion Quarterly,* 1960, 24, 1: 12-18.

2293 Siepmann, Charles A. *Radio, Television and Society.* New York: Oxford University Press, 1950.

2294 Sigel, Roberta S. "Effect of Partisanship on the Perception of Political Candidates." *Public Opinion Quarterly,* 1964, 28, 3: 483-496.

2295 _____ . "Political Socialization: Its Role in the Political Process." *Annals of the American Academy of Political and Social Science,* 1965, 361, September.

2296 _____ . "Television and the Reactions of School Children to the Assassination." In B. S. Greenberg and E. B. Parker (eds.), *The Kennedy Assassination and the American Public.* Stanford, Calif.: Stanford University Press, 1965: 199-219.

2297 Silverman, L. T. "The Effects of *Sesame Street* Programming on Cooperation Between Preschool Children." Doctoral Dissertation, Institute for Communication Research, Stanford University, 1975.

2298 Silverman, R. E. "Short-Term Effects of Television Viewing on Aggressive and Psychophysiological Behavior of Adults and Children." Doctoral Dissertation, State University of New York at Buffalo, 1972.

2299 Silvey, Robert. "Methods of Viewer Research Employed by the British Broadcasting Corporation." *Public Opinion Quarterly,* 1951, 15, 1: 89-104.

2300 _____ . "Television Viewing in Britain." *Public Opinion Quarterly,* 1950, 14, 1: 148-150.

2301 _____ . *Who's Listening?: The Story of BBC Audience Research.* London: Allen and Unwin, 1974.

2302 Simmons, Robert E., Kent, Kurt, and Mishra, Vishwa M. "Media and Developmental News in Slums of Ecuador and India." *Journalism Quarterly,* 1968, 45: 698-705.

2303   Simmons, W. R. "Violence on Television." *Media/Scope,* 1969, 12: 36-78.

2304   Simon, H. A. and Stern, F. "The Effect of Television Upon Voting Behavior in Iowa in the 1952 Presidential Election." *American Political Science Review,* 1955, 49, 2: 470-477.

2305   Simon, Rita James and Eimermann, Thomas. "The Jury Finds Not Guilty: Another Look at Media Influence on the Jury." *Journalism Quarterly,* 1971, 48, 2: 343-344.

2306   Simons, C. W. and Pilavin, J. A. "Effect of Deception on Reactions to a Victim." *Journal of Personality and Social Psychology,* 1972, 21: 56-60.

2307   Simonson, H. M. "The Relationship of Television Program Content and Socioeconomic Status to Aggressive Behavior." Doctoral Dissertation, Columbia University, 1972.

2308   Simpkins, John D. and Smith, Jack A. "Effects of Music on Source Evaluation." *Journal of Broadcasting,* 1974, 18, 3: 361-367.

2309   Singer, Aubrey. "Television: Window on Culture or Reflection in the Glass." *American Scholar,* 1966, 35, 2: 303-309.

2310   Singer, Benjamin D. "Mass Media and Communication Processes in the Detroit Riot of 1967." *Public Opinion Quarterly,* 1970, 34, 2: 236-245.

2311   _____ . "Mass Society, Mass Media and the Transformation of Minority Identity." *British Journal of Sociology,* 1973, 24, 2: 140-150.

2312   _____ . "Television and the Riots." Department of Sociology, University of Western Ontario, London, Ontario, 1968.

2313   _____ . "Violence, Protest and War in Television News: The U.S. and Canada Compared." *Public Opinion Quarterly,* 1970, 34, 4: 611-616.

2314   _____ ·, Osborn, Richard W., and Geschwender, James A., *Black Rioters: A Study of Social Factors and Communication in the Detroit Riot.* Lexington, Mass.: Heath, 1970.

2315   Singer, D. L. "Aggression Arousal, Hostile Humor, Catharsis." *Journal of Personality and Social Psychology,* 1968, Monograph Suppl., 8, 1: 1-16.

2316   _____ , Gollob, H. F., and Levine, J. "Mobilization of Inhibitions and the Enjoyment of Aggressive Humor." *Journal of Personality,* 1967, 35, 4: 562-569.

2317   Singer, Jerome L. *The Child's World of Make-Believe.* New York: Academic Press, 1973. A review and original theoretical integration of the significance and the psychopathological and practical implications of childhood fantasy. The role of the media in fantasy behavior is discussed.

2318   _____ , ed. *The Control of Aggression and Violence: Cognitive and Physiological Factors.* New York: Academic Press, 1971. Good background material for understanding the physiological and inhibition aspects of aggressive behavior.

2319   _____ . "The Influence of Violence Portrayed in Television or Motion Pictures Upon Overt Aggressive Behavior." In J. L. Singer (ed.), *The Control of*

Aggression and Violence: Cognitive and Physiological Factors. New York: Academic Press, 1971: 19-60.

2320   Skornia, Harry. *Television and Society: An Inquest and Agenda for Improvement.* New York: McGraw-Hill, 1965.

2321   Slater, John w. and McCombs, Maxwell E. "Some Aspects of Broadcast News Coverage and Riot Participation." *Journal of Broadcasting,* 1969, 13, 4: 367-370.

2322   Small, William J. *Political Power and the Press.* New York: W. W. Norton, 1972.

2323   Smart, Reginald B. and Krakowski, Mark. "The Nature and Frequency of Drug Content in Magazines and on Television." *Journal of Alcohol and Educat'on,* 1973, 18, 3: 16-23.

2324   Smith, B. L. and Smith, C. M. *International Communication and Political Opinion: A Guide to the Literature.* Princeton, N.J.: Princeton University Press, 1956.

2325   Smith, David M. "Mass Media as a Basis for Interaction: An Empirical Study." *Journalism Quarterly,* 1975, 52: 44-49, 105.

2326   _____ . "Some Uses of Mass Media by 14-Year-Olds." *Journal of Broadcasting,* 1971-1972, 16, 1: 37-50. Investigates the extent to which mass media are used for (1) interaction with peers, (2) withdrawal from interaction, (3) problem avoidance, and (4) boredom.

2327   Smith, Don C. "Books on Broadcasting in the Library of Congress: Programming and Audience Research." *Journal of Broadcasting,* 1966, 10: 83-92.

2328   _____ . "Music Programming of Thirteen Los Angeles AM Radio Stations." *Journal of Broadcasting,* 1964, 8, 2: 173-184.

2329   _____ . "The Selectors of Television Programs." *Journal of Broadcasting,* 1961-1962, 6: 35-44.

2330   Smith, Don D. "The U.S. Audience for International Broadcasts." *Journalism Quarterly,* 1970, 47, 2: 364-366.

2331   Smith, F. A., et al. "Health Information Druing a Week of Television." *New England Journal of Medicine,* 1972, 286: 516-520.

2332   Smith, James R. "Television Violence and Driving Behavior." *Educational Broadcasting Review,* 1969, 3, 4: 23-28.

2333   _____ and McEwen, William J. "Effects of Newscast Delivery Rate on Recall and Judgement of Sources." *Journal of Broadcasting,* 1974, 18, 1: 73-78.

2334   Smith, M. Dwayne and Matre, Marc. "Social Norms and Sex Roles in Romance and Adventure Magazines." *Journalism Quarterly,* 1975, 52: 309-315.

2335   Smith, R. G. "Issues and Images." In S. Kraus (ed.), *The Great Debates.* Bloomington: Indiana University Press, 1962: 289-312.

2336   Smith, Roger H., ed. *The American Reading Public: What it Reads, Why it Reads.* New York: R. R. Bowker, 1964.

2337 Smith, Terry and Levin, Jack. "Social Change in Sex Roles: An Analysis of Advice Columns." *Journalism Quarterly,* 1974, 51, 3: 525-527.

2338 Smythe, D. "Mass Communications and Cultural Revolution: The Experience of China." In G. Gerbner, L. Gross and W. Melody (eds.), *Communications Technology and Social Policy: Understanding the New "Cultural Revolution."* New York: Wiley, 1973: 441-466.

2339 _____. "Reality as Presented by Television." *Public Opinion Quarterly,* 1954, 18, 2: 143-156. Synthesizes early content analyses to reveal trends. Demonstrates extent of stereotyping but emphasizes the viewer's perceptions as more important than straight content in assessment of television "reality."

2340 Snare, Austin, Bednall, David H. B., and Sullivan, Lyndall M. "Relationship Between Liking and Watching TV Programs." *Journalism Quarterly,* 1972, 49, 4: 750-753.

2341 Snow, Robert P. "How Children Interpret TV Violence in Play Context." *Journalism Quarterly,* 1974, 51, 1: 13-21.

2342 Soderlund, Walter C. and Wagenberg, Ronald H. "A Content Analysis of Editorial Coverage of the 1972 Electoral Campaigns in Canada and the United States." *The Western Political Quarterly,* 1975, 28: 85-107.

2343 Solis Quiroga, Héctor. "Influencia de la Televisión en la Conducta Infantil y del Adolescente" [The Influence of Television on Child and Adolescent Behavior]. *Revista Interamericana de Sociología,* 1967, 1, 4, April-June: 41-58.

2344 Sonenschein, D., et al. "A Study of Mass Media Erotica: The Romance or Confession Magazine." In *Technical Report of The Commission on Obscenity and Pornography: The Consumer and the Community* (vol. 9). Washington, D.C.: Government Printing Office, 1972: 99-164.

2345 Sparks, Kenneth R. *A Bibliography of Doctoral Dissertations in Television and Radio.* Syracuse University School of Journalism, 1971.

2346 Spitzer, Stephen P. "Mass Media vs. Personal Sources of Information About the Presidential Assassination: A Comparison of Six Investigations." *Journal of Broadcasting,* 1964-1965, 9, 1: 45-50.

2347 Spradley, James P., ed. *Culture and Cognition: Rules, Maps, and Plans.* San Francisco: Chandler, 1972.

2348 Sprafkin, Joyce N., Liebert, Robert M., and Poulos, Rita W. "Effects of a Prosocial Televised Example on Children's Helping." *Journal of Experimental Child Psychology,* 1975, 20: 119-126. Watching television helping scene increased children's willingness to help.

2349 Stamm, K. R. "Environment and Communication." In F. G. Kline and P. J. Tichenor (eds.), *Current Perspectives in Mass Communication Research.* Beverly Hills: Sage, 1972: 265-294.

2350 Stanton, Frank. *Mass Media and Mass Culture.* New York: Columbia Broadcasting System, 1962.

2351 Starck, Kenneth. "Media Credibility in Finland: A Cross-National Approach." *Journalism Quarterly,* 1969, 46, 4: 790-795.

2352 Staub, E. "Effects of Persuasion and Modeling on Delay of Gratification." *Developmental Psychology,* 1972, 6: 166-177.

2353 Steilen, Charles F. "The Impact of Environmental Change on Consumer Behavior." *Dissertation Abstracts International,* 1971, 32 (1-A): 27.

2354 Stein, A. H. "Imitation of Resistance to Temptation." *Child Development,* 1967, 38: 157-169.

2355 _____. "Mass Media and Young Children's Development." In I. J. Gordon (ed.), *Early Childhood Education II.* Chicago: The University of Chicago Press, 1972.

2356 _____ and Bailey, M. M. "The Socialization of Achievement Orientation in Females." *Psychological Bulletin,* 1973, 80, 5: 345-366.

2357 Stein, A. H., and Friedrich, L. K. "Television Content and Young Children's Behavior." In J. P. Murray, E. A. Rubinstein, and G. A. Comstock (eds.), *Television and Social Behavior: Television and Social Learning* (vol. 2). Washington, D.C.: Government Printing Office, 1972: 202-317.

2358 Stein, G. M. and Bryan, J. H. "The Effect of a Television Model Upon Rule Adoption Behavior of Children" *Child Development,* 1972, 43: 268-273. Relates cheating and ability to correctly verbalize the rules of a game to the observation of a peer model doing the same.

2359 Stein, Robert. *Media Power: Who is Shaping Your Picture of the World?* Boston: Houghton Mifflin, 1972. An experienced journalist discusses the picture of the world we all carry in our heads, who put it there, why, how, and under what circumstances. Considers advertising, McLuhan and Agnew, the public's right to know, the role of news, and freedom of expression.

2360 Steiner, Gary A. "The American Mass Media Audience." In B. Berelson and M. Janowitz (eds.), *Reader in Public Opinion and Communication* (2nd ed.). New York: Free Press, 1966: 331-338.

2361 _____. "The People Look at Commercials: A Study of Audience Behavior." *Journal of Business,* 1966, 9: 272-304.

2362 _____. *The People Look at Television: A Study of Audience Attitudes.* New York: Knopf, 1963. See R. T. Bower, 1973, for the 10 year update.

2363 Steinfeld, Jesse L. "Statement of the Surgeon General Concerning Television Violence." Statement before the Subcommittee on Communications of the Committee on Commerce, U.S. Senate. Washington, D.C.: Government Printing Office, 1972. Reprinted in V. B. Cline (ed.), *Where Do You Draw the Line?: An Exploration into Media Violence, Pornography, and Censorship.* Provo, Utah: Brigham Young University, 1974: 177-178.

2364 Steinmann, M. F. *Massenmedien und Werbung* [Mass Media and Advertising]. Freiburg im Breisgau: Verlag Rombach, 1971.

2365 Stempel, Guido H. "Comic Strip Reading: The Effect of Continuity." *Journalism Quarterly,* 1956, 33, 3: 366-367.

2366 _____. "Visibility of Blacks in News and News-Picture Magazines." *Journalism Quarterly,* 1971, 48, 2: 337-339.

2367 _____ . "Selectivity in Readership of Political News." *Public Opinion Quarterly,* 1961, 25, 3: 400-404.

2368 Stemple, Diane and Tyler, Jane E. "Sexism in Advertising." *American Journal of Psychoanalysis,* 1974, 34, 3: 271-273.

2369 Stephens, Lowndes F. "Media Exposure and Modernization Among the Appalachian Poor." *Journalism Quarterly,* 1972, 49, 2: 247-257, 262.

2370 Stephenson, William. "The 'Infantile' vs. the 'Sublime' in Advertisements." *Journalism Quarterly,* 1963, 40, 2: 181-186.

2371 _____ . *The Play Theory of Mass Communication.* Chicago, Ill.: University of Chicago Press, 1967.

2372 Sterba, Richard F. "Some Psychological Factors in Pictorial Advertising." *Public Opinion Quarterly,* 1950, 14, 3: 475-483.

2373 Sterling, Christopher H., ed. *Broadcasting and Mass Media: A Survey Bibliography* (5th ed.). Philadelphia: Temple University, 1974.

2374 _____ . "Mass Communication Texts and Readers: An Overview for 1974/75." *Mass Comm Review,* 1974, 2, 1: 24-40.

2375 _____ . "Mass Media Books: Quantity/Quality; Trends/Needs." *Mass Comm Review,* 1973, 1, 1: 9-17.

2376 _____ . *The Media Sourcebook: Comparative Reviews and Listings of Textbooks in Mass Communication.* Washington, D.C.: National Association of Educational Broadcasters, 1974.

2377 Stern, S. L. "Television and Creativity: The Effect of Viewing Certain Categories of Commercial Television Broadcasting on the Divergent Thinking Abilities of Intellectually Gifted Elementary Students." Doctoral Dissertation, University of Southern California, 1973.

2378 Sternglanz, Sarah H. and Serbin, Lisa A. "Sex-Role Stereotyping in Children's Television Programs." *Developmental Psychology,* 1974, 10, 5: 710-715.

2379 Steuer, F. B., Applefield, J. M., and Smith, R. "Televised Aggression and the Interpersonal Aggression of Preschool Children." *Journal of Experimental Child Psychology,* 1971, 11: 442-447.

2380 Stevenson, Harold W. "Television and the Behavior of Pre-School Children." In J. P. Murray, E. A. Rubinstein, and G. A. Comstock (eds.), *Television and Social Behavior: Television and Social Learning* (vol. 2). Washington, D.C.: Government Printing Office, 1972: 346-371.

2381 Stewart, Janice S. "Content and Readership of Teen Magazines." *Journalism Quarterly,* 1964, 41: 580-583.

2382 Stimson, Gerry V. "The Message of Psychotropic Drug Ads." *Journal of Communication,* 1975, 25, 3: 153-160.

2383 Stoessel, R. E. "The Effects of Televised Aggressive Cartoons on Children's Behavior." Doctoral Dissertation, St. John's University, 1972.

2384 Stoll, Clarice S. *Female and Male: Socialization, Social Roles, and Social Structure.* Dubuque, Iowa: Wm. C. Brown, 1974.

2385 Stone, Vernon A. "Attitudes Toward Television Newswomen." *Journal of Broadcasting,* 1974, 18, 1: 49-62.

2386 _____ . "Individual Differences and Innoculation Against Persuasion." *Journalism Quarterly,* 1969, 46, 2: 267-273.

2387 _____ and Chaffee, Steven H. "Family Communication Patterns and Source-Message Orientation." *Journalism Quarterly,* 1970, 47, 2: 239-246.

2388 Strainchamps, Ethel, ed. *Rooms With No View: A Woman's Guide to Man's World of the Media.* New York: Harper & Row, 1974.

2389 Streicher, Helen W. "The Girls in the Cartoons." *Journal of Communication,* 1974, 24, 2: 125-129.

2390 Streicher, Lawrence H. and Bonney, Norman L. "Children Talk About Television." *Journal of Communication,* 1974, 24, 3: 54-61. Six to twelve-year-olds specify types of preferred programs, which are most realistic, and who controls program selection.

2391 Stricker, George. "The Operation of Cognitive Dissonance on Pre- and Post-Election Attitudes." *Journal of Social Psychology,* 1964, 63, 1: 111-119.

2392 Strong, E. C. "The Effects of Repetition in Advertising: A Field Experiment." Doctoral Dissertation, Stanford University, 1972.

2393 Strouse, James C. *The Mass Media, Public Opinion, and Public Policy Analysis.* Columbus, Ohio: Charles Merrill, 1975.

2394 Stumphauzer, Jerome S. and Bishop, Barbara R. "Saturday Morning Television Cartoons: A Simple Apparatus for the Reinforcement of Behavior in Children." *Developmental Psychology,* 1969, 1, 6: 763-764.

2395 Sturm, H., Haebler, R., and Helmreich, R. "Medienspezifische Lerneffekte" [Media-Specific Learning Effects]. Munchen: TR-Verlagsunion, Buchdruckerei Josef Bosch, Landshut, 1972.

2396 Suchy, John T. "British Television and Its Viewers." *Journalism Quarterly,* 1954, 31, 4: 466-472.

2397 _____ . "How Does Commercial Television Affect British Viewing?" *Journalism Quarterly,* 1958, 35, 1: 65-71.

2398 Sulzer, Elmer and Johnson, George. "Attitudes Toward Deception in Television." *Journal of Broadcasting,* 1960, 4, 2: 97-109.

2399 Summers, Harrison B. "Qualitative Information Concerning Audiences of Network Television Programs." *Journal of Broadcasting,* 1961, 5, 2: 147-160.

2400 Summers, R. E. and Summers, H. B., *Broadcasting and the Public.* Belmont, Calif.: Wadsworth Publishing Co., 1966.

2401 Sunderlin, S., ed. *Children and TV.* Washington, D.C.: Association for Childhood Education International, 1967.

2402 Surlin, Stuart H. "Black-Oriented Radio: Programming to a Perceived Audience." *Journal of Broadcasting,* 1972, 16, 3: 289-298.

2403 _____ . "Black-Oriented Radio's Service to the Community." *Journalism Quarterly,* 1973, 50: 556-560.

2404 _____ and Dominick, Joseph R. "Television's Function as a 'Third Parent' for Black and White Teenagers." *Journal of Broadcasting,* 1971, 15, 1: 55-64. Notes that blacks and low-income teens tend to prefer programs featuring a family group.

2405 Surlin, Stuart and Kosak, H. H. "The Effect of Graphic Design in Advertising on Reader Ratings." *Journalism Quarterly,* 1975, 52: 685-691.

2406 Survey Research Center. *The Public Impact of Science in The Mass Media. A Report on a Nationwide Survey for the National Association of Science Writers.* Ann Arbor: Institute for Social Research, University of Michigan, 1958.

2407 Swanson, Charles and Jones, Robert. "Television Owning and Its Correlates." *Journal of Applied Psychology,* 1951, 35, 5: 352-357.

2408 Sweetser, Frank L., Jr. "Home Television and Behavior: Some Tentative Conclusions." *Public Opinion Quarterly,* 1955, 19, 1: 79-84.

2409 Swinehart, James W. and McLeod, Jack. "News About Science: Channels Audiences and Effects." *Public Opinion Quarterly,* 1960, 24, 4: 583-589.

T

2410 Tadros, S. S. "An Investigation of the Impact of Television Upon the Maturing Process of the Adult." Doctoral Dissertation, Indiana University, 1960.

2411 Taggart, K. "Symposium: Moral and Spiritual Values in TV." In *This is Television,* Report of Provincial Conference, Regina, Saskatchewan, Canada, April 27-28, 1956: 56.

2412 Takeshima, Y. "Children and Television: Main Findings from Shizuoka Survey, 1967." Tokyo: Japan Broadcasting Corporation, Radio and Television Culture Research Institute, 1971.

2413 Tankard, James W. "Eye Contact Research and Television Announcing." *Journal of Broadcasting,* 1971, 15, 1: 83-90.

2414 Tannenbaum, Percy H. "The Effect of Headlines on the Interpretation of News Stories." *Journalism Quarterly,* 1953, 30, 2: 189-197.

2415 _____ . "Effect of Serial Position on Recall of Radio News Stories." *Journalism Quarterly,* 1954, 31, 3: 319-323.

2416 _____ . "Emotional Arousal as a Mediator of Communication Effects." In *Technical Report of The Commission on Obscenity and Pornography: Erotica and Social Behavior* (vol. 8). Washington, D.C.: Government Printing Office, 1971: 326-356.

2417 _____ . "Music Background in the Judgement of Stage and Television Drama." *Audio-Visual Communication Review,* 1956, 4, 2: 92-101.

2418 _____ . "Public Communication of Science Information." *Science,* 1963, 140, May: 579-583.

2419 _____ . "Studies in Film and Television Mediated Arousal and Aggression: A Progress Report." In G. A. Comstock, E. A. Rubinstein, and J. P. Murray (eds.), *Television and Social Behavior: Television's Effects: Further Explorations* (vol. 5). Washington, D.C.: Government Printing Office, 1972: 309-350.

2420 _____ . "What Effect When TV Covers A Congressional Hearing?" *Journalism Quarterly,* 1955, 32, 4: 434-440.

2421 _____ and Gaer, E. P. "Mood Change as a Function of Stress of Protagonist and Degree of Identification in a Film Viewing Situation." *Journal of Personality and Social Psychology,* 1965, 2: 612-616.

2422 Tannenbaum, Percy H. and Greenberg, B. S. "Mass Communication." *Annual Review of Psychology,* 1968, 19: 351-386.

2423 Tannenbaum, Percy H. and Kerrick, Jean. "Effect of Newscast Item Leads Upon Listener Interpretation." *Journalism Quarterly,* 1954, 31: 33-37.

2424 Tannenbaum, Percy H. and Lynch, M. "Sensationalism: The Concept and its Measurement." *Journalism Quarterly,* 1960, 37, 3: 381-392.

2425 _____ . "Sensationalism: Some Objective Message Correlates." *Journalism Quarterly,* 1962, 39, 3: 317-323.

2426 Tannenbaum, Percy H. and McLeod, Jack. "On the Measurement of Socialization." *Public Opinion Quarterly,* 1967, 31, 1: 27-37.

2427 Tannenbaum, Percy H. and Zillmann, D. "Emotional Arousal in the Facilitation of Aggression Through Communication." In L. Berkowitz (ed.), *Advances in Experimental Social Psychology* (vol. 8). New York: Academic Press, 1975: 149-152. Reviews the evidence relating general arousal level to aggressive response, regardless of stimulus content.

2428 Tannenbaum, Percy H., Greenberg, B. S., and Silverman, F. "Candidate Images." In S. Kraus (ed.), *The Great Debates.* Bloomington: Indiana University Press, 1962: 271-288.

2429 Taylor, Charles Lewis. "Communications Development and Political Stability." *Comparative Political Studies,* 1969, 1, 4: 557-564.

2430 Taylor, Wilson L. "Gauging the Mental Health Content of the Mass Media." *Journalism Quarterly,* 1957, 34, 2: 191-201.

2431 Tedesco, Nancy S. "Patterns of Prime Time." *Journal of Communication,* 1974, 24, 2: 119-124.

2432 Television Advertising Representatives, Inc. *Psy-color-gy: A Study of the Impact of Color Television.* New York: Television Advertising Representatives, Inc., 1966.

2433 Television Bureau of Advertising, Inc. *How to Research People: Report on Audience Composition.* New York: Television Bureau of Advertising, 1959.

2434 Television Information Office. *Television and Education: Bibliography.* New York: Television Information Office, 1972.

2435 _____ . "Television in Government and Politics: A Bibliography." New York: Television Information Office, 1964.

2436   Television Research Committee. *Second Progress Report and Recommendations.* Leicester, England: Leicester University Press, 1969.

2437   _____ . *Problems of Television Research: A Progress Report.* Leicester, England: Leicester University Press, 1966.

2438   Thayer, John R. "The Relationship of Various Audience Composition Factors to Television Program Types." *Journal of Broadcasting,* 1963, 7, 3: 217-225.

2439   Thayer, L. *Communication: Ethical and Moral Issues.* New York: Gordon and Breach, 1973.

2440   _____ . *Communication and Communication Systems.* Homewood, Ill.: Irwin, 1968.

2441   Thelen, M. H. and Soltz, W. "The Effect of Vicarious Reinforcement on Imitation in Two Social-Racial Groups." *Child Development,* 1969, 40: 879-887.

2442   Thelen, M. H., McGuire, D., Simmonds, D. W., and Akamatsu, T. J. "Effect of Model-Reward on the Observer's Recall of the Modeled Behavior." *Journal of Personality and Social Psychology,* 1974, 29: 140-144. Observation of a rewarded model increased imitation and recall.

2443   Thomas, D. L., et al. *Family Socialization and the Adolescent: Determinants of Self-Concept, Conformity, Religiosity and Countercultural Values.* Lexington, Mass.: Lexington Books, 1974.

2444   Thomas, Margaret H. and Drabman, Ronald S. "Toleration of Real Life Aggression as a Function of Exposure to Televised Violence and Age of Subject." *Merrill-Palmer Quarterly,* 1975, 21, 2: 227-232.

2445   Thomas, Sally A. "The Role of Cognitive Style Variables in Mediating the Influence of Aggressive Television Upon Elementary School Children." Los Angeles: Early Childhood Research Center, University of California, 1972.

2446   _____ . "Violent Content in Television: The Effect of Cognitive Style and Age in Mediating Children's Aggressive Responses." *Proceedings of the Annual Convention of the American Psychological Association,* 1972, 7: 97-98. Of children in the same age group, those who were more cognitively complex were less likely to react aggressively following an aggressive stimulus.

2447   Thompson, Charles A. H. *Television and Presidential Politics.* Washington, D.C.: The Brookings Institution, 1956.

2448   Thomson, R. J., ed. "Television Crime Drama: A Report." Sydney: Australian Broadcasting Control Board, 1972.

2449   _____ . *Television-Crime-Drama: Its Impact on Children and Adolescents.* Melbourne, Australia: F. W. Cheshire, 1959.

2450   Thornberry, T. P. and Silverman, R. A. "Exposure to Pornography and Juvenile Delinquency. The Relationship as Indicated by Juvenile Court Records." In *Technical Report of the Commission on Obscenity and Pornography; Preliminary Studies* (vol. 1). Washington, D.C.: Government Printing Office, 1971: 175-180.

2451   Thorne, Frederick, C. "Television Talk Shows and Actualization Neuroses." *Journal of Community Psychology,* 1975, 3, 2: 165-174.

2452   Tichenor, Phillip J., Donohue, George A., and Olien, Clarice N. "Mass Communication Research: Evolution of a Structural Model." *Journalism Quarterly,* 1973, 50, 3: 419-425.

2453   _____ . "Mass Media Flow Differential Growth in Knowledge." *Public Opinion Quarterly,* 1970, 34, 2: 159-170.

2454   Tichenor, Phillip J., Rodenkirchen, J. M., Olien, C. N., and Donohue, G. A. "Community Issues, Conflict, and Public Affairs Knowledge." In P. Clarke (ed.), *New Models for Mass Communication Research.* Beverly Hills: Sage, 1973: 45-80.

2455   Tiemens, Robert K. "Some Relationships of Camera Angle to Communicator Credibility." *Journal of Broadcasting,* 1970, 14, 4: 483-490.

2456   Tipton, L. P., Haney, R. D., and Basehart, J. R. "Media Agenda-Setting in City and State Campaigns." *Journalism Quarterly,* 1975, 52, 1: 15-22.

2457   Toch, Hans H. and MacLean, Malcolm S. "Perception, Communication and Educational Research: A Transactional View." *Audio-Visual Communication Review,* 1962, 10, 5: 55-77.

2458   Toch, Hans H. and Schulte, W. H. "Readiness to Perceive Violence as a Result of Police Training." *British Journal of Psychology,* 1961, 52: 389-393. Recruits were more likely to see violence in a stimulus following their police training than before.

2459   Toch, Hans H., Allen, Terrence M., and Lazer, William. "Effects of the Cancer Scares: The Residue of News Impact." *Journalism Quarterly,* 1961, 38, 1: 25-34.

2460   Tolley, H., Jr. *Children and War: Political Socialization to International Conflict.* New York: Teachers College Press, Columbia University, 1973. Television was the dominant source of information about the Vietnam War for children 7-15 years old but parental attitudes toward the war were instrumental in determining the child's attitude.

2461   Toomey, Timothy C. "Alteration of a Perceptual Mode Correlate Through a Televised Model." *Journal of Experimental Research in Personality,* 1972, 6: 52-59.

2462   _____ . "The Effect of a Televised Model in Altering a Behavioral Correlate of Field Dependence and Field Independence." *Dissertation Abstracts International,* 1972, 32 (7-B): 4231-4232.

2463   Topping, Malachi C. "The Cultural Orientation of Certain "Western" Characters on Television; A Content Analysis." *Journal of Broadcasting,* 1965, 9, 4: 291-304.

2464   Torney, J. V. "The Influence of Current Affairs Broadcasting Upon Pupil Attitudes Toward Politics." In *Television and World Affairs Teaching in Schools.* London: Atlantic Educational Publications, 1972: 12-18.

2465 Towers, I. M. Goodman, L. A., and Zeisel, H. "A Method of Measuring the Effects of Television Through Controlled Field Experiments." *Studies in Public Communication,* 1962, 4: 87-110.

2466 Trager, R. E. "Adolescent Audience System Reactions to Mass Media Messages Regarding Drug Education." Doctoral Dissertation, University of Minnesota, 1972.

2467 Treacy, David P. "The Effects of Mass Communication: A Survey and Critique." *Dissertation Abstracts,* 1967, 27 (7-A): 2128.

2468 Trenaman, J. *Communication and Comprehension.* London: Longmans, Green & Co., 1967.

2469 _____ and McQuail, D. *Television and the Political Image: A Study of the Impact of Television on the 1969 General Election. London: Methuen & Co., 1961.*

2470 Tripi, Gabriele. "Considerazioni sull' Importanza dei Fattori Ambientali nella Profilassi dell' Aggressivita: I Films di Violenza nel Determinismo dell' Aggressivita" [Considerations on the Importance of Environmental Factors in the Profile Analysis of Aggressiveness: I. Films of Violence in Determination of Aggressiveness]. *Archivio de Psicologia, neurologia e Psichiatria,* 1968, 29, 5-6: 557-561.

2471 Troldahl, Verling C. "A Field Test of a Modified 'Two-Step Flow of Communication' Model." *Public Opinion Quarterly,* 1966, 30, 4: 609-623.

2472 _____ . "Studies of Consumption of Mass Media Content." *Journalism Quarterly,* 1965, 42, 4: 596-603.

2473 _____ , Robeck, George B., and Costello, Daniel E. *Bibliography of Mass Communication Research.* Dept. of Communication, Michigan State University, April 1965.

2474 Tsai, Micheal Kuan. "Some Effects of American Television Programs on Children in Formosa." *Journal of Broadcasting,* 1970, 14, 2: 229-238.

2475 Tuchman, Sam and Coffin, Thomas E. "The Influence of Election Night Television Broadcasts in a Close Election." *Public Opinion Quarterly,* 1971, 35, 3: 315-326. Indicates that election night exposure has no effect on voting.

2476 Tumin, Melvin M. "Exposure to Mass Media and Readiness for Desegregation." *Public Opinion Quarterly,* 1957, 21, 2: 237-251.

2477 Tunstall, J., ed. *Mass Communicators and Audience: A Reader.* London: Constable, 1969.

2478 _____ . *Media Sociology: A Reader.* Urbana: University of Illinois, 1969.

2479 Turner, Charles W. and Berkowitz, Leonard. "Identification with Film Aggressor (Covert Role Taking) and Reactions to Film Violence." *Journal of Personality & Social Psychology,* 1972, 21, 2: 256-264.

2480 Turner, Mary Alice. "News Reading Behavior and Social Adjustment." *Journalism Quarterly,* 1958, 35, 2: 199-204.

2481 Turow, Joseph. "Advising and Ordering: Daytime, Prime Time." *Journal of Communication,* 1974, 24, 2: 138-141. Men tend to be dominant in giving advice and orders during prime-time, but men and women are nearly equal in daytime programming.

2482 _____ . "Talk Show Radio as Interpersonal Communication." *Journal of Broadcasting*, 1974, 18, 2: 171-180.

2483 Twyman, W. A. "A Review of Research into Viewership of Television Commercial Breaks." London: Institute of Practitioners in Advertising, 1971.

2484 Tyler, I. K. *Television for World Understanding.* Washington, D.C.: National Education Association, 1970. A brief (80 pp.) look at television's potential role in the development of world understanding, with an emphasis on the young viewer.

2485 Tyler, Parker. *Screening the Sexes: Homosexuality in the Movies.* Garden City, N.Y.: Anchor, 1973.

U

2486 Udry, J. R. *The Media and Family Planning.* Cambridge, Mass.: Ballinger, 1974.

2487 _____ , Clark, Lydia T., Chase, Charles L., and Levy, Marvin. "Can Mass Media Advertising Increase Contraceptive Use?" *Family Planning Perspectives,* 1972, 4, 3: 37-44. Demonstrated marked increases in awareness but no effect on use.

2488 UNESCO. "Mass Media in Society: The Need of Research." *Reports and Papers on Mass Communication, No. 59.* Paris: UNESCO, 1970.

2489 United States Congress. *Hearings Before Senate Select Committee on Nutrition and Human Needs: Nutrition Education—1973, Parts 3-5: TV Advertising of Food to Children.* 93rd Congress, 1st session. March 5-12, 1973. Washington, D.C.: Government Printing Office, 1973.

2490 _____ . Hearings Before Senate Select Committee on Nutrition and Human Needs. *Nutrition Education—1973. Part 8. Broadcast Industry's Response to TV Ads.* 93rd Congress, 1st session. June 11, 1973. Washington, D.C.: Government Printing Office, 1973.

2491 _____ . House Committee on Interstate and Foreign Commerce. Hearings and report. *Investigation of Radio and Television Programs.* 82nd Congress, 2nd session. June 3–Dec. 5, 1952. Washington, D.C.: Government Printing Office, 1952.

2492 _____ . House Committee on Interstate and Foreign Commerce. Hearing Before the Subcommittee on Communications and Power. *Films and Broadcasts Demeaning Ethnic, Racial, or Religious Groups.* 91st Congress, 2nd session. September 21, 1970. Washington, D.C.: Government Printing Office, 1970.

2493 _____ . House Committee on Interstate and Foreign Commerce. Hearings Before the Subcommittee on Communications and Power. *Films and Broadcasts Demeaning Ethnic, Racial, or Religious Groups.* 92nd Congress,

1st session. April 27-28, 1971. Washington, D.C.: Government Printing Office, 1971.

2494 _____ . Senate Committee on Commerce. Hearings Before the Subcommittee on Communications. *Projections, Predictions of Election Results and Political Broadcasting.* 90th Congress, 1st session. July 18-20, 1967. Washington, D.C.: Government Printing Office, 1967.

2495 _____ . Senate Committee on Commerce. *Hearings Before the Subcommittee on Communications: Surgeon General's Report by the Scientific Advisory Committee on Television and Social Behavior.* 92nd Congress, 2nd session. March 21-24. Washington, D.C.: Government Printing Office, 1972.

2496 _____ . Senate Committee on Commerce. *Hearings Before the Subcommittee on Communications: Violence on Television.* 93rd Congress, 2nd session. April 3-5, 1974. Washington, D.C.: Government Printing Office, 1974.

2497 _____ . Senate Committee on Commerce. Report. *Predictions and Projections of Election Results.* Washington, D.C.: Government Printing Office, August 30, 1967.

2498 _____ . Senate Committee on Commerce. Staff Report for the Subcommittee on Communications. *Analysis of the Character of Violence in Literature and Violence as Expressed Through Television.* 91st Congress, 1st session. Washington, D.C.: Government Printing Office, 1969.

2499 _____ . Senate Committee Hearings Before the Subcommittee to Investigate Juvenile Delinquency. *Juvenile Delinquency: Part 10: Effects on Young People of Violence and Crime Portrayed on Television.* 87th Congress, 1st and 2nd sessions. June 8, 1961–May 14, 1962. Washington, D.C.: Government Printing Office, 1963.

2500 _____ . Senate Committee on the Judiciary. *Hearings Before the Subcommittee to Investigate Juvenile Delinquency: Juvenile Delinquency (Television Programs.)* 83rd Congress, 2nd session, June 5–Oct. 20, 1954. Washington, D.C.: Government Printing Office, 1955.

2501 _____ . Senate Committee on the Judiciary. *Hearings Before the Subcommittee to Investigate Juvenile Delinquency: Juvenil Delinquency (Television Programs).* 84th Congress, 1st session. April 6-7, 1955. Washington, D.C.: Government Printing Office, 1955.

2502 _____ . Senate Committee on the Judiciary. *Report of Subcommittee to Investigate Juvenile Delinquency: Television and Juvenile Delinquency (with Bibliography).* 84th Congress, 1st session. Washington, D.C.: Government Printing Office, 1956.

2503 _____ . Senate Committee on the Judiciary. Hearings Before the Subcommittee to Investigate Juvenile Delinquency. *Juvenile Delinquency. Part 10. Effects on Young People of Violence and Crime Portrayed on Television.* 87th Congress, 1st and 2nd sessions. June 8, 1961–May 14, 1962. Washington, D.C.: Government Printing Office, 1963.

2504 _____ . Senate Committee on the Judiciary. Hearings Before the

Subcommittee to Investigate Juvenile Delinquency. *Juvenile Delinquency, Part 16. Effects on Young People of Violence and Crime Portrayed on Television.* 88th Congress, 2nd session. July 30, 1964. Washington, D.C.: Government Printing Office, 1965.

2505 _____ . Senate Committee on the Judiciary. *Hearings Before the Subcommittee to Investigate Juvenile Delinquency: Television and Juvenile Delinquency.* 88th Congress, 2nd session, and 89th Congress, 1st session. October 15, 1965. Washington, D.C.: Government Printing Office, 1966.

2506 U.S. Surgeon General's Scientific Advisory Committee on Television and Social Behavior. *Television and Growing Up: The Impact of Televised Violence.* Washington, D.C.: Government Printing Office, 1972.

2507 Unwin, Stephen, J. F. "How Culture, Age, and Sex Affect Advertising Response." *Journalism Quarterly,* 1973, 50, 4: 735-743.

2508 Utz, W. J., Jr. "The Comparative Effect of Color and Black and White Film Clips Upon Rated Perception of Reality." Doctoral Dissertation, University of Illinois, 1968.

V

2509 Vaillancourt, P. M. "Stability of Children's Survey Responses." *Public Opinion Quarterly,* 1973, 37: 373-386.

2510 Van Tubergen, G. Norman and Friedland, Karen. "Preference Patterns for Comic Strips Among Teenagers." *Journalism Quarterly,* 1972, 49: 745-750.

2511 Verna, Mary Ellen. "The Female Image in Children's TV Commercials." *Journal of Broadcasting,* 1975, 19, 3: 301-309. Analyzed advertisements in which males and/or females appeared, for the activity involved in the ad, the male-female orientation, mood, and sex presented in the voice-over and audio track.

2512 Vidmar, Neil and Rokeach, Milton. "Archie Bunker's Bigotry: A Study in Selective Perception and Exposure." *Journal of Communication,* 1974, 24, 1: 36-47. Indicates that different viewers may be getting different messages from the program, depending on which major character they identify with.

2513 Vinyard, Dale and Sigel, Roberta S. "Newspapers and Urban Voters." *Journalism Quarterly,* 1971, 48, 3: 486-493.

2514 Vitar, Zoltan. "A Televizionzas Nehany Szocialpszichologiai Vonat-koozasa" [Some Social-Psychological Implications of Television Watching]. *Pszichologiai Tanulmanyak,* 1968, 11: 111-124.

2515 Vlahlijska, L. "On the Problem of Free Time in Old Age and Certain Types of Activity for Elderly and Old People." In D. Mateeff, et al. (eds.), *Problems of Gerontology and Geriatrics* (vol. 4). Sofia: Medicina i Fizkultura, 1969.

2516 Voos, H. *Information Needs in Urban Areas: A Summary of Research and Methodology.* New Brunswick, N.J.: Rutgers University Press, 1969.

W

2517 Wackman, Daniel B., Reale, Greg, and Ward, Scott. "Racial Differences in Response to Advertising Among Adolescents." In E. A. Rubinstein, G. A. Comstock, and J. P. Murray (eds.), *Television and Social Behavior: Television in Day-to-Day Life: Patterns of Use* (vol. 4). Washington, D.C.: Government Printing Office, 1972: 543-553.

2518 Wade, Serena E. "Adolescents, Creativity, and Media: An Exploratory Study." *American Behavioral Scientist,* 1971, 14, 3: 341-351.

2519 _____. "Media Effects on Changes in Attitudes Toward the Rights of Young People." *Journalism Quarterly,* 1973, 50, 2: 292-296, 347.

2520 _____. "Media and the Disadvantaged: A Review of the Literature." Stanford: ERIC Clearinghouse, 1969.

2521 _____ and Schramm, Wilbur. "The Mass Media as Sources of Public Affairs, Science, and Health Knowledge." *Public Opinion Quarterly,* 1969, 33, 2: 197-209. Television comes through as the dominant medium with print being used primarily by the upper income/education groups.

2522 Waisensen, F. B. and Durlak, J. T. "Mass Media Use, Information Source Evaluation, and Perception of Self and Nation." *Public Opinion Quarterly,* 1967, 31: 399-406.

2523 Walker, C. E. "Erotic Stimuli and the Aggressive Sexual Offender." In *Technical Report of The Commission on Obscenity and Pornography: Erotica and Antisocial Behavior* (vol. 7). Washington, D.C.: Government Printing Office, 1972: 91-148.

2524 Wall, W. D. and Simson, W. A. "The Emotional Responses of Adolescent Groups to Certain Films: Part I." *British Journal of Educational Psychology,* 1950, 20: 153-163.

2525 _____. "The Responses of Adolescent Groups to Certain Films, Part II." *British Journal of Educational Psychology,* 1951, 21: 81-88.

2526 Wallace, D. "Obscenity and Contemporary Community Standards: A Survey." *Journal of Social Issues,* 1973, 29, 3: 53-68.

2527 _____, Wehmer, G. and Podany, E. "Contemporary Community Standards of Visual Erotica." In *Technical Report of The Commission on Obscenity and Pornography: The Consumer and the Community* (vol. 9). Washington, D.C.: Government Printing Office, 1972: 27-88.

2528 Walters, Judith K. and Stone, Vernon A. "Television and Family Communication." *Journal of Broadcasting,* 1971, 15, 4: 409-414. Examines family interaction as it is mediated by the television context. Does not provide clear evidence that TV hampers family interaction.

2529 Walters, R. H. "Implications of Laboratory Studies of Aggression for the Control and Regulation of Violence." *Annals of the American Academy of Political and Social Science,* 1966, 364: 60-72.

2530 _____ and Parke, R. D. "Influence of Response Consequences to a Social Model on Resistance to Deviation." *Journal of Experimental Child Psychology,* 1964, 1, 3: 269-280.

2531 Walters, R. H. and Thomas, E. L. "Enhancement of Punitiveness by Visual and Audiovisual Displays." *Canadian Journal of Psychology,* 1963, 17, 2: 244-255.

2532 Walters, R. H. and Willows, D. C. "Imitative Behavior of Disturbed and Nondisturbed Children Following Exposure to Aggressive and Nonaggressive Models." *Child Development,* 1968, 39, 1: 79-89. Both disturbed and nondisturbed children imitated aggressive behavior witnessed on television.

2533 Walters, R. H., Leat, M., and Mezei, L. "Inhibition and Disinhibition of Responses Through Empathetic Learning." *Canadian Journal of Psychology,* 1963, 17: 235-243.

2534 Walters, R. H., Parke, R. D., and Cane, V. A. "Timing of Punishment and Observation of Consequences to Others as Determinants of Response Inhibition." *Journal of Experimental Child Psychology,* 1965, 2: 10-30.

2535 Walters, R. H., Thomas, E. L., and Acker, C. W. "Enhancement of Punitive Behavior by Audio-Visual Displays." *Science,* 1962, 136: 872-873.

2536 Waltzer, Herbert. "In the Magic Lantern: Television Coverage of the 1964 National Conventions." *Public Opinion Quarterly,* 1966, 30, 1: 33-53.

2537 Wanat, John. "Political Broadcast Advertising and Primary Election Voting." *Journal of Broadcasting,* 1974, 18, 4: 413-422.

2538 Wand, Barbara. "Television Viewing and Family Choice Differences." *Public Opinion Quarterly,* 1968, 32, 1: 84-94.

2539 Wangermee, Robert. "Publics et Culture en Television" [Television: Audiences and Culture]. *Etudes de Radio-Television,* 1968, 14: 3-15.

2540 _____. "Television et Politique" [Television and Politics]. *Etudes de Radio-Television,* 1965, 10: 2-19.

2541 Waniewicz, Ignacy. *Broadcasting for Adult Education: Guidebook to World-Wide Experience.* Paris: UNESCO, 1972.

2542 Ward, Scott. "Children's Reactions to Commercials." *Journal of Advertising Research,* 1972, 12, 2: 37-45.

2543 _____. "Consumer Socialization." *Journal of Consumer Research,* 1974, 1, 2: 1-14.

2544 _____. "Effects of Television Advertising on Children and Adolescents." In E. A. Rubinstein, G. A. Comstock, and J. P. Murray (eds.), *Television and Social Behavior: Television in Day-to-Day Life: Patterns of Use* (vol. 4). Washington, D.C.: Government Printing Office, 1972: 432-451.

2545 _____. "Kids' TV-Marketers on Hot Seat: Research Evidence Helps Clarify Burning Consumerist Issue of Children's Television Advertising." *Harvard Business Review,* 1972, 50: 16-18.

2546 _____ and Robertson, Thomas S. "Adolescent Attitudes Toward Television Advertising: Preliminary Findings." In E. A. Rubinstein, G. A.

Comstock, and J. P. Murray (eds.), *Television and Social Behavior: Television in Day-to-Day Life: Patterns of Use* (vol. 4). Washington, D.C.: Government Printing Office, 1972: 526-543.

2547 _____ , eds. *Consumer Behavior: Theoretical Sourcebook.* Englewood Cliffs, N.J.: Prentice-Hall, 1973.

2548 _____ . "Family Influences on Adolescent Consumer Behavior." Cambridge, Mass.: Marketing Science Institute, 1970.

2549 Ward, Scott and Wackman, Daniel B. "Children's Information Processing of Television Advertising." In P. Clarke (ed.), *New Models for Mass Communication Research,* Beverly Hills: Sage, 1973: 119-146.

2550 _____ . "Children's Purchase Influence Attempts and Parental Yielding." *Journal of Marketing Research,* 1972, 9: 316-319.

2551 _____ . "Effects of Television Advertising on Consumer Socialization." Cambridge, Mass.: Marketing Science Institute, 1973.

2552 _____ . "Family and Media Influences on Adolescent Consumer Learning." In E. A. Rubinstein, G. A. Comstock, and J. P. Murray (eds.), *Television and Social Behavior: Television in Day-to-Day Life: Patterns of Use* (vol. 4). Washington, D.C.: Government Printing Office, 1972: 554-567.

2553 _____ . "Television Advertising and Intra-Family Influence: Children's Purchase Influence Attempts and Parental Yielding." In E. A. Rubinstein, G. A. Comstock, and J. P. Murray (eds.), *Television and Social Behavior: Television in Day-to-Day Life: Patterns of Use* (vol. 4). Washington, D.C.: Government Printing Office, 1972: 516-525.

2554 Ward, Scott, Levinson, David, and Wackman, Daniel B. "Children's Attention to Television Advertising." In E. A. Rubinstein, G. A. Comstock, and J. P. Murray (eds.), *Television and Social Behavior: Television in Day-to-Day Life: Patterns of Use.* Washington, D.C.: Government Printing Office, 1972: 491-516.

2555 Ward, Scott, Reale, Greg, and Levinson, David. "Children's Perceptions, Explanations, and Judgements of Television Advertising: A Further Exploration." In E. A. Rubinstein, G. A. Comstock, and J. P. Murray (eds.), *Television and Social Behavior: Television in Day-to-Day Life: Patterns of Use* (vol. 4). Washington, D.C.: Government Printing Office, 1972: 468-490.

2556 Ward, Scott, Wackman, Daniel B., and Seale, Greg. "Racial Differences in Responses to Advertising Among Adolescents." In *Effects of Television Advertising on Children and Adolescents.* Cambridge, Mass.: Marketing Science Institute, 1971.

2557 Ward, Scott, Wackman, D. B., Faber, R., and Lesser, G. S. *Effects of Television Advertising on Consumer Socialization.* Cambridge, Mass.: Marketing Science Institute, 1974.

2558 Warner, W. Lloyd, Henry, William E., Moore, Harriet B., and Friedson, Eliot. *Television and Children,* Chicago: Social Research, 1954.

2559   Warneryd, Karl-Erik and Nowak, K. "Mass Communication and Advertising." Stockholm: The Economic Research Institute at the Stockholm School of Economics, 1968.

2560   Warren, D. I. "Mass Media and Racial Crisis: A Study of the New Bethel Church Incident in Detroit." *Journal of Social Issues,* 1972, 28: 111-131.

2561   Wartella, Ellen and Ettema, James S. "A Cognitive Developmental Study of Children's Attention to Television Commercials." *Communication Research,* 1974, 1, 1: 69-88.

2562   Watt, James H. "Television Viewing and Aggression; An Examination of the Catharsis, Facilitation and Arousal Models." Doctoral Dissertation, University of Wisconsin, 1973.

2563   Wayne, Ivor. "American and Society Themes and Values: A Content Analysis of Pictures and Popular Magazines." *Public Opinion Quarterly,* 1956, 20, 1: 314-320.

2564   Weaver, D., McCombs, M. E., and Spellman, C. "Watergate and the Media: A Case Study of Agenda-Setting." *American Politics Quarterly,* October, 1975.

2565   Webb, E. J. and Campbell, D. T. "Experiments on Communication Effects." In I. de Sola Pool and W. Schramm (eds.), *Handbook of Communication.* Chicago: Rand McNally, 1973: 938-952.

2566   Weigel, Russell H. and Jessor, Richard. "Television and Adolescent Conventionality: An Exploratory Study." *Public Opinion Quarterly,* 1973, 37, 1: 76-90. Time spent with television was positively related to conventionality of values, attitudes, and behavior.

2567   Weinberger, Marvin. "Do People Know How Susceptible They Are to Television Advertising?" *Public Opinion Quarterly,* 1962, 26, 2: 262-265.

2568   Weintraub, N. T. "Some Meanings Radio Has For Teenagers." *Journal of Broadcasting,* 1971, 15: 147-152.

2569   Weisenborn, R. E. "An Experimental Study of the Effects of Communication Media on Source Credibility." Doctoral Dissertation, Michigan State University, 1968.

2570   Weiss, W. "Effects of the Mass Media of Communication." In G. Lindzey and E. Aronson (eds.), *The Handbook of Social Psychology: Applied Social Psychology* (vol. 5). Reading, Mass.: Addison-Wesley, 1969: 77-195.

2571   _____ . "Mass Communication." *Annual Review of Psychology,* 1971, 22: 309-336.

2572   Weitzman, L. J., Eifler, D., Hokoda, E., and Ross, C. "Sex-Role Socialization in Picture Books for Preschool Children." *American Journal of Sociology,* 1972, 77: 1125-1150.

2573   Wells, Alan F. *Picture-Tube Imperialism?: The Impact of U.S. Television on Latin America.* Maryknoll, N.Y.: Orbis Books, 1972. Stems from the author's doctoral dissertation dealing with "Development, Consumerism and Television in Latin America."

2574 Wells, William D. "Children as Consumers." In J. Newman (ed.), *On Knowing the Consumer.* New York: Wiley, 1966.

2575 _____. "Communicating with Children." *Journal of Advertising Research,* 1965, 5, 2: 2-14.

2576 _____. "Television and Aggression: Replication of an Experimental Field Study." Chicago: Graduate School of Business, University of Chicago, 1973.

2577 Werner, A. "Barn of Fjernsyn: Fritidssysler Flytteonsker og Yrkesplaner Blant Skoleelever i Finnmark for og etter Inforingen av Fjernsyn" [Children and Television: Leisure Pursuits, Wishes to Move and Vocational Plans Among School Pupils in Finnmark Before and After the Introduction of TV]. Oslo: Universitetsforlaget, 1972.

2578 _____. "A Case of Sex and Class Socialization: The Effects of Television on Children and Adolescents." *Journal of Communication,* 1975, 25, 4: 45-50.

2579 _____. "Children and Television in Norway." *Gazette,* 1971, 17, 3: 133-151.

2580 _____. "A Comparison of Methods of Measuring TV Viewing Time." *Journalism Quarterly,* 1972, 49, 1: 136-140.

2581 Werner, Norma. "A Study of Personality Factors in Children's Thematic Apperception of their Favorite (Child Orientated) Television Programs." Doctoral Dissertation, University of Chicago, 1965.

2582 Wertham, Frederic. "Is TV Hardening Us to the War in Vietnam?" In Otto Larsen (ed.), *Violence and the Mass Media.* New York: Harper and Row, 1968: 50-54.

2583 _____. "School for Violence." In Otto Larsen (ed.), *Violence and the Mass Media.* New York: Harper and Row, 1968: 36-39.

2584 _____. "School For Violence, Mayhem in the Mass Media." In V. B. Cline (ed.), *Where Do You Draw the Line?* Provo, Utah: Brigham Young University Press, 1974: 157-175.

2585 _____. "The Scientific Study of Mass Media Effects." *American Journal of Psychiatry,* 1962, 119, 4: 306-311.

2586 _____. *Seduction of the Innocent.* New York: Holt, Rinehart, Winston, 1953. Explores the effects of aggression as presented in comic books on children's attitudes and behaviors and on television's imitation of comic content.

2587 _____. *A Sign for Cain: An Exploration of Human Violence.* New York: Macmillan, 1966.

2588 Westley, Bruce and Barrow, Lionel C. "An Investigation of News-Seeking Behavior." *Journalism Quarterly,* 1959, 36, 4: 431-438.

2589 _____ and MacLean, Malcolm S. "A Conceptual Model for Communications Research." *Audio-Visual Communications Review,* 1955, 3, 1: 3-12.

2590 _____. "A Conceptual Model for Communications Research." *Journalism Quarterly,* 1957, 34, 1: 31-38.

2591 Westley, Bruce H. and Mobius, Joseph. "A Closer Look at the Non-Television Household." *Journal of Broadcasting,* 1960, 4, 2: 164-173.

2592 Westley, Bruce H. and Severin, Werner J. "Some Correlates of Media Credibility." *Journalism Quarterly,* 1964, 41, 3: 325-335.

2593 Whale, J. *The Half-Shut Eye: Television and Politics in Britain and America.* New York: St. Martin's Press, 1969.

2594 Whan, Forest. "Attitude of Iowans Toward Radio Music." *Journal of Broadcasting,* 1958, 2, 1: 44-54.

2595 Wheatley, John J. "Assessing TV Pretest Audiences." *Journal of Advertising Research,* 1971, 11, 1: 21-25.

2596 _____. "Influence of Commercial's Length and Position." *Journal of Marketing Research,* 1968, 5: 199-202.

2597 Wheeler, S. "Crime and Violence." In F.T.C. Yu (ed.), *Behavioral Sciences and the Mass Media.* New York: Russell Sage Foundation, 1968: 131-150.

2598 White, B. L. and Watts, J. C. *Experience and Environment: Major Influences on the Development of the Young Child.* Englewood Cliffs, New Jersey: Prentice-Hall, 1973.

2599 White, David Manning. "Mass-Communication Research: A View in Perspective." In L. A. Dexter and D. M. White (eds.), *People, Society, and Mass Communications.* New York: Free Press, 1964: 521-546.

2600 _____ and Averson, R. *The Celluloid Weapon: Social Comment in the American Film.* Boston, Beacon Press, 1972.

2601 White, W. J. "An Index for Determining the Relative Importance of Information Sources." *Public Opinion Quarterly,* 1969, 33, 4: 607-610.

2602 Whitehead, Paul C. "Sex, Violence, and Crime in the Mass Media." *Canada's Mental Health,* 1970, 18, 2: 20-23.

2603 Whitehouse, M. *Cleaning-Up TV: From Protest to Participation.* London: Blanford Press, 1967.

2604 Whiteside, Thomas. *Selling Death: Cigarette Advertising and Public Health.* New York: Liveright, 1973.

2605 Whiting, Gordon C. "Empathy: A Cognitive Skill for Decoding the Modernization Import of the Mass Media." *Public Opinion Quarterly,* 1971, 35: 211-219.

2606 _____ and Stanfield, J. David. "Mass Media Use and Opportunity Structure in Rural Brazil." *Public Opinion Quarterly,* 1972, 36, 1: 56-68.

2607 Whiting, J. W. M., et al. *Field Guide for a Study of Socialization.* New York: John Wiley, 1966.

2608 Wiebe, Gerhardt, D. "Mass Communications." In E. Hartley and R. Hartley (eds.), *Fundamentals of Social Psychology.* New York: Knopf, 1952: 159-195.

2609 _____. "Mass Media and Man's Relationship to His Environment." *Journalism Quarterly,* 1973, 50, 3: 426-432, 446.

2610 ———. "Merchandising Commodities and Citizenship on Television." *Public Opinion Quarterly,* 1951, 15, 4: 679-691.

2611 ———. "Responses to the Televised Kefauver Hearings: Some Social Psychological Implications." *Public Opinion Quarterly,* 1952, 16: 179-200.

2612 ———. "Two Psychological Factors in Media Audience Behavior." *Public Opinion Quarterly,* 1969, 33, 4: 523-537. The factors are, to avoid coping with others, and to avoid expending effort.

2613 Wiggins, X. R. "Drug Education Through the Mass Media." In N. R. Benchley and P. G. Hammond (eds.), *The Media and Drug Abuse Messages.* Washington, D.C.: Special Action Office for Drug Abuse Prevention, Monograph Series D, no. 1, 1974: 79-83.

2614 Wight, Robin. *The Day the Pigs Refused to be Driven to Market: Advertising and the Consumer Revolution.* New York: Random House, 1974.

2615 Wilcox, L. D. et al. *Social Indicators and Societal Monitoring: An Annotated Bibliography.* San Francisco: Jossey-Bass, 1972.

2616 Wilder, Alec. *American Popular Song: The Great Innovators, 1900-1950.* New York: Oxford University Press, 1972.

2617 Wilhelmsen, D. and Bret, J. *Telepolitics: The Politics of Neuronic Man.* Plattsburgh, N.Y.: Tundra Books, 1972. Discussion of TV effects relative to brain and neural functioning. An extension of the McLuhan philosophy.

2618 Wilkie, W. L. *Assessment of Consumer Information Processing Research in Relation to Public Policy Needs.* Washington, D.C.: Government Printing Office, 1975.

2619 Willey, George A. "The Soap Operas and the War." *Journal of Broadcasting,* 1963, 7, 4: 339-352.

2620 William, D. C., Ogilivie, P. J., and Ogilivie, J. C. "Mass Media, Learning, and Retention." *Canadian Journal of Psychology,* 1957, 11, 3: 157-163.

2621 Williams, Dwight A., Jr. "Mass Media Preference Patterns: A Cross-Media Study." Doctoral Dissertation, Ohio State University, 1971.

2622 Williams, Frederick. "A Factor Analysis of Judgements of Radio Newscasters." *Journal of Broadcasting,* 1963, 7, 2: 135-143.

2623 ———. "Social Class Differences in How Children Talk About Television." *Journal of Broadcasting,* 1969, 13, 4: 345-358.

2624 ——— and Lindsay, Howard. "Ethnic and Social Class Differences in Communication Habits and Attitudes." *Journalism Quarterly,* 1971, 48, 4: 672-678.

2625 Williams, Frederick and Natalicio, D.S. "Evaluating 'Carrascolendas': A Television Series For Mexican-American Children." *Journal of Broadcasting,* 1972, 16: 299-309.

2626 Williams, Frederick, Valenzuela, N., and Knight, P. "Prediction of Mexican-American Media Habits and Attitudes." Austin: Center for Communication Research, University of Texas, 1973.

2627 Williams, Raymond. *Television: Technology and Cultural Form.* New York: Schocken Books, 1975.

2628 Williams, S. *Climate For Change.* San Francisco, Calif.: Committee on Children's Television, 1972.

2629 Williams, T. R. *Introduction to Socialization, Human Culture Transmitted.* Saint Louis: Mosby, 1972.

2630 Willis, E. E. "McLuhanism, Television, and Politics." *Quarterly Journal of Speech,* 1968, 54, 4: 404-409.

2631 Wilson, Bryan. "Mass Media and the Public Attitude to Crime." *Criminal Law Review,* 1961, June: 376-384.

2632 Wilson, James Q. "Violence, Pornography and Social Science." In V. B. Cline (ed.), *Where Do You Draw the Line?: An Exploration into Media Violence, Pornography, and Censorship.* Provo, Utah: Brigham Young University, 1974: 293-308.

2633 Wilson, R. W. *The Moral State: A Study of the Political Socialization of Chinese and American Children.* New York: Free Press, 1974.

2634 Wilson, W. C. "Facts vs. Fears: Why Should We Worry About Pornography?" *The Annals of the American Academy of Political and Social Science,* 1971, September, 105.

2635 _____ . "Law Enforcement Officers' Perceptions of Pornography as a Social Issue." *Journal of Social Issues,* 1973, 29, 3: 41-52.

2636 _____ . "Pornography: The Emergence of a Social Issue and the Beginnings of Psychological Study." *Journal of Social Issues,* 1973, 29, 3: 7-18.

2637 Wilson, W. C. and Abelson, H. I. "Experience With and Attitudes Toward Explicit Sexual Materials." *Journal of Social Issues,* 1973, 29, 3: 19-40

2638 Wind, Y. and Denny, J. "Multivariate Analysis of Variance in Research on the Effectiveness of TV Commercials." *Journal of Marketing Research,* 1974, 11: 136-142.

2639 Windlesham, Lord. "Television as an Influence on Political Opinion." *Political Quarterly,* 1964, 35: 375-385.

2640 Winick, Charles. "Censor and Sensibility: A Content Analysis of the Television Censor's Comments." *Journal of Broadcasting,* 1964, 5, 2: 117-135.

2641 _____ . "A Content Analysis of Drug Related Films Released During 1971." In National Commission on Marihuana and Drug Abuse, *Drug Use in America: Problem in Perspective: Social Responses to Drug Use* (vol. 2). Washington, D.C.: Government Printing Office, 1973: 709-717.

2642 _____ . "A Content Analysis of Drug Related Network Entertainment Prime-Time Programs 1970-72." In National Commission on Marihuana and Drug Abuse, *Drug Use in America: Problem in Perspective: Social Responses to Drug Use* (vol. 2). Washington, D.C.: Government Printing Office, 1973: 698-708.

2643 _____ . "Mass Communications and Drug Dependence." In C. Winick (ed.), *Sociological Aspects of Drug Dependence.* Cleveland: CRCO Press, 1974, 77-99.

2644 _____ . "Some Observations on Characteristics of Patrons of Adult Theaters and Bookstores." In *Technical Report of the Commission on Obscenity and Pornography: The Marketplace: Empirical Studies* (vol. 4). Washington, D.C.: Government Printing Office, 1971: 225-244.

2645 _____ . "Television and the Culture of the Child." In P. D. Hazard (ed.), *TV as Art.* Champaign, Ill.: National Council of Teachers of English, 1966: 137-156.

2646 _____ . "Tendency Systems and the Effects of a Movie Dealing with a Social Problem." *The Journal of General Psychology.* 1963, 68: 289-305.

2647 Winick, Charles and Winick, Mariann Pezzella. "Courtroom Drama on Television." *Journal of Communication,* 1974, 24, 4: 67-73.

2648 _____ . "Some Uses of Home Television Viewing in the Elementary Classroom." *Childhood Education Bulletin,* 1963, 9-A: 27-40.

2649 Winick, Charles, Williamson, Lorne G., Clizmir, Stuart F., and Winick, Mariann Pezzella. *Children's Television Commercials: A Content Analysis.* New York: Praeger, 1973.

2650 Winston, Don C. "Some Motivational Factors in the Serious Music Audiences." *Journalism Quarterly,* 1956, 33, 3: 364-366.

2651 Winthrop, Henry. "Focus on the Human Condition: Sexual Revolution or Inner Emptiness: Portents of Brave New World: II. The Skin Trade Versus Holistic Balance in Sexuality." *Journal of Human Relations,* 1970, 18, 2: 924-938.

2652 Wittenborn, J. R., Smith, J. P., and Wittenborn, S. A., eds. *Communication and Drug Abuse.* Springfield, Ill.: Thomas, 1970. Contains the proceedings of the second Rutgers symposium on drug abuse, covering attitude change, sources of drug information, drug education and communication programs, drug law considerations, and the role of public opinion in drug abuse problems.

2653 Witty, P. A. "Children of the Television Era." *Elementary English,* 1967, 44: 528-535, 554.

2654 _____ . "Some Research on TV." In S. Sunderlin, (ed.), *Children and TV: Television's Impact on the Child.* Washington, D.C.: Association for Childhood Education International, 1967.

2655 _____ . "Studies of the Mass Media, 1949-1965." *Science Education,* 1966, 50: 119-126. Examines this 16-year period for trends in children's use of media and the media's effects on and relationships to other activities and childhood skills.

2656 _____ . "Televiewing by Children and Youth: Eleven Years of Surveys and Studies." New York: Television Information Office, 1961.

2657 _____ and Kinsella, Paul. "Children and the Electronic Pied Piper." *Education,* 1959, 80, 1: 48-56.

2658 Woelfel, Joseph, Woelfel, John, Gillham, James, and McPhail, T. "Political Radicalization as a Communication Process." *Communication Research,* 1974, 1, 3: 243-263.

2659 Wolf, T. M. "A Developmental Investigation of Televised Modeled Verbalizations and Behavior on Resistance to Deviation." *Developmental Psychology,* 1972, 6: 537.

2660 _____ . "Effects of Televised Modeled Verbalizations and Behavior on Resistance to Deviation." *Developmental Psychology,* 1973, 8: 51-56.

2661 _____ and Cheyne, J. A. "Persistence of Effects of Live Behavioral, Televised Behavioral, and Live Verbal Models on Resistance to Deviation." *Child Development,* 1972, 43: 1329-1436.

2662 Wolfe, G. Joseph. "Some Reactions to the Advent of Campaigning by Radio." *Journal of Broadcasting,* 1969, 13, 3: 305-314.

2663 Wolfgang, M. E. "Youth and Violence." Washington, D.C.: Department of Health, Education, and Welfare, 1970.

2664 Women on Words and Images. *Dick and Jane as Victims.* Princeton, N.J.: Educational Testing Service, 1972.

2665 Woods, Donald J. "Repression-Sensitization, Attitude Towards Emotionality, and Response to a Threatening and Non-Threatening Film." *Dissertation Abstracts International,* 1972, 32 (9-B): 5464-5465.

2666 Worchel, S., Andreoli, V., and Eason, J. "Is the Medium the Message?: A Study of the Effects of Media, Communicator, and Message Characteristics on Attitude Change." *Journal of Applied Social Psychology,* 1975, 5, 2: 157-172. An experimental test of the interaction of medium, message, and source in a newscast situation.

2667 Worden, J. K. "A Systematic Method for Creating New Ideas for Television Programs From Audience Interest in Leisure Activities." Doctoral Dissertation, Syracuse University, 1971.

2668 Worth, Sol. "The Uses of Film in Education and Communication." In D. Olson (ed.), *Media and Symbols: The Forms of Expression, Communication, and Education.* Chicago: University of Chicago Press, 1974: 271-302.

2669 _____ and Adair, John. *Through Navajo Eyes: An Exploration in Film Communication and Anthropology.* Bloomington: University of Indiana Press, 1972.

2670 Wotring, C. E. "The Effects of Exposure to Television Violence on Adolescents' Verbal Aggression." *Dissertation Abstracts International,* 1972, 32 (12-A): 7025.

2671 _____ and Greenberg, B. S. "Experiments in Televised Violence and Verbal Aggression: Two Exploratory Studies." *Journal of Communication,* 1973, 23: 446-460.

2672 Wright, C. R. "Evaluating Mass Media Campaigns." *International Social Science Bulletin,* 1955, 7, 3: 417-430.

2673 _____ . "Functional Analysis and Mass Communication." *Public Opinion Quarterly,* 1960, 24: 605-620.

2674 _____ . "Functional Analysis and Mass Communication Revisited." In J. G. Blumler and E. Katz (eds.), *The Uses of Mass Communication: Current Perspectives on Gratifications Research.* Beverly Hills: Sage, 1974: 197-212.

2675 _____ . *Mass Communication: A Sociological Perspective* (2nd ed.). New York: Random House, 1975. An update of the 1959 classic with a new chapter on the sociology of the mass communicator. Also includes chapters on the nature and functions of mass communication, mass communications as social institutions, sociology of the audience, cultural content of the media, and social effects.

2676 _____ . "Social Structure and Mass Communications Behavior: New Directions for Audience Research." In L. Coser (ed.), *The Idea of Social Structure: Papers in Honor of Robert K. Merton.* New York: Harcourt Brace Jovanovich, 1975.

2677 _____ . "Television and Radio Program Ratings and Measurements: A Selected and Annotated Bibliography." *Journal of Broadcasting,* 1961, 5, 2: 165-186.

2678 _____ and Cantor, Muriel. "The Opinion Seeker and Avoider: Steps Beyond the Opinion Leader Concept." *Pacific Sociological Review,* 1967, 10, 1: 33-43.

2679 Wright, C. R. and Turk, H. "Introductory Comments on the Socialization of Adults." *Sociological Inquiry,* 1967, 37: 3-10.

2680 Wright, John S. and Mertes, J. E., eds. *Advertising's Role in Society.* St. Paul, Minn.: West Publishing, 1974.

2681 Wright, Peter L. "Analyzing Media Effects on Advertising Responses." *Public Opinion Quarterly,* 1974, 38, 2: 192-205.

2682 Wright, Russell W. "Mass Media as Sources of Medical Information." *Journal of Communication,* 1975, 25, 3: 171-173.

2683 Wright, William. *Six Guns and Society: A Structural Study of the Western.* Berkeley: University of California Press, 1975.

2684 Wurtzel, Alan H. and Dominick, Joseph R. "Evaluations of Television Drama: Interacting of Acting Styles and Shot Selection." *Journal of Broadcasting,* 1972, 16, 1: 103-110.

2685 Wyckoff, Gene. *The Image Candidates: American Politics in the Age of Television.* New York: Macmillan, 1968.

Y

2686 Yankelovich, D., Inc. "Mother's Attitudes Toward Children's Television Programs and Commercials." Newtonville, Mass.: Action for Children's Television, 1970.

2687 _____ . "A Report on the Role and Penetration of Sesame Street in Ghetto Communities" [Bedford-Stuyvesant, East Harlem, Chicago, and Washington, D.C.]. New York: Daniel Yankelovich, Inc., 1973.

2688 Yates, G.C.R. "Influence of Televised Modeling and Verbalization on Children's Delay of Gratification." *Journal of Experimental Child Psychology,* 1974, 18: 333-339.

2689 Yin, R. K. "The Workshop and the World: Toward an Assessment of the Children's Television Workshop." Santa Monica, Calif.: The Rand Corporation, October, 1973.

2690 Young, Ruth. "Television in the Lives of Our Parents." *Journal of Broadcasting,* 1969-1970, 14, 1: 37-46.

2691 Yu, F.T.C., ed. *Behavioral Sciences and the Mass Media.* New York: Russell Sage Foundation, 1968.

Z

2692 Zagona, S. and Kelly, M. "The Resistance of the Closed Mind to a Novel and Complex Audio-Visual Experience." *Journal of Social Psychology,* 1966, 70: 123-131.

2693 Zajonc, Robert. "Some Effects of Space Serials." *Public Opinion Quarterly,* 1954, 18: 367-374.

2694 Ziegler, Edward. "Social Class and the Socialization Process." *Review of Educational Research,* 1970, 40, 1: 87-110.

2695 Ziegler, Sherilyn Kay. "Attention Factors in Televised Messages: Effects on Looking Behavior and Recall." *Journal of Broadcasting,* 1970, 14, 3: 307-315.

2696 Zigler, E. F. and Child, I. L., eds. *Socialization and Personality Development.* Reading, Mass.: Addison-Wesley, 1973.

2697 Zillmann, D. "Emotional Arousal as a Factor in Communication-mediated Aggressive Behavior." Doctoral Dissertation, University of Pennsylvania, 1969.

2698 _____ . "Excitation Transfer in Communication-Mediated Aggressive Behavior." *Journal of Experimental Social Psychology,* 1971, 7: 419-434.

2699 _____ and Johnson, R. C. "Motivated Aggressiveness Perpetuated by Exposure to Aggressive Films and Reduced by Exposure to Nonaggressive Films." *Journal of Research in Personality,* 1973, 7: 261-776.

2700 Zillmann, D., Hoyt, J. L., and Day, K. D. "Strength and Duration of the Effect of Aggressive, Violent, and Erotic Communications on Subsequent Aggressive Behavior." *Communication Research,* 1974, 1, 3: 286-306.

2701 Zillmann, D., Mody, B., and Cantor, J. R. "Empathetic Perception of Emotional Displays in Films as a Function of Hedonic and Excitatory State Prior to Exposure." *Journal of Research in Personality,* 1974, 8: 335-349.

2702 Zillmann, D., Johnson, R. C., and Hanrahan, J. "Pacifying Effect of Happy Ending of Communications Involving Aggression." *Psychological Reports,* 1973, 32: 967-970.

2703 Zurcher, L. A., Kirkpatrick, R. G., Cushing, R. G., and Bowman, C. K. "Ad Hoc Antipornography Organizations and Their Active Members: A Research Summary." *Journal of Social Issues,* 1973, 29, 3: 69-94.

2704 Zusne, L. "Measuring Violence in Children's Cartoons." *Perceptual and Motor Skills,* 1968, 27: 901-902.

SUBJECT INDEX

INDEX OF NONPRIMARY AUTHORS

Since all references in the bibliography are in alphabetical order, no author index for primary authors is needed. The author index to follow lists only nonprimary authors.

ABOUT THE EDITORS

Thomas F. Gordon

Dr. Gordon is currently an Associate Professor of Communications at Temple University, Philadelphia. He earned the Ph.D. degree from Michigan State University's Communication Department in 1973. His M.A. degree is from the Television-Radio Department at Michigan State University and the B.S. degree is from the Film and Television Department, Montana State University. Dr. Gordon was Book Review Editor for the *Journal of Broadcasting* from 1972-1976 and remains on the Editorial Board for that journal. His teaching and research interests emphasize communication theory, research methods, and socialization effects of the media. Besides contributions to numerous convention paper sessions, he has published articles in *Journalism Quarterly, Journal of Advertising, Journal of Broadcasting, Broadcasting Monographs,* and *Gazette,* and coauthored three research papers in the Surgeon's General's violence series, *Television and Social Behavior.* Dr. Gordon is currently Editor of *Communication Abstracts.*

Mary Ellen Verna

Ms. Verna obtained her Bachelor of Science degree, Cum Laude, from Temple University's School of Communications and Theater in 1974, after three years of course work. During her college stay, she worked as a research assistant of Professor Gordon. She has conducted research on sex-role images in the media and published a research article in the *Journal of Broadcasting.* Ms. Verna gave up a graduate school opportunity in TV research to pursue a professional broadcasting career. Since her graduation she has worked at WCAU-TV in Philadelphia as a news writer and as news talent with WMID, Atlantic City and WPEN, Philadelphia. Ms. Verna is currently a newscaster with WCAU-FM, Philadelphia.